*with the best
of good wishes!
Love, Pat*

THE GIRL FROM COW NECK

Patricia Collins Schof

ISBN: 1977877729
ISBN 13: 9781977877727
Library of Congress Control Number: 2017915510
CreateSpace Independent Publishing Platform
North Charleston, South Carolina

For Ellie and all my boys—Bobby, Matty, Dominic,
Jake, Bud, Peter, Joey, Tim, and William—and
for the Forest Hills Women's Club Writers and
the Manhasset Scribes

CHAPTER ONE

July 9, 1776

Just after dawn, the shrill cry of the Rhode Island red rooster woke me from my fitful sleep, and right away, my stomach began to pitch about like a rowboat in a rainstorm. I threw the summer blanket away from me on my rope bed and crept out to the front porch of our mansion in my shift, barefoot, where a family of cats lay sleeping in the rocking chair, their fur lifting and falling gently. Watching their slow, steady breaths, I felt calmer and leaned over the whitewashed porch railing to gaze out over the cornfields. The green stalks stood as still as sentries; in the fields beyond, wheat swayed in a soft breeze. The hard dirt road outside our front yard was clear of wagons, animals, and workmen. Nothing could be heard in the quiet morning but the beats of my heart.

It was much too early to be out on the porch, waiting for a horse and rider, but I had to be there when Mr. Matthew Douglas, our town's storekeeper, returned from his night ride into York City to General Washington's camp for the paper that would change our lives forever. The Declaration of Independence. It frees us from our mother country, England, and her greedy King George III, who rules his colonies in America in a strangling grip. The Document unites us into a nation: the United States of America, and today, my papa, Philip Scott, judge of the Queens County Court, will read the Document out loud among the pines on top of Shepherd's Hill. Our whole town will be there to listen to Papa proclaim Mr. Jefferson's words at 5 o'clock. Then, we'll have a great Liberty Feast to celebrate. Even this early in the morning I can smell the fragrance of an ox roasting in the pit our town's sawyer and grave digger dug in the meadow last evening. It takes a whole day and night to roast an ox. The Feast will begin in the meadow outside the pine grove just as soon as papa reads the Declaration. Mr. Douglas is expected to arrive carrying the Declaration in his saddlebag this very morning, on our front grass—what a day! What a day! What a day it will be!

There'll be music and dancing and fireworks and food. But first, Mr. Douglas has to get back from York City. He said he would ride all night so he could be here early this morning. But one never knows, what with the roads being muddy from the downpour last night. He could be hours away or he could be riding his horse, Bucyrus, into our front yard right now. I must wait. I hate waiting. It is so boring. I have no idea how I shall pass the time.

I'm Cassandra, Phil's daughter; some say, Phil's beautiful daughter, which always pleases me to hear, immensely. I especially want to look my most beautiful today for everyone in town, and, of course, my beau, David Van Essen. I am so excited. I have a new gown. Well, not truly new, but one of Mama's favorite gowns from Paris. I can wear it now I am sixteen and tall enough to fit it. Mama loved this gown. Today I shall feel the royal-blue taffeta slide over my shoulders, and shall admire myself in mama's gown, especially the delicate red rosebuds embroidered into the neckline. Mama always slipped her feet easily into her silky, soft shoes when she wore this gown, but I am much taller than my mama. So I will stuff my big clodhopper's feet into mama's shoes and try to ignore the tightness since they match the gown. Anyway, I've seen it in print in my French book that one must take pains to be beautiful. I do truly wish that Mama were here to celebrate this day with Papa and me. But sadly, she died in '73 from the fever. I know she is with us still. I just know it. She is looking down at us from heaven. I know that she will like to see me in her gown and shoes. How perfect I shall look. Voilà!

I love French expressions like *voilà*—and *n'est ce pas,* which I think means "Isn't it so?" I learn these words from the French book of ladies' fashions Papa brought home from one of his trips to New Rochelle, for his new wife, Hannah. French is a favored language in that city and many people speak it. Hannah doesn't look at the book much; I never see her look at the pictures. But I do. I love the book, and I use my French at Saturday-afternoon gatherings on the Thayer's front grass. Lifting my tea cup, I say "tres bien fait, Mrs. Thayer," which sounds so polished, and means 'well done'. I use those words if the cake tastes very fine, too. I do love French and everyone likes to hear this pretty bunch of words.

But then Papa, being who he is, tells me I should study French, not just recite French phrases from the book. He even bought me a French grammar book. I truly do not want to study the book. I don't. But in the New Rochelle book, there is a drawing of a young girl with long golden hair just like mine, which she has twisted up just at the ends and clipped with a diamond barrette, a very elegant way to wear the hair, I must say. Right now, I don't have a diamond barrette, but I have fixed my hair in this style by holding a brick that I warmed up in the kitchen hearth to the edges of my hair, so that they turn up nicely, without searing one lock, and I've clipped my hair with my pearl barrette. I do think my beau, David, will like this new way I will wear my hair today. He likes to hold strands of my hair out to the sunlight to watch it glow, and I do like him to feel its silkiness.

Papa does not have much patience with hairstyles or dresses from Paris anymore since Mama's been gone from us. He did buy my new stepmother, Hannah, a shimmering dark-green gown to wear today to the celebration. I remember how my mama used to dress in her favorite shifts and gowns of the day and how I loved to talk to her about them. Since yesterday, Papa has been telling me "As a matter of plain fact, Cassie, the gown you plan to wear today was your mama's favorite." I'm glad he still remembers because now that he has married Hannah from Ireland, he seems besotted with her, which I can say is a large thorn in my side, being that I loved my mother in life and still do. Anyway, after Papa reads the Declaration, we'll start the Liberty Feast. Later, there will be dancing on the green—lively hornpipes, fast-moving quadrilles, reels and jigs, and stately minuets. It is all just too exciting and wonderful.

But where is Mr. Matthew Douglas? He is late; he should be here by now. As the sun moves higher in the sky, I am worried. What if he's not coming? What if he fell off his horse? What if he lost the paper the Declaration is written on? What if? What if? *What if?* The morning is fast wearing away with no sign of Mr. Douglas.

I shall have to wait. I hate waiting. How shall I spend the time? What shall I do with myself until Mr. Douglas rides onto our front grass? I know. I shall practice walking in Mama's shoes and see if I can stretch them so they won't pain me so much when I dance at the Liberty Feast. I wonder if Hannah and Papa will dance. Mama loved to dance, but Hannah would look odd dancing because she is so tall.

Besides, Hannah comes from a small farm in Ireland and is used to cooking for her three brothers, and feeding pigs and hogs scraps of leftovers. What a dreary life she must have led in Ireland; was there dancing at all? I doubt it. Mayhap that's why she left and came to America. She ended up in Mrs. Curry's Boarding House and Restaurant jutting out from a wharf on the North River, working as a servant. Papa met her there one night after working late, so he told me. They talked while he ate his supper, waiting for the ferry to Cow Neck. Now they are married, and I am so unhappy. I don't like Hannah; I don't like her loud voice and her bossy way of speaking to me. There is nothing I like about Hannah. Nothing. When she scrubs the floor, she bellows out her Irish country songs for all the neighbors to hear—as far away as Mr. Douglas's store! She never speaks softly; she yells for me to do something, as though I'm some sort of servant and not the daughter of the house.

Hannah is the opposite of my mother, who was soft-spoken, with brown wavy hair and a pretty smile. Every day I tell Mama the latest outrage from Hannah. In the little graveyard halfway up the hill outside our mansion I feel closer to Mama, and when I leave and shut the gate behind me, I have forgotten for a while that I have a stepmother.

Not that I ever want to forget Papa; the thing about Papa is, he listens to everybody who has a grievance or complaint—except me.

But to get back to *me*, there are those in town who go on and on about me, I am very content with their description of me being tall, with fair hair, and blue, blue eyes. I do try hard, though, not to go on about myself.

Lately, Papa is mighty sorry that he ever brought that French book home. From it, he says I am much too eager to show myself to advantage—that I primp my hair too much and I am always looking in the glass to see myself. What I mind the most is that Papa says these things to me in front of Hannah. "Oh, Papa, how tiresome!" I tell him.

I suppose the thing that most upsets Papa is that I have a natural tendency toward strong opinions—just like he does, especially about the British—which leads him to scold me into keeping quiet about the king. I try but it is something I can't seem to do.

There is much bitterness in our town just now between Patriots like me and Papa who are willing to fight for the right to govern ourselves and Tories, or Loyalists, as they like to call themselves, who remain loyal to the king. They are just as devoted to their cause as we Patriots are to ours. There are fights in the streets and in the lanes. Some people have been dragged from their homes and beaten up for their Loyalist sympathies; rocks are thrown. Tories have been ridden out of town on rails, which is quite horrible to watch. Some persons are set upon and punched out because they voice their Patriot feelings in the town square.

"Don't argue with Tories in the streets, Cassie. Don't take sides in this fight. One of these days you're going to get hurt. Wait. Wait quietly. Our day will come," Papa tells me.

I tell Papa not to worry about me. It is too hard to wait and not take sides, because I am an extreme Patriot. Often on travels about town, I stand on the steps of a building and tell young people like me their loyalty to King George is senseless. I do get young people like myself to listen to me, especially when I am dressed up in my finery, standing outside of Mr. Douglas's store or in the town square. People listen to me when I speak to them in my dress-up gowns from Paris, which is a good reason for Papa to buy me more gowns from Paris, I tell him. It does no good though. Papa simply delivers another lecture to me.

I'm not Papa's only worry, though. Papa holds secret midnight meetings of the Committee of Safety in our parlor with Patriots willing to fight for separation from England. The men arrive in the dark of night and tie up their horses to hitching posts some distance from one another on our property; they then walk silently into our parlor to sit in a tight circle lit by the gloom of a single candle. Papa is chairman of the committee that keeps track of Tories' schemes. Last week Tories planned to disable Patriot boats by cutting down their sails. The plan failed because Papa found out about it, and he and his friends hid their boats in a cove out Huntington way moving them back to Cow Neck and loading them up in the middle of the night and sailed to York City with their produce.

As I leaned over the whitewashed porch railing, I imagined David whirling me 'round to the music of the Allemande, the hornpipe, and the formal minuet. How my gown would flare and flow!

I jolted upright from the porch rail. My stepmother Hannah opened the door and let it bang shut behind her. Jangling her keys, she managed to send the cats skittering across the porch in a flurry of yowls and flying fur.

"Cassie, go to the springhouse and bring back my apple pie, peach pie and my cherry pie, also the dish of black and red currants. Be very careful with them." Not "Good Morning, Cassie," just instructions and directions. I gritted my teeth. Hannah stood almost six feet in height, taller than any of the women in town and, most likely, taller than any of the women in Ireland, I do believe. At this early hour, to my absolute astonishment, she wore the shimmering green silk gown Papa bought for her in York City for today's festivities. The gown made a vivid contrast with her flaming red hair and was the same color green as her eyes. I tried not to stare. *What is she doing so early in the morning dressed in this beautiful shimmering gown? I just despair of Hannah. Don't say anything. Don't even ask her why she would be dressed in her finery at dawn.* Sticking out from under her gown were the tips of the muddy brown boots she wore the day Papa married her and brought her home to Scott Mansion, a year and a half ago. And who knew why he married her in the first place? I was doing perfectly well cooking for Papa before she came along. She had worn those boots every day since she came to us. I was trying to get used to her ways, not trying very hard, I admit, but didn't she have any pretty shoes? *Do not stare at her feet*, I told myself.

"Cassie, you're building castles in the sky again. Now, there are chocolates in a dish along with the pastries. Bring them too. Be very careful. Chocolate is hard to come by these days and costs much."

As if I don't know that. But my papa is rich and can afford all the chocolate we can eat.

Hannah smiled down at me as though she were the queen and I was the tiny cat looking up at her. "Go now, Cassie, if you please."

I did not please. Hannah handed me a big, flat basket. I snatched the keys from her hand and walked across the grass, wet from morning dew, to where Papa had built the springhouse resting on sticks over the running brook, where we kept our milk, butter, and baked goods cold and protected from the animals.

Muttering to myself, I didn't see the tree root sticking up almost at the water's edge. I tripped and fell over it, more annoyed than hurt. Hannah's keys dropped from my fingers into the rushing water. They skipped along the rocks of Berry creek and flowed fast in its downward pitch. If I didn't hurry after them, they would empty out into our vast Long Island Sound. All this I thought in a second. Plunging into the cold water, trying to hold my shift up to my knees so it wouldn't get wet, I slipped and slid over small pebbles, whirlpools, and over rocks in my bare feet. Drenched to my knees, I reached down and pulled the keys out of the water just before they lurched into deeper waters. My feet were cut and bloody. How would I dance later? But I told myself I would find a way. I generally did.

The wet springhouse key wouldn't turn in the lock at first, but after two more tries, I was able to wrench the door open. I lifted the pies off the shelf and laid them in the basket and then took out the dish of currants. There was the chocolate lurking in the back of the pies. I jammed it into the by now full basket. Carrying the basket was hard work because it was unbalanced, but I walked slowly through the wet morning grass to the porch.

Hoofbeats! I felt them in the ground before I actually saw Bucyrus gallop into our front yard. Mr. Douglas jumped down from his horse, not even bothering to tie him up to the post. Grabbing a rolled-up paper sticking out of his saddlebag, he ran across the yard and up the porch steps. The Declaration!

I picked up my shift and tried to run, gripping the basket in my other arm. Mr. Douglas was halfway up the porch steps. When I got to the porch, I set the basket down on the bottom step. I ran up two steps at a time and caught the door before it slammed on Mr. Douglas's back. I was in Papa's study almost on the heels of Mr. Douglas.

There was the Document, spread out across Papa's desk. I put my hands on it and helped Papa and Mr. Douglas smooth it out. Papa then reached into the bottom drawer of his desk and lifted up a bottle of rum.

"I propose a toast, Matthew, to Mr. Jefferson and to our Congress! Imagine, Cassie, to compose such a document. Why, it is a work of such clear thinking and precise writing that no American can fail to see the English king as a damned tyrant." Papa handed Mr. Douglas a glass, and they toasted.

"Now, a toast to you, Matthew, for bringing back the document to us!" They clinked glasses again and drank. Rivulets of sweat and grime ran down Mr. Douglas's face from riding hard all night long, but his mouth moved into a wide smile. Dark fingerprints smudged his glass. I was filled with admiration for our messenger. *He's a true Patriot. If I could only do something brave for my country I would, yet I shall. I vow to myself I shall.*

"Matthew, after I read out this copy of the document to the people, we should put it in a public space so everyone can see it again and again."

"On the wall over the pickle barrel in my store, Judge."

"The perfect place," Papa said.

It was then I heard a rumbling, followed by loud, angry yells. I ran out of the room and out to the porch, bumping into the rail, not believing what I saw on the grass.

Hannah stood flailing pie plates leaking apple slices and red currant juice. Chunks of chocolate, peach pie, and cherry juice smeared and clung to the front of her shimmery green gown as she tried to pull the crumbling mixture from the maws of our cows. But Jamie and Jubie didn't even brush her away, just kept filling their slobbering tongues with apple slices and peach crusts and the sweet cherries. Broken pie crusts slid down their maws; chocolate dripped from their tongues. Our dog, Benjamin, trotted over and tore into the bowl of currants. Hannah hit him over the nose with a pie plate. He only stopped chewing long enough to look up and gnash his purple teeth at her. Meanwhile, Bucyrus, and our horse, Star, trotted over, between them edging Hannah out of the way with their flanks; together, they lapped up half-pies themselves. When I saw the front of Hannah's gown Papa had bought for her in York City especially for today, its beads and buttons and its lacey inserts stained with apple slices, peach and cherry syrup, purple currant juice, and sticky brown chocolate, all of it running down the front of her beautiful green silk gown, I could hardly look. I covered my face with my hands and peeked out through the spaces in my fingers. Just then a swarm of high-flying bees dove down and circled Hannah, landing on Bucyrus's nose. The horse butted his head into the cows' flanks, and the cows, startled and stung, backed up into Hannah, knocking her to the ground. Having finished eating, Benjamin ambled away from the whole business to rest in the morning sunshine.

Hannah's face, when she was able to stand, was red, splotchy with tears. Her ripped gown showed part of her shoulder. When she saw Papa, Mr. Douglas, and me rooted to the porch floor, staring down at her in the grass, she gathered her gown around her ankles, stood up tall, and climbed the steps slowly. When she got to the top, she turned and looked at me. "Why, Cassie? Why?"

"I'm sorry, Hannah." I stood mute as a milepost. *It was my fault.*

The gown Papa had bought for Hannah in York City was ruined. She stood at the door for a few seconds and then walked past Papa and went into the house. Papa followed Hannah into the house and did not come out while I ran to the well to draw pails of water to throw on the porch steps. Mr. Douglas stepped gingerly down the steps, gave me a tilt of his head, got back on his horse, and rode home.

CHAPTER TWO

Four thirty in the afternoon

The sun stumbled along the horizon, so bright it tricked the dull pewter plates and tankards into shiny silver objects. Behind me on the wide meadow, ladies carried jars of jam and pitchers of lemon water to tables decked out in red-checked cloths. Standing in the flat meadow looking down, I watched thousands of water diamonds sparkle on our Long Island Sound below; looking up, I saw a cloudless sky, bluer than indigo.

People stepped out of their cottages and cabins and walked past their kitchen gardens of lettuce, parsley, rosemary, and dill, past their fences bordered with primroses, to make the long climb up the path to the meadow on Shepherd's Hill. Mr. Ferguson, our fiddler, played a wild hornpipe to welcome folks as they stepped off the dirt path and onto the grass. I almost could not keep from dancing. But I remembered it just wouldn't be seemly for the judge's daughter to be doing a jig on the green. Also, I felt sadness inside myself every time I thought of Hannah's stained, ripped new gown and the look on her face when she turned and asked me, "Why,

Cassie?" Later, I heard her crying in the room she shared with Papa. She only came out to fill her teacup every now and then. It had taken a good while before Papa would speak to me and then only to tell me Hannah would not come to the reading, nor the Liberty Feast. He said Hannah did not want to wear her everyday muslin gown. It was a quiet mansion in the morning. I could see the sadness in Papa's eyes.

I went to her. "Hannah, please open the door. I didn't mean for anything bad to happen to your baked goods. Please forgive me."

She opened the door a crack. "I won't be coming. That's all, Cassie," she said and shut the door firmly.

In a way, I did think luck was with Hannah when her pastries got ruined; she couldn't bake, anyway. Her biscuits were brittle. She always left some ingredient out of her pies. Yet my brothers Max and Ernest liked her cooking and her baking, or at least they pretended to. They laughed and joked with her. They talked to her and even gave her a kiss when they came home after working outside.

Papa was very angry with me as we walked together up the steep path. I knew what he was thinking. *Cassie, you've done it again.*

Yes, I had. But I didn't mean to do it. It wasn't something I had planned. It all happened so fast: Mr. Douglas came into the yard. I dropped the pastries on the step; I didn't think. I was in such a rush to see the Declaration. It just happened. I didn't mean it to happen. But it did.

Anyway, I had to get over feeling awful. We all were here to hear Papa proclaim our independence from England, and even if Hannah were standing in the meadow now wearing her green silk gown, new and pretty and unstained, I would not dance. *This is a serious day,* I reminded myself; *there is plenty of time to dance after Papa reads out the Declaration. I am the daughter of the judge, after all; Papa has not disowned me, at least not yet, and I'm not without a conscience. Besides, I shall dance later at the Liberty Feast with David Van Essen. I shall forget all that has happened so far today. I will try hard to please Papa.* "We shall speak of this later, Cassie" was the last thing he said to me on the path up the hill. His voice was his court voice: stern. Even so, Papa never stayed mad for long. After all his years as judge, he gave second chances to people who broke the law. Would he give me a second chance? When it came to Hannah, I just didn't know.

It was too hot on the hill. I fanned myself with Mama's Watteau fan Papa had bought for her in Paris. David would be here any minute. I wished I could take my mobcap off before he climbed the hill. It was ruining my French hairstyle. No use reminding myself that girls who didn't wear the mobcap were thought of as conceited showoffs. Nonsense! It was too hot to wear this stifling cap. I pulled it from my head. I was free and cool, and my hair bounced. What a lovely feeling! Suddenly, I felt all better. If Hannah chose to stay home because of her dirty, ripped gown, that was her choice.

There they all came! Townspeople—excited, happy, talking, laughing, clinging to the hands of children, neighbors, and friends. They waved and smiled at me when they turned off the path into the meadow. Many stopped to chat with me until I was more than fair pleased.

"Cassie, you look lovely in that gown," Miss Hoary, the town schoolteacher praised me. Suzie Mancks and I worked as her assistants in the schoolhouse. Talk was that when she was young Miss Hoary fell in love with someone. We didn't know who. They never married. It was a sad time for her. Now she was older and beyond the first flush of beauty, as Papa would say. I told her how pretty she looked in her new blue calico gown that had a blossom green velvet ribbon as a sash around its waist.

There came sour Mrs. Comerford, who never said anything nice unless it was steeped in vinegar. "Look at you, Cassie Scott, a grown-up young lady, with your gown. I ain't never seen that gown on you before. I'm thinkin' it's your mama's, and your hair all turned up on the bottom? You should be wearin' your cap. It ain't proper, you know, for a young lady like yourself, to go without. I'll bet you got some color from roses on those fat cheeks of yours."

"Thankee," I said through gritted teeth. "I'm proud to wear my mama's gown, Mrs. Comerford. And I did rub my cheeks with roses. You look a sight for sore eyes yourself," I said with a smile and a curtsy, *as though "sore eyes" would even look at her,* I thought.

"Hmph! Who are you to tell me what I look like?" Mrs. Comerford turned on me. "I always did think you Scotts acted uppity. " Mrs. Comerford quitted me, obviously offended.

I guess she thought I was putting on airs, which was something Papa was always telling me not to do. "Try to make friends, Cassie. It don't do to act superior." *Now I've done it. If I could just keep my mouth shut.* Later, I would go to Mrs. Comerford and say something nice to compliment her. It was getting late; David was not walking up the path yet. Why, it was past five o'clock.

Along came Mr. Bailey, the blacksmith, for whom David worked in his forge, one of the last persons to climb up the hill. *Was David with you today? Did he go home to change his clothes?* He smiled and tilted his hat to me, and then he walked on, and my questions remained unasked. I was too proud to show I was troubled.

There were my brothers, Ernest and Max, horsing around now under the shade of a sycamore tree with a crowd of militia boys, all friends. David was not with them. I looked across at Papa. He was in the pine grove smiling, chatting to people.

Our sawyer and gravedigger had managed to turn the huge ox on its iron spit, and the aroma from across the meadow made my mouth water. But that was just the beginning: How could I keep myself from dancing! It was not possible, no matter how badly my feet ached in Mama's blue shoes, no matter how mean I felt about Hannah. I still wanted to dance.

So much bustle in the meadow. The cold potato salad, the pickle relish, pies, pastries, and cobblers, all of it looking so delicious! The ladies unpacked them all in ice as I watched. A queue of men set up a barrel of hard beer under the sycamore tree; there would be small beer for the ladies. Where was David? I wished he would get here. Papa had put on his spectacles; he was almost ready to read the Declaration.

CHAPTER THREE

"No. No!" This could not be happening. Plodding up the hill came Hannah with old Eban, the town handyman, her only friend, whose wife Sally had died only months ago. Eban was lonely; he loved to talk, and he found a good listener in Hannah. He was now too old to fix roofs, but he did the odd job here and there and gossiped with all the wives. He held a pitchfork in one hand and a glass of cider beer in the other. Hannah walked beside him, resting her fingers lightly on his wrist.

Hannah had not changed her gown. It was still covered with stains. The rip in her sleeve had split open; her arm lay bare from her shoulder down to her elbow. Her hair was a mess, matted and full of crumbs and pieces of piecrust. How could she? She looked so wretched. Eban, wearing his all-weather 'coon skin hat in the heat, whispered comforting words in her ear as they drew near. Her light touch on Eban's wrist became a clutching grip.

I ran down the hill to stop them. "Hannah! What are you doing here?"

"As you see, I've come for the reading of the Declaration and the Liberty Feast," she said. The two of them had not stopped walking, even though I planted myself in front of them.

"But, Hannah, look at your gown, so messy and dirty from the animals this morning. You must go home and change. You will embarrass Papa. Your sleeve is ripped. Your shoulder is showing. You must change. Please, Hannah." I walked alongside them, trying to reason with Hannah.

Hannah stopped and brought herself up to her full height. "I'll do no such thing. Your father gave me this gown to wear for the reading and the celebration, and I'm proud to wear it."

"But you can't go to hear Papa read the Declaration looking like you've been dragged through mud."

"And whose fault is that, Cassie?" Hannah said, reaching up to push a sticky clump of hair back from her forehead.

"I've said I'm sorry, and I am. What will people think if you come to the reading as you are? Can't you understand it was an accident? I just didn't think."

"You didn't think. I am thinking. I'm thinking 'twas no accident. I see your father is getting ready to read. Shall we go on, Eban?"

"Eban," I pleaded, putting a hand on his shoulder. "Can you not persuade Hannah to go home and change?" But it was useless. Eban stayed mute, and the two walked together into the pine grove. I turned once, looked for David one last time, and then followed some yards behind the two of them.

In the shade of the pines, people looked at Hannah and then looked again. Their looks expressed surprise and more than that distaste. Hannah held her head high. She walked with Eban through the crowd of townsfolk, not looking to her left or right until the two of them had made their way into the crowd a few feet in front of Papa's circle of mounded earth. Hannah's eyes were still wet and red from crying. I felt the color rise in my cheeks. *How could Papa have married this crazy woman?* But Papa's look and his smile at Hannah showed only his pleasure at seeing her standing there in front of him.

Eban shook hands and greeted people near him, acting as though he were out on the green after church service on Sunday. Hannah stood silently by his side. After a while, people nodded to Hannah, half smiling to acknowledge her presence but quickly looking away, not wanting to embarrass her in her stained clothes. Chattering people inside the pine grove turned interested, hopeful faces toward Papa, who waited on the mound of dirt for silence. Everyone quieted as he picked up the paper in both hands. In that moment, a shaft of sunlight shot through the trees onto Papa's shoulders, and a slight breeze flapped his collar, tossing his sandy hair this way and that. He looked out at the crowd of people standing before him. Then a deep shade encircled us from the tops of the trees down to the carpet of pine needles under our feet. It was quiet as a church except for the sighing of the wind. Curious, the cows had gathered outside the pine grove and gaped into the trees, their great maws methodically chewing chunks of green grass. David was nowhere. Hannah looked like a large mistreated orphan, and I, who had started out this day with such wonderful expectations, felt my face crumple into tears.

Papa began to read. When he got to the second paragraph, he stopped and looked out at the crowd, leaned forward, and pronounced each word slowly and with great expression.

"We hold these truths to be self-evident, that all men are created equal, that they are endowed by their creator with certain unalienable Rights, that among these are Life, Liberty and the pursuit of Happiness . . ."

Cheers, whistling, clapping. The crowd roared approval. Old Eban waved his pitchfork up and down in one hand and sloshed his glass of cider beer into the air with the other. Miss Hoary, our schoolteacher, always so reserved, jumped up and down and did a bit of a jig. My goodness! I couldn't believe my eyes. Papa picked up the document and began to read again. An expression of outrage settled on his face so strong it strengthened his words until Papa seemed as fierce as that fiery Patriot in Massachusetts, Sam Adams. He rang out the words with the outrage we all felt against this evil ruler. "The King has kept standing armies in our towns." Catcalls, curses, grumblings, called down upon the king from all of us inside the pine grove.

"For quartering large bodies of armed troops among us." Whistles and jeers filled the summer air.

"If I could only get me hands on the scoundrel," Nathanial Thayer, Nate's father, spoke slowly, grinding the words out of his mouth in as loud and menacing a tone as he could muster, "he'll wish he was already dead." I shivered. I knew Mr. Thayer meant what he said. His bull-like arms had wrestled many a wolf to the ground and killed it with a swipe of one arm.

"For imposing Taxes on us without our consent."

"Aye, and he keeps us poor while he enriches himself!" James Fanshawe, our next-door neighbor, spat out in a loud, bitter burst.

"No more!" the crowd yelled out. Papa stopped reading, waiting for silence. "No more!" the people yelled back in one voice. It was an outcry that could be heard over in Cedar Grove on the next peninsula.

"He has plundered our seas, ravaged our coasts, burnt our towns, and destroyed the lives of our people," Papa yelled out over the noise of the crowd.

"War!" the men chanted, lifting muskets, poles, pikes, and pistols up to the sky. "War! War!" Papa waited for silence a long minute.

After the furious cry subsided, he continued in a subdued voice, "He has taken us Captives on the high Seas." At this, the people were silent. Many Long Island fishermen had perished upon capture by British ships invading waters along our coast. Those men were missed.

"My friends," my father said, "this be our resolve."

"[T]hese United Colonies are, and of Right ought to be Free and independent States; that they are Absolved from all Allegiance to the British Crown, and that all political connection between them and the State of Great Britain, is and ought to be totally dissolved, and that as Free and independent States, they have full Power to levy War, conclude Peace, contract Alliances, establish Commerce...[W]ith a firm reliance on the protection of divine Providence, we mutually pledge to each other our Lives, our Fortunes and our sacred Honor."

"Huzzah! Huzzah! Huzzah!" burst out from the townsfolk. Our militia shot off a volley of precious bullets into the air. Bonfires erupted into flames. Sparkle wheels made points of blue and red light. Sky rockets burst into colors. And amid the hubbub, church bells pealed in triumph all across our peninsula. I could hardly hear myself cheer in the noise. Everyone crowded around Papa to shake his hand, slap him on the back, and hold the document for themselves. Passed from hand to hand for all to see and touch, the paper made its way through the crowd. It was Jubilation Day!

Hannah stood alone and silent in the whirl of noise and commotion surrounding us. She watched as Papa was lifted onto the shoulders of several brawny men and carried aloft. Again, wild cheers rippled through the crowd. Eban shook every extended hand and pummeled every man's shoulder, lifting his glass over and over in salutes to our newly born nation. If I chose this minute to speak to Hannah softly, would she forgive me and go home to change her gown?

I walked through the pine needles to get to her. I spoke softly, right next to her ear. "Please believe me, Hannah, I never meant any harm. I just forgot everything when I saw Mr. Douglas ride into our yard with the Declaration. I was desperate to see it."

Hannah looked at me as though she had bitten into a lemon. She didn't answer. Her face was set in stone. I walked away.

Mrs. Fanshawe came by and spoke under her breath to me, "Well, what just happened?"

"Hannah's pies got ruined this morning," I said, mopping my eyes.

"Mind you, that's no tragedy." Mrs. Fanshawe, like the other ladies on our lane, did not much like Hannah. Whether it was her loud Irish voice, which always put me in mind of a commander giving orders, or her loud singing of hymns while she washed clothes in the big pail outside the kitchen, or mayhap it was because she didn't spin cloth or do embroidery or give teas or make quilts as the other ladies did. I didn't know but I supposed it was really because Hannah was so different from the others.

"It wouldn't be, except it was I who ruined them."

"Well, don't trouble yourself. I'm sure you didn't intend it to happen. Come on, I hear Mr. Ferguson's fiddle and Miss Place's flute. Look! Mr. Fanshawe is waving to me. I do believe he wants to dance with me. Glory!"

Mrs. Fanshawe picked up her gown and ran to Mr. Fanshawe, who grabbed her waist and pulled her into a circle of dancers just starting a quadrille. Then it seemed as if all the ladies on our lane were up dancing. I turned back and looked once more at Hannah. She was gazing at the dancers with envy on her face. Not that anyone would want to dance with her looking as downcast and dirty as she did. Hannah was looking on from the outside.

But then, Hannah was used to standing on the outside looking in. On Tuesday afternoons, the ladies walk past the mansion to Mrs. Fanshawe's house for their quilting party. Hannah always managed to be out in the garden when the ladies passed by. She waved to them, and they waved back, but they kept walking. At the Liberty Feast today, she was hoping that her baked goods would smooth the way to making friends with the town ladies. Hannah didn't tell me, but I knew it from the way she acted. Every morning after Papa left for work this past week, she had held up her new green gown to the glass and admired herself. Then she would practice her good manners. 'Isn't it warm out today?" she would say into the glass, pretending her own image staring back at her was a finely dressed town lady. 'My blood is curdling inside of me from the heat!" I watched Hannah practice being social, and I knew that her attempts would land like bricks on the women's ears. I wondered would the ladies have liked her any better if they had tasted her pastries. I didn't think so.

Papa finally remembered Hannah. He walked to her and put his jacket around her shoulders. He didn't seem embarrassed. Tables filled up. People talked and laughed across the plates of food and tankards of beer and lemon water. I walked out of the shade into the sunlight back to the edge of the meadow. No one climbed the path. My heart sank. David had said he would meet me here before Papa spoke. Why wasn't he here?

But my brother Max and Suzie Mancks, my best friend, were. And they walked toward me out of the pines. Suzie wore a yellow gown, the color of buttercups. She had made it from muslin bought from Jasper Deecke, the Tory, in his Dry Goods store, from whom no Patriot in town bought anything since it was found out that Mr. Deecke had been seen practicing drills with Tories in Sunken Meadow. Now, Mr. Deecke wanted to take his family up to Montreal, where he could sell his notions and dry goods and live unchallenged under the king's rule. Other families had already left for Montreal; David Van Essen had said good-bye to his mother and father a month before in the middle of the night; he was devastated when they left. Though he stayed in Cow Neck and threw his lot in with the rebels, he missed his parents terribly, I knew. His father had deeded the cottage over to David before he left Cow Neck, and so it was a final parting from his family.

Suzie had incurred the town's anger, and the uptown ladies were quick to start a gaggle of backyard gossip. In kitchens, over wash lines, in the lanes, and in Mr. Douglas's store, townsfolk expressed their opinions. People shouted "Tory" at Suzie, turning their backs to her, refusing to say "hello." Some women spat at her feet. It was all horrible for Suzie; I was afraid for her, but at the same time she was wrong to do what she did. I never said so to her face, but I'm sure she knew. I walked her home from the schoolhouse every day while the two of us constantly looked behind us on the path.

My brother Max heard the news first that James Ellmore, neither Patriot nor Tory—just a home-grown troublemaker—had thrown a rock, missing Suzie by a hair. My brother Max was angry. He appeared outside James Ellmore's front door.

"Come out, you coward! I'll beat the stuffing out of you," Max shouted. The boy who had thrown the rock at Suzie would not answer the door. "Come out!" Max banged on the door. The front door opened, and Mrs. Ellmore appeared in her apron.

"Send him out here while I give him the beating he wants," Max yelled.

"He ain't home. He didn't do anything," Mrs. Ellmore shouted back at Max, "only spoke against that Tory girl, Suzie Mancks."

"That right? Well, I can see him hidin' behind that door. You hear me, James? You better not show your face outside this house 'cause I'll fix you good if you do."

I noticed James and his mother were not here on Shepherd's Hill today.

Mr. Deecke was open about his plan to move his family to Montreal. Everyone in town knew. At a midnight meeting of the Committee of Safety, Mr. Isaac Harkens, Sarah Harkens's father, the richest man in town, stood up, scraping his chair on the floor. I listened hard with my ear stuck against the stem of one of Mama's wine goblets against the wall separating my bedroom from the parlor.

"Jasper Deecke has been drilling with a Loyalist unit for two months. Now he wants to move up to Canada. I say he deserves a good dose of Patriot justice, Judge."

"I say he don't," Papa objected.

But before he could get out another word, Mr. Harkens was on his feet again; I heard the chair scrape the floor. "He don't deserve to leave peacefully. He could go up to Canada and double back here with a Loyalist unit with arms to take up against us. I say, let's give him something to remember." I heard Mr. Harkens's fist hit the table.

"Another knock on the table, Isaac, and you'll be out of here for good," Papa said. "Jasper's been friend to us for all these years. He wants to leave with his family and move up to Montreal to make a new start," Papa said. I heard his gavel hit the table. "We'll not shame him or humiliate him, Isaac. Jasper will leave for Montreal with his family in peace."

"Judge, you're too soft. What say all here? Let's give Jasper Deecke a bath in hot pitch tar and stick him with feathers and then ride him out of town on a rail. That'll fix him."

"That will not happen, Isaac," Papa spoke in his court voice.

"Judge, you ain't in the courtroom right now. Let's take a vote."

There was silence for a minute. "All right," Papa said. "Let's take a vote. All those in favor of Jasper taking his family up to Montreal peacefully, say 'aye.'" There was a chorus of whispered "ayes."

"Unanimous except for you, Isaac. The ayes have it," Papa said. "Jasper Deecke takes his family to Montreal without incident, and Godspeed to him." The next minute there was the bang of a chair falling backward and angry boots striding across the parlor. Outside, Mr. Harkens unhitched his horse and rode away in the night.

Early the next morning, Papa rode over to the Deecke cottage and helped load up the big farm wagon with belongings. He rode all the way to Flushing with the family in case anyone would accost them. I was proud of Papa that day, too.

Today, a new day had dawned for us and for Suzie; she was happy. She held hands with Max, and the two of them seemed deep in conversation walking toward me. The slurs and rude remarks were over, and here she was, present for the reading of the document. It was hard for Suzie to face the town. But with Max at her side, she had more confidence.

"You look so pretty in your new gown, Suzie," I said, smiling at her.

Max looked at her with the light of love in his eyes. She pirouetted in front of him, and he caught her around the waist, lifted her up, so that her gown billowed in the breeze, and then set her down firmly. "That should hold you," he said.

"That'll do me fine, thank you, Max!" Suzie said with a pert smile. "I'm glad you like my gown, Cassie." We three stood in the sunshine. "Your papa gave a wonderful reading of the document, Cassie. But it true scared me, even so, with the people yelling, 'War!'" Susan said.

"It did me too," I admitted.

"You girls are always painting the devil on the walls! There will be war, but it'll be over by Christmas Day. General Washington will send the redcoats packing. Don't you fret." Max sounded so convinced I almost believed him.

"My papa will lead the militia. I'm afraid for him." A cloud passed over Suzie's face. "And for you too, Max, and Ernest."

"There's none better to lead us than your pa, Suzie," Max said, putting an arm around her shoulders. "Your father is unafraid and a true leader. All the boys trust him."

"They say British ships sail into New York Bay more and more every day. The *Globe* said there were so many British ships in the

Narrows that one couldn't see the opposite shore." Suzie's face clouded.

"Yes, I read that too, and I heard that a man standing on the Brooklyn shoreline said it looked like all of London was afloat in New York Bay. Imagine what a sight. It does make one fearful," I said.

"Not me," Max said. "I don't care if they've got the whole British navy in the bay. We'll fight, and we'll win." But then he lightened. "And when we win, you and I will get married, Suzie, as we plan to do."

Suzie's cheeks colored. "That's right, Cassie. When Max comes back from the fighting, he and I will wed."

"Truly?" For answer, they both beamed smiles at me.

"Will you help me sew up a wedding dress, Cassie?" Suzie asked.

"Yes, I will. It'll be fun taking the ferry down to York City and buying material there. Then we'll have lunch at City Tavern. I knew someday you two would get married." I was thrilled for my brother and Suzie, but even as I said it, I felt a pang in my heart. *David isn't here. Where is my beau?*

"Wait a minute, you two! Let's take one thing at a time. The feast is ready. Let's go eat for now." Max's nose was in the air, sniffing the good smells.

"You go ahead," I told them. "I'll just wait a while longer for David." The two of them drifted across the grass. Miss Hoary handed Max a heavy platter of ox meat to set down on a nearby table and Suzie a bowl of gravy. It was good to see that people welcomed Suzie.

CHAPTER FOUR

"What a day! What a day! But where's your beau, Cassie?" Sarah Harkens called out to me from across the green.

"Hey, Sarah." Here came the princess, Suzie's name for her. How much did I not want to talk to Sarah today of all days? I'd heard her stories over and over again: how her precious ancestors came to America on the *Mayflower*. How proud she was to tell us the family had been in Cow Neck four generations after moving from Boston. How her father, Isaac Harkens, made a fortune trading furs for the West India Company; how he had built the best house in the town; and on and on and on.

Yet Sarah's father, Isaac Harkens, who had been warm for giving Mr. Deecke a bath in pitch tar and feathers, was not here today with Mrs. Harkens. Everyone knew he was a not-so-secret Tory just as we all knew he was welcomed into the Committee of Safety just so he could be fed wrong information to report back to the British soldiers in their camp at Bowling Green.

Sarah was dressed today in one of her Paris shifts made of dense blue material with a good many ribbons and bows attached. A glittery necklace of an orange hue hung from her crowded bodice, and lacey inserts were everywhere.

"He certainly makes himself scarce, don't he?" Sarah craned her neck to take in the green meadow.

"Who?" I said, taking in the whole confusing jumble of colors and jewels.

"David Van Essen, your beau. That's who."

"Sarah," I said, out of patience with her, "why don't you get a beau for yourself? There's a nice-looking boy standing by the pie table. Go, say hello."

"Don't go managing my business, Cassie."

"Then don't manage mine." I had to get rid of her. I was not in the mood for jousting with Sarah; she was always jealous of my friendship with David. She always wanted David for herself. *If he doesn't get here soon, she can have him. Mayhap it's good riddance.*

Sarah dragged me from my thought. "By the by, Cassie, I heard every word your Papa read to us from the Declaration, all so unnecessary since my family read it in the *Globe* last week."

"Well, now we heard it for ourselves. Shouldn't you find a seat at some table or another, Sarah?" Snapping back was the only way I knew of to get rid of her. And yet, she still stood.

"What do you mean, sending me off? I'm not done talking. My papa is the biggest landowner here in Cow Neck. He should have read out the Declaration."

"And my father is the judge." Sarah had no answer for that. She turned and walked with her head up toward Max and Suzie's table, where she plopped down with a thud next to Suzie, and promptly pushed hard against her, moving Suzie off the bench onto the ground. She sat down hard. I looked through slatted fingers to see what would happen next.

"There now! We have the bench all to ourselves." Sarah smiled over at Max. Max gave Sarah a look too dark for words.

"Oh no. You don't." Suzie got up with Max's help and sat down again giving Sarah a good, solid push; then Suzie turned her face toward Max, who began to brush reverently away at the dirt smudges on her face and her shoulders, which held odd blades of grass and bits of dirt. Nobody helped Sarah get up, and she had to brush herself off. *Good for Suzie.*

"Hello, pretty girl."

"Where were you?" I turned, forgetting Sarah and Suzie, and stood face-to-face with David. I tried to be angry, but it was hard. He looked so handsome and tall with that shock of blond hair falling over his forehead; I instantly forgave him, but I had to show some pique.

"Out on Berry Creek, fishing."

"Fishing? The day of the Declaration?"

"Yeah. The blues were running," he said, looking up at the sky.

"But you said you would be here for the reading."

"I just told you the blues were running," he said, not looking at me but gazing over the grass at the tables.

"And the Declaration you weren't here for?"

"I read the whole thing. And I'm here. Come on. The food's out. Let's catch up with Max and Suzie."

"But..."

"I'll tell you later, Cassie."

"Tell me what?" I did not enjoy running to keep up with David's strides across the meadow. David waved to Max. We slid into the empty seats opposite him and Suzie. Sarah had now managed to slide into the seat next to my brother Ernest, the seat he was saving for Betsy Rose Thayer, the girl he walked out with in the early evenings. Betsy Rose was just coming across the meadow with her mother and father. I waved and she waved back.

Betsy Rose looked at our table for a few seconds with a confused expression on her face. Seeing Sarah seated at Ernest's elbow, she was unsure of whether to approach. She sat down at the table with her parents.

Ernest was angry. He leaned over and spoke low to Sarah, "I was saving that seat for Betsy Rose." His face was rock solid.

"It isn't that I wanted to sit next to you," she replied. "I'd much rather sit next to Max."

"You should have." Ernest got up, walked over to Betsy Rose, took her hand, and brought her over to our table. Sarah had no choice. She moved. But Ernest and Betsy Rose sat closer together by choice, and Sarah ended up with more room than she needed so that it was terribly obvious to everyone that she didn't have a partner as we all did. *Sometimes I did feel sorry for Sarah. Not this time though.*

My brother Ernest and my beau David were best friends, but Ernest knew how to rile David up. He got a sly look on his face. "I shot a nice, plump hen quail yesterday right on the path to your place, David."

David exploded, "You dog! I was fattenin' up that quail for a good meal."

"That quail made a real nice stew Hannah put up last night." David looked like he was going to strangle Ernest.

"Nah, breathe easy, David." Ernest laughed. "I didn't shoot that bird. I just caught myself a rabbit. It weren't even on your property."

"Well, then, you're welcome to it. I ain't worried about no rabbit. We got hundreds running around."

I turned to David and whispered, "Why were you fishing while my father read the document?"

Again he ignored me. He shouted across the table to Ernest, "I'll catch that bird tomorrow, so it don't haunt you no more."

Ernest grinned. "Better get up early."

"That ain't no problem," David shot back.

I couldn't stand the wrangling between those two. Hard to believe they were best friends. "Please pour me a glass of cider, David." I finally had his attention. "What do you have to tell me?" I asked as he set the cider down in front of me.

"Later, Cassie."

I was supposed to be content with that answer. But I was not happy with it. I drank my cider, concentrating on the summer breezes filled with colors and rich smells. The ladies wore their best day gowns that had been taken out of their linen covers. They had shaken out the pale blue, yellow, rose, and apple blossom green gowns from their wraps and wore them proudly. They set platters of sliced-up, roasted ox and dishes of cabbage slaw and hot breads on the tables. Urns of hot, sweet coffee sat on each table. I looked over at Hannah sitting next to Papa, across from Eban. Papa had put his jacket around Hannah's shoulders. They seemed to all be talking, and even Hannah, still begrimed, spoke spiritedly to Papa and Eban. Her copper color hair shone in the sunlight, and her face brightened; somehow, even her green gown, where it wasn't trampled on by the animals, glowed.

Should I go there? No. I should not. There will be no more apologies from me. Mr. Ferguson played softly with his fiddle, and Miss Place, betrothed to Mr. Ferguson, made sweet music with her flute to accompany our meal. The talking was muted now, and we saw the sun slowly fall behind the rim of the world in the western sky. Coffee was poured into pewter cups. At our table, we ate our desserts and drank our cider with gusto. I was content for the moment.

"Come on, girls!" Mr. Ferguson struck his fiddle. I felt the ground shake as boys and girls and men and women, too, surged to the open part of the green. Muskets, the odd rifle, poles, pikes, and fowling pieces were shoved against trees. Boys in homespun grabbed girls in flounce gowns, and a loud, fast reel started up. I felt myself pulled into the fray. David and I skipped madly through a long line of arched arms to add our own outstretched arms across the end of the column while still another couple streaked through the arches.

Breathless, I slipped away from David and landed gasping for breath on a flat-topped boulder. David dropped down beside me. Neither of us could speak. When my heart slowed, I sat back and saw that twilight was beginning. I turned to him. "Were you really fishing while Papa read the document?"

"No." His face turned stony again.

"Where were you?" He turned from me and was silent.

On the meadow, some families still sat chatting to each other. Still, David did not look at me; I felt my heart sink. "Why won't you tell me? Don't you trust me?"

He spun around, his eyes black as coals, his voice harsh. "Because it's hard to tell you. That's why. Now, can't you leave me alone for a minute? You've been after me all afternoon."

"I haven't even seen you till after Papa proclaimed the Declaration today."

"All right, I'll tell you." He looked straight at me. "I won't be fighting."

"What do you mean?"

"I won't go to war against my king. I don't believe in the Patriot cause."

"You don't believe in the Patriot cause?" I sounded stupid even to myself, repeating his words. "I don't understand."

He looked me straight in the eyes. "I owe my loyalty to King George. Can I be clearer?"

"You're a Patriot. You practiced drills with all the militia boys right here on this meadow. What about the Sons of Liberty? You go to their meetings."

"I changed my mind. I owe my allegiance to my king. If you think about it, you do too, Cassie."

"I? I owe the king nothing. I belong to a free, independent nation. I belong to these new united states of America, as Mr. Jefferson says in the document—same as you belong. The Declaration has freed us from all ties with England."

David laughed. "A piece of paper freed you! You're going to stack that up against over seventeen hundred years of English history?"

"Yes. I am, David."

"I'm not. I'm leaving Cow Neck, Cassie, to visit my parents in Montreal. They write to me they are much happier since leaving Cow Neck. They like living in the English way, far from all these rowdies stirring up trouble. Then I shall leave Montreal and put on the red coat to serve my king."

I drew back like I had been punched in the stomach. "You're a coward!"

"I'm no coward. I shall fight for my king. Listen, Cassie." David grabbed my hand and held it tightly in his own. "Someday, this war coming to us will be over, and we shall be settled under peaceful English rule again. You and I will pick up where we left off."

I pulled my hand away. "No, we won't. I'll never pick up with a damned turncoat. That's what you are, David Van Essen, a turncoat and a coward."

David's eyes took on a dark cast. He clenched and unclenched his hands, which ever since we were children helped me bridle a horse, pull an ox, and gut a fish. We had built so many rafts together and sailed the Sound so often.

But he was no longer looking at me. He was looking out to the water and hadn't even heard me. His eyes were locked on the water.

"What is that speck on the horizon?" I almost feared to ask.

CHAPTER FIVE

The black speck loomed larger on the water.

"She's a British man-of-war, the HMS *Vulture*, ship of the line, about to make the turn into Berry Cove. See, the king's colors fly from her top mast." The pride in David's voice was unmistakable.

"What does she want?" I couldn't breathe easily.

"Probably just taking a look. Do you ken those two sixty-four-pounders aimed from the portside?"

"Aye."

"What a beauty!" Still some way out, the *Vulture* approached swiftly on the last of the incoming tide. The ship was huge, even this far off. When she made the turn from the river into our secluded bay, her sailors hauled ropes and chains across her deck and lowered an anchor out in the channel.

It became quiet on the meadow. Slowly, faces turned toward the water, and all chatting stopped as glasses were held halfway to lips. By now, everyone in the meadow had seen the ship, its rigging, masts, and mighty hull so out of place among our people's fishing boats. We could see the red coats of the officers standing on the

deck and the helmsman steering the wheel. There was much movement on the *Vulture*'s decks. Sailors lowered a rowboat. An officer
sat in its prow while two oarsmen rowed toward our shore. By now,
the sun had sunk below the horizon. People seemed to fade into
the twilight. I turned; David was not at my side. He had gone as
silently as he had appeared hours before.

Close to shore, the officer jumped down and waded to the
banks of Berry Cove. Our men aimed their muskets directly at
the officer. Seeing our men with their guns aimed at their leader,
British sailors aimed their rifles back at us. I held my breath. There
was not a sound on the hillside. I feared all our blood would spill
out over the green hillside on the very first day of our independence celebration.

The British officer climbed the path up to the meadow, and his
sailors followed in single file, holding their rifles in front of them.

"I am Colonel Daniel Braithwaite, Commander of HMS *Vulture*
standing at anchor in your harbor. I do not come as an enemy.
There is no need for a show of guns."

"Then have your men disarm," Papa shot back.

The colonel turned to his crew. "Guns down, men." The company of sailors lowered their guns to their sides.

Papa nodded and said, "How come you to be here?"

"Our maps and charts failed us. We sailed the ocean and turned
into this bay looking for the North River. We are due in York City.
We are quite lost and have run out of vittles."

"Spying, Judge! That's why they're here." The yeller was Eban,
now deep into his cups, weaving from side to side.

Some of his old friends took up the chant. "Spying. Grab them,
take them prisoners!"

It was almost dark. Only a thin rim of scarlet pierced the western sky.

"Stop!" Papa barked at Eban and his friends. He turned to the
British officer. "We shall give you food and water. Lower your guns,

boys," Papa said. At first no one moved. There was a moment of indecision among the men. I watched my brothers lower their guns. Others followed. Quietly, the ladies packed food onto trays, and put them into the hands of waiting British sailors. If we doubted their story of hunger, we soon became believers. The men almost skipped up the rope ladder, carrying the platters as though each was a gold brick. Not a crumb fell into the water. They made three trips carrying food back and forth from their ship to the ladies on shore carrying the food. Just about to climb up the rope ladder, the cry went up.

"Fire!" An uneven, jagged voice screaming in panic reached us, coming from a British sailor. A glow, more orange than the sun, crept raggedly round the edges of the *Vulture*'s decks, illuminating her gunwales and crawling up the sides of the ship, becoming a sheet of flame reaching out into the ship's rigging. In the orange brightness, a burly man plunged headfirst from the crow's nest into the sea. Broad-shouldered and tall, in an instant he was gone.

Shapes and shadows of redcoats splashed about in the water, swimming toward their ship. Thrown buckets by sailors on deck, they contrived to pass them up the ladder hand over hand from one sailor to the other filled with water to fight the flames. Eventually the redcoats made headway against the fire. The ship's sails were damaged and bent but they managed to row the ship out of the cove toward the open waters of the Sound, helped by the outgoing tide. Black smoke clouded the sky amid the dying flames. We townsfolk watched the British ship enter the deeper waters, all thoughts of our Liberty Feast fled. As the ship receded and became smaller and smaller, Eban aimed his flintlock at it and fired! We waited for an answering shot. But none came.

"Too busy rowing since their sails are useless," Ernest crowed. Everyone laughed. Yet, among us, the feeling of celebration was at an end. The last of the tablecloths was gathered up. We walked down the path to town and then through the woods back home.

Night fell, and there was no moon. I was the last person down the path. I kept hoping that David would come back, but though I looked behind me twice, the hill remained dark and empty. I caught up with the others.

"Papa, did you see the man who set the fire?" Ernest asked, a few steps ahead of me.

"Yep."

"Who was he?"

"That'd be Caleb Brewster, the whaleman."

"Well, them lobsterbacks be gone now, and we gave them a good dousing. 'Twere cold, too, that water in July." Max's words got a smattering of laughter, but then we were solemn again all the way home.

Papa and Hannah walked hand-in-hand home.

CHAPTER SIX

Hannah stood over the hearth, ready to take the pan of boiling water off the hob and pour it over the tea inside the warmed-up teapot. She had finally changed from her stained gown into a pink shift and brushed her hair up into a washerwoman's knot on top of her head. Papa sat at the table, and as I walked in the door, I saw that now the two of them were talking in the glow of the candle lamp just as Papa and Mama used to do when she was alive. The only thing different was the way Hannah poured her hot tea from the cup into the saucer, then picked up the saucer, blew on the tea, and finally sipped it from the saucer. It was a ritual she performed every night as she and Papa sat down for their last talk of the day and every morning when she sat alone for her elevenses tea.

In the daytime, she would mutter to herself over her tea. I heard her say she would leave and go back to Mrs. Curry's boarding house "if it comes to it." "How a body stays content here I don't know, what with the women who don't invite me to the quilting parties; even if I don't know how to quilt, I could learn. And them what passes me on the road without even a wave. Just keep lookin' down at the dirt, they do as I pass. I'll just go back to Mrs. Curry's where I had a friend. I miss Molly Anderson, the Swede. We had our tea together. I have money, and if it comes to it, I shall leave this place, as much as I love Philip." I had seen her chin jut up and her face turn resolute.

But tonight, she was all sweetness. "Have tea with us, Cassie." Papa stirred cream into his cup of tea. He looked up at me. "You've been crying, Cassie. What's happened?" He laid his spoon down on the table and waited. But if I told him, I would cry again.

"Nothing, Papa. I'll go to bed now."

"Cassie, Hannah understands you didn't mean to let her pastries get ruined. Don't you, Hannah?"

"Yes, I do." But she didn't look me in the eye when she said it. She looked away.

"There, Cassie. You see? It's all over now." Papa got up and pulled a chair out for me.

"Good night, Papa, Hannah." I turned and went upstairs to my room.

CHAPTER SEVEN

Earlier in June

A hot night in June 1776. A muffled knock on the kitchen door. David Van Essen opened his eyes from a tossing, turning attempt at sleep in his cot a few feet from the hearth. At first, he thought he had dreamed there was a knock. But then came a louder knock. It took some seconds before he could rub the sleep from his eyes and allow himself to believe that the tall man who sat across from him on the hard, dented wooden chair was Major William Tallmadge of the Continental army. The Major's words filled David's head with waves of excitement as he struggled to understand snatches of what he was saying. "I've observed you. I know of your midnight trips crossing the East River and then rowing to Bowling Green to meet with the Sons of Liberty. It takes courage to cross the river in daytime. You row over it at night."

"I've spent my whole life on boats, sir."

The lieutenant nodded, almost smiling. "We know," he said. "The Sons give us excellent reports about your bravery. You were part of the attack on the British installation on Bowling Green.

You are not given to promiscuous speech, and you are skillful in your handling of people. You are resourceful, and I have it from the Sons of Liberty—brave. In short, you're the kind of person we need."

David felt his cheeks get hot to think that the commander in chief would even know his name. *What does the major require of me?* His mind was a jumble of misgivings and anticipation.

"We need information. The general does not know when the enemy will be on the move to do battle. We need to know British troop strength, and we need an accurate count of British ships in York Bay, according to their classes: men-of-war, ships of the line, frigates, schooners, sloops. How many men does each ship carry? How many and what classes of guns?" He stopped speaking, looking at David's face in the shaft of moonlight measuring its way across the kitchen.

David stayed silent, looking intently at the major who now leaned forward, his hands folded across his knees. "You will be in a position to find out this information." He waited a few seconds. "You will be assigned to the First Loyalist camp on Staten Island. You may refuse. This is dangerous work. Know that if you're caught, you will be killed. You must think carefully before you decide. Think very carefully." When the major stood up, he dwarfed the kitchen. He held out his hand to the boy, and they shook.

"I'll be proud to do it," David said.

"Don't decide yet. But if you do make up your mind to come in with us, you may be sure of your country's undying appreciation." The lieutenant lowered his head in the kitchen doorway.

"I shall do it. I don't need any more time," David said.

"All right. You'll make a valuable addition, I know. Wait here. You will be contacted." Opening the door, Major Tallmadge turned. "Good fortune to you, my boy." He grasped David's hand. "Until freedom!" And he was gone into the night.

CHAPTER EIGHT

July 23, 1776

David Van Essen sat on his porch alone in the twilight. He wiped waves of sweat from his face. The hardest part was having to lie to Cassie. He hadn't seen her since Independence Day. His fear of being caught spying on the British and then hanged from a tree—a fear he felt constantly in the pit of his stomach—possessed him: posing as a redcoat terrified him. But worse was the sadness pulling at his gut at the look on Cassie's face when he had told her he would wear the red coat. It was contempt.

"You're a coward," she had spat out at him. Now it was done. He shouldn't have told her. Yet she would have known soon enough. Part of the plan for David was to make it known around town he would turn traitor to the Patriot cause. There were many Loyalist soldiers from Long Island in the First Loyalist camp on Staten Island. If he were to be recognized by someone from Cow Neck as a dedicated Patriot, he would be turned in and shot at dawn. He must convince them all he had gone over to the British before leaving Cow Neck. It was the only way he could carry out his mission to spy for the Americans in safety.

David's absence from the drills conducted on the commons by Mr. Mancks was noticed and commented on. After a while, his friends had mostly deserted him. Ernest and Max still talked to him, but no one else did. Nate Thayer and Mr. Fanshawe avoided him on the lanes. Mr. Bailey told him not to show up at the forge any longer. Shopkeepers, farmers, and dairymen—people he'd known all his life—turned their backs on him. All saw him now as a traitor. Townspeople treated him as an outcast in the same way they had treated Jasper Deecke. It was only a matter of time until he would be waylaid on the road and grabbed by thugs—Patriots in name—their strength important to the cause, but brutes. David knew they would splash his naked back with hot pitch tar and then stick him with feathers. Imagining himself balancing his legs across a high rail for the humiliating ride out of town, he felt he would rather die before he would have Cassie see that spectacle. The longer he stayed in Cow Neck, the more his uneasiness grew into heart-stopping fright.

But how long would he have to wait? He had sat outside his cottage this night as he had done every night since that fateful evening in June, waiting, looking down at the moonlit water of Berry Creek. Just then he heard a soft splash of a canoe paddle. A minute later, Caleb Brewster tied up the canoe to a thick sapling on the bank of the creek and walked along the soft grass to David's porch. David held the door to the cottage open. Caleb was a big man, wide around the middle. Sitting across from David at the kitchen table, his voice was thick in his throat as he spoke. "Good to see you, David. Haven't seen you since we raided the British camp on Cedar Street with the Sons. That was a blast, wasn't it?"

"Sure was, Caleb. They scattered fast. We made a good haul of their guns."

Caleb sat back in his chair, gazing directly into David's eyes with his own shrewd, dark eyes. "Got coffee, boy? Cold and black is good."

David got up and poured the last of his supper coffee into a china cup with a thin, tiny imperfection; a rose painted on the porcelain had a missing petal. His mother had left it behind on her and his father's journey up to Montreal. His parents were loyal to King George; they were English to the core. An older couple, they sensed thug revenge from overzealous Patriots, and they were anxious to get up to Montreal to live in the approved English way. The cup brought back the moment of their leave-taking, and David saw in that instant his mother's tearful face as she kissed him good-bye. Would he not change his mind and come with them? He couldn't, he said. He was a Patriot. He had to stay and fight for liberty. The vision passed.

"Pretty soon we won't be able to get our hands on coffee, so thanks." David poured the dregs for himself, cold and black to show he was just as much a man as Caleb, even though he hated it cold without milk.

"What's wrong, boy? You look a little green around the gills."

"Nothing. I'm fine."

"I take it Lieutenant Tallmadge was here?"

"Yes."

"And you're with us?"

"Yes."

"And you're scared."

"I guess."

Caleb sat back in his seat. "I was full of fear, and I had plenty of bad nights and second thoughts," he said. "After I signed on to work for the general's intelligence service, I worried day and night them redcoats would catch me throwing bombs and torching the decks of His Majesty's men-of-war on the Sound. I'm out there in my whaleboat with my crew roaming alongside the hulls of those ships in the dark, their masts sky high. Fifty to sixty pounders aimed at my boat. You bet I worried. You bet I was scared. I'm still scared; they ain't caught me yet, me and my crew. We've sunk plenty of their ships. They want me more than they want others." Caleb smiled. "They find my activities objectionable."

"Yeah. I am scared." It was a relief to admit it to Caleb.

"You can change your mind, David. Even now. You can stay here and work with the Sons against the king's men."

"I said I'm scared. I didn't say I'm quitting. I'm in."

"Nicely said, David." Caleb took a long sip of his coffee. He stood up. "Got to get going. It's dangerous to stay in one place too long."

"Thanks, Caleb. Wait." David paused. "Were you sent here by way of testing my will?"

"Something like that. I told Tallmadge you'd be true." They clasped hands. "Until freedom, David."

David heard Caleb's paddle dip and move through the water and pass the turn of the creek, where he would tie up the canoe to his whaleboat hidden in the shelter of Drowned Man's Cove adjacent to Berry Cove.

CHAPTER NINE

Midnight. A brushing noise. Alert, David listened. He jumped out of bed, reached for his musket, aimed it at the door, and flattened himself against the wall. Quiet. He waited a minute more and then looked through the window. No one. He opened the door. On the porch, a paper lay at his feet on the floor.

Tomorrow, take the ferry at Whitestone bound for Bowling Green. There, switch to ferry running to Staten Island. Wait on the dock for a redcoat to meet you. He will be wearing a sprig of green vine in his helmet. He will instruct you further.

David lay down on his cot, but sleep was impossible. He got up and reread the paper. A soft glow suffused the sky at dawn. He dressed in a faded, long-sleeved work shirt and homespun knickers; through washing up, he gathered his rucksack and opened the door of the small cottage he had lived in all his life. Quietly, he latched it behind him and began to walk. He had one matter to attend to before he would take the Northern Road to Whitestone.

CHAPTER TEN

Next morning I was in my bedroom sorting out my keepsakes, something I liked to do while the air was fresh and cool. The day's heat had already begun to settle like a blanket over the room. The sheer white curtains on my windows hung limp. The morning, with its brilliant blue sky and playful puffs of cloud, looked deceptively cool and inviting, but it was hot and damp, a typical Long Island July day. I pushed the sweaty ringlets of hair back from my forehead.

In the quiet of the morning, I heard Papa and Eban wall up a space in the chicken coop amid the squawks of the hens. A new shipment of guns must have come in during the night. Since Mr. Harkens had tried to furnish the British the old hiding place in the shack, Papa looked for a new place to hide stores of guns from Connecticut. The chicken coop was an inspiration; Mr. Harkens would never think of it as a safe place to hide stores of guns to be smuggled to General Washington's troops in Brooklyn.

How I knew about the new hiding spot was because I was in the right place at the right time. I had risen at the rooster's first crow and gone out to the barn to feed the animals. When I heard voices carry up from the banks of the creek, I hid in the barn and watched through cracks in the wood. Papa, Eban, and Mr. Fanshawe spoke in low tones on the shingle of sand; Mr. Fanshawe's boat lay at anchor in the bay. Voices carried in the early-morning air. While I scattered chicken feed in handfuls on the grass for the rooster, I heard whispers among the three men to remove the shipment of rifles from the chicken coop tomorrow night and load them onto Jim Fanshawe's wagon under a large stack of hay bales. The guns would be taken to encampments at Red Hook and the heights of Brooklyn, places it was thought the British might land in advance of the battle. Just where the British would attack was the question. "Can't take chances. Deliver a packet down to Bowling Green as well." Papa had whispered.

Hammering and doweling outside almost forced me to close my window. Hannah burst through my bedroom door, speaking in her own shrill noise, "David Van Essen waits downstairs for you."

"I have nothing to say to him." I held a pretty garnet ring up to the sunlight, enjoying its sparkle.

Hannah stood in the doorway, her arms folded at her ample chest, her mane of copper hair falling free from her shoulders onto her printed calico gown. "Your papa asks that you say a civil good-bye to David."

"I shan't say good-bye to that traitor." I laid the garnet down gently into the satin-lined jewelry box. "If Papa wants to, that's his business."

"I shall tell David to wait." She smiled sweetly at me.

I picked up a pearl necklace and then laid it down on the bedspread. "All right," I yelled after her. "I'll come down. I shall say good-bye, but that's all I'll say and naught else." I turned. Hannah had gone.

I moved the edge of the curtain and peeked out. David stood under the branches of a huge elm. He looked up as I looked down, and our eyes met. All of a sudden, my heart beat faster, and my throat tightened. I quickly changed from my barn clothes into a mint-green linen shift for the hot day, ran down the back stairs, and opened the door.

David was looking out at the rows of ripening corn. He half smiled and tilted his head toward me, a gesture I knew well. I had not seen him since the afternoon of the Liberty Feast on Declaration Day, when he disappeared and didn't even have the grace to say good-bye to me.

"Well?" I tried to make my voice severe, but it sounded trembly in my ear.

He took his cap off and rolled it in his hands. "I…leave this morning. I wanted to say good-bye to you, Cassie."

"Good-bye, then." I kept my nose up.

"Can we walk down to the cove? It's less noisy there."

"You must be on your way, mustn't you?" I hoped he'd say no.

"I've some time. Come on."

We walked down to the shore without speaking. I felt my feet crunch through the first of the dead maple leaves already littering the grass on this hot July day. The tide was high, and it was cool here near the sound of rushing, slapping water.

"I shall miss this place." He picked up a stone and threw it. It went skipping across the water. "Remember when we paddled out that day and the canoe sprung a leak? We had to swim back to the shore."

"I remember it. You kept watching me to make sure I didn't go under."

"Yeah." David looked down at me. He tried to smile, I think, but it didn't come off so well. Somehow, I just couldn't speak after that.

"That was a good day out on the water," David said.

"It was fun," I said.

"Cassie, I want you to know that I'm not going because I want to." David looked down at the ground.

"Then don't go. Stay and fight with us; fight for your country with Max and Ernest and all of your militia friends."

"I must go."

"Why must you?" I demanded to know.

He shook his head. "I must leave."

"Go then, if you're so afraid!"

"I'm not afraid."

"Yes, you are. You turned your coat!"

"I did."

I folded my arms and tried to keep the tears from falling. We both stood, not talking. David looked out at the water.

"I have something that I want to leave with you." David unclenched his fist, and I saw lying across his palm a gold ring with an opal at its center, glowing pink and purple in the shaft of a sunbeam.

"It glows like a sunset," I whispered.

"Will you wear it until I come back? We can make our plans then."

"I could never marry a turncoat, David."

"Can you kiss one?"

"I can." And I did. I kissed David again and again, and I must say I liked it too.

"I'm coming back," he said.

I didn't want to argue anymore, but I had to say it. "We Patriots will win. Do you think you will be welcomed back after you turned coat?"

"I don't know. But I give you my word; I'll come back home." I looked into David's eyes. There was resolve there.

"I shall wear the ring," I said, twisting it around my finger, watching the colors glow, not really noticing them anymore.

"I shall like to think of you wearing my mother's ring." David grasped my hand in his.

We walked back up the hill. David stopped at the shack to shake hands with Papa and Eban. He turned around and waved at me. "Good-bye, Cassie." He walked on, tightening the rucksack on his back.

I walked over to Papa. He knew about David's about-face. But quick enough, he had wiped his hand on his knickers and shook hands with him. "Oh, Papa, he's gone over to the enemy. He might not come back."

"He's a brave boy, Cassie."

"How can you say that, Papa? To be going over to the British is brave?"

Papa didn't answer. He picked up his hammer and set to work.

CHAPTER ELEVEN

August 4, 1776

"Bye, son."
"Keep safe, Willy."
"Godspeed, fellows."

Our boys left home this morning to join General Washington's army in Brooklyn, preparing for war. Mothers and fathers stood in their dooryards, leaning on fences. Children played marbles in the dirt. Young girls threw wild flowers in front of our soldiers as they marched. Danny Thayer piped "Johnny Is Gone for a Soldier." The music sounded mournful to our ears. We all knew he played it for his big brother, Nate. Mr. Fanshawe's boy, Jeb, played a soft accompaniment on the drums. Papa held his coat sleeve up to his eyes. Hannah cried huge tears. My two brothers, the outside two on the pivot turning into the Northern Road, passed close to Suzie and me. I tried to smile, but I felt hot tears run down my cheeks. I blew kisses to Max and Ernest. Suzie blew kisses to both of them, but especially to Max. She ran to the front of the line to give her father one last kiss. We waved, and we waited until we lost sight of the boys, and still we heard the music and the roll of the drums until they faded away. The last sound we heard was the fading of their marching boots on the dry, hot ground.

Afterward, people went inside their homes. Papa, Hannah, and I walked back to the mansion without speaking. On the way, Suzie and Eban fell into step with us.

"Come in and have tea with us, Eban, Suzie." Papa held the door open.

We followed Hannah through the quiet rooms. We all tried our best to keep up, but everyone fell to their own thoughts. I did not realize how much my brothers meant to me. I missed them even now, only an hour after they had left for Brooklyn. I could only imagine how Suzie felt, having to say good-bye to her father and her husband-to-be at the same moment.

Hannah poured black tea and set a plate of scones on the kitchen table. Papa managed to get one down by taking huge swallows of tea. Eban chewed for a long time on a couple of bites. "Redcoats will occupy us if the general don't win, Judge." He sat forward after swallowing the very last piece of hard scone, his beard almost dripping into his cup of tea. "I ain't aimin' to walk around without my shotgun."

"I think that's wise, Eban," Papa said. "From what I'm reading in the *Globe* and *Rivington's Gazette*, the British have amassed a huge armada from the Narrows in Brooklyn all the way out to Gravesend."

My skin prickled with goosebumps. "Will the army come to us, to Cow Neck, Papa?"

"We have to be prepared, and hope it won't happen. If they do settle in here, they'll come to every town on Long Island, and they will take up living in the best houses."

"That would be ours and Sarah Harkens's houses," I said.

"Yes, and Harkens is a strong Tory himself. They'll think twice before they take his house."

I felt a shiver run down my spine. "That leaves us."

Papa sat back in his chair. "We have to rely on General Washington to carry the day."

CHAPTER TWELVE

August 15, 1776

On this warm morning, newly promoted Corporal David Van Essen of the New York Volunteers, First Loyalist Regiment, was at his post as porter to General Sir William Howe, the commander in chief of the British Forces in America, in what had been the birthing room in the Morgan house for over a century. A room no larger than an oversized cupboard, it shared the same view of New York Bay, brilliant in morning sunshine as the general himself enjoyed from the spacious parlor, which was now his office.

David had been quartered here in Staten Island for three weeks, occupied with menial jobs and mostly twiddling his thumbs. General Howe, except to briefly shake hands on meeting him, had avoided his door other than to request meals from the kitchen. David had been given no tasks other than to fetch servants and make handwritten copies of documents. Obviously, Sir William's preference would have been for a British aide-de-camp and not an American turncoat to the king's cause. Yet David Van Essen had been recommended by a man highly placed in British Intelligence in London, whom King George knew and trusted. General Howe could not block the assignment, nor did he try; he chose to simply ignore his young aide. There was important work to do in advance of the coming battle, and he didn't need this fellow Van Essen cluttering up his office. This morning, General Sir William Howe walked over to his floor-to-ceiling windows and, for the moment, indulged himself in admiring the sun shining off the masts of the *Eagle*, a beautiful sight in the bay. Thinking of his brother, Lord Admiral Richard Howe, who would visit him shortly, General William Howe felt his spirits rise. He felt immensely relieved. At last Dick was here to share some of the planning.

Eagle, a British man-of-war, a formidable fifty-eight-gun ship of the line, of the Repulse Class, was the flagship of Lord Admiral Sir Richard Howe, commander of the British Fleet in America and brother to Sir William. "Black Dick" was the admiral's nickname, given to him by his own sailors in gritty tribute to his leadership and sailing skills. His ship, *Eagle*, dwarfed every other sailing vessel in New York Bay this morning. The king's colors flapped and smarted from the top gallant of her mains'il. Sunlight shone off the metal of her menacing guns, as it did the guns of the flotilla of ships of the line anchored behind her in the bay. The splendid sight of *Eagle* in the bay inspired fear and wonder among early risers on both the Brooklyn and the Staten Island shoreline.

David leaned forward over his desk. *How many ships all together do the British anchor in the bay? How many troops are on those ships? Where do the British intend to put in to shore? Where would they strike first? York City? A point on Long Island? The Brooklyn shoreline would be logical.* The questions burned in his mind. Answers were most eagerly desired by the commander in chief of the Continental army, General George Washington.

Success would hinge on whether or not David could hear the Howe brothers' plans or, even better, could capture something in writing. How was he to accomplish it all when he knew General Howe didn't trust him as a turncoat? There might be documents inside Sir William's office, but Sir William had a hard-and-fast rule: his door was shut unless he opened it or gave permission to enter. Sir William trusted only one servant to carry messages. Could David somehow contrive to open the door, even an inch?

Earlier than usual this morning, Sir William made his way down the hall in full military dress to await his brother Richard's visit. The general for the first time in two days blocked David's doorway, addressing him firmly and without warmth: "I'm expecting Lord Admiral Sir Richard Howe at ten. Have a tray with coffee and cake and a bottle of Jamaican rum sent to my office by my personal servant just after Lord Admiral Sir Richard Howe is piped aboard."

"Yes, sir." David pulled the cord of a bell attached to the wall. Within seconds a liveried servant strode into his office. David delivered the general's instructions while he kept his gaze steady on the *Eagle*. "Bring the tray to me, please," he told the servant. "I shall deliver the tray personally."

"I can't do that, sir. I am the general's personal servant. I serve him in his office."

"The general specifically asked me to bring it to him." David out-stared the servant and waited until he was well out the door.

While he waited for supplies, David kept his spyglass trained on the *Eagle*. An unmarked and unnamed sloop sailed alongside the *Eagle*. When the sloop maneuvered close enough to the *Eagle's* massive hull, a knot of sailors standing on the main deck dropped bulging crates onto the foredeck of the sloop. The crates landed heavily; some of them splitting their boards on impact, releasing an avalanche of dull green uniforms on the deck. The crates were clearly marked: Hessians. The sloop then headed for the tip of Long Island with split crates of uniforms. David could not write fast enough. The arrival of the uniforms pointed to Hessians making camp along the southern part of the island. This news would greatly interest the general.

As David watched, a tender was lowered from the *Eagle.* Lord Admiral Sir Richard Howe descended the rope ladder and climbed unassisted into the tender, where he stood for the short ride to the shoreline of Staten Island. Once there he refused the offer of a hand and lifted one long leg over the side of the boat, then the other, and hurried along the sand to the porch of the house.

General Sir William Howe stood between the two white pillars of the porch while his brother Richard took the steps two at a time to greet him. A bugler sounded a welcome flourish for Lord Admiral Sir Richard Howe who greeted his brother, the general, with a bear hug and a firm, long handshake. The two walked quickly to the general's office. David opened the door for the brothers, and Sir William reached around and slammed it shut.

A minute later, the servant entered David's office, balancing a tray containing a silver coffee service, slices of cake, and an amber bottle of rum with two crystal glasses resting in silver holders.

"Set the tray down. You may leave." David gave the soldier a quick smile, but he remained surly, casting his eyes down, refusing to make eye contact with David. "The general likes his morning draft, sir, with his coffee. He depends on me to bring in the rum."

"I take full responsibility. Don't concern yourself. It will be fine." The servant turned on his heel and left. A moment later, David heard the heavy stamp of General Howe's boots approach his door. He steeled himself for the general's displeasure. Sir William's eyes flashed sparks. "I specifically ordered these supplies to be brought to my office. What are they doing here?"

"Just arrived, sir. I was about to bring them to you."

"Do so." The general walked away, treating David to a heavy slam of his own door.

"Yes, sir."

On David's knock, a bark came from the general to enter. Jollity prevailed in the general's office. David set the glasses down in front of the two men, but his hands shook so that the bottle and glasses trembled. The general looked up quickly, but said nothing. The admiral kept talking about a past old time, smiling at his brother.

"Shall I pour, sir?"

Instead of answering, Sir William inclined his head. David poured two fingers of rum into each glass. Immediately, the two men hoisted their glasses. There was no toast; they drank. The admiral resumed his story. David quickly interrupted, "Would you care for anything else, sir?" David stood before the general.

"No. Leave."

The admiral finished his story. There was hearty laughter from Sir William. David made his way to the door as slowly as he could. Sir William poured more rum into the waiting glasses. David walked through the door, leaving it open about an inch and a half. When he got to his own desk, it took a few minutes for his breathing to return to normal.

At first, he could only hear the rise and fall of voices. The two men spoke in tones too low to hear from across the hall in David's office, but after a while, the talk between the brothers grew more animated as splashes of rum were poured into glasses. David kept his head bent to an account ledger book, his quill in hand.

The social talk was over. The men were getting down to business. "How many men do you have, Dick?" The general's tone was somber.

"I have nine thousand sailors in ships waiting on Long Island Sound and one thousand Hessians still on ships in New York bay." The admiral sounded confident.

General Sir William said, "I have twenty thousand troops. Commodore William Hotham arrived with some seven thousand

Hessians under the command of General von Heister, giving us thirty-seven thousand troops. How many ships do you bring, Dick?"

"Four hundred and twenty-nine ships, counting the flotilla I brought here last night, and twelve hundred cannons." David could hear the scratch his own quill made as he frantically copied down numbers.

"We should see a quick, successful end to this encounter with the rebels and be home for autumn in London. I'm planning on Christmas dinner at the palace; how about you, Dick?"

Admiral Howe smiled. "William, if King George should so honor us, I shall be delighted."

Sir William said, "These rustics have nowhere near the troop strength we have, and their guns are to laugh at! My spies tell me they drill with poles and pikes."

"It'll be a good show, won't it, William? When will we be in a position to strike?"

"A few days less than a fortnight, I'm thinking, enough time for you to get your flat-bottom boats ready for troop landings to some point on the shoreline.

"My men will start building them today."

"There's still the question: Where will we put into shore? I have not yet decided." There was silence after this. David picked up his ears. Where would the British strike? David could hear parchment crinkle. He heard a map being unscrolled. He waited, his quill stopped in midair. Nothing for a time—then a whispered mingling of voices he could not decipher. A chair squeaked, as if a large body had lowered its weight into it. Voices became speculative, as though the brothers had settled into a chat.

"Seems a shame, Dick, don't it, to squash the Americans? I thought when the king appointed us peace commissioners, we could talk some sense into these roughnecks." Black Dick's voice seemed to hold a trace of sadness. "I thought we had a chance for peace. I liked Ambassador Franklin. I never thought he'd go to war. I'll say this for them: they're a stiff-necked lot. I always liked 'em though."

"I haven't got much stomach for this war myself," Sir William agreed. "But you know, Dick, orders is orders."

In the hall, David heard the brothers exchange good-byes. He opened his door fully to witness final handshakes. Ten minutes later, Admiral Richard Howe climbed up the rope ladder to the *Eagle's* deck. He waved to his brother one final wave. The general, standing on the porch of the Morgan house, waved back and returned to his office once the admiral was piped on board.

David sat in his tiny cubicle, almost not believing his luck. Reading his scribbled numbers, he copied them in a more orderly fashion. He wrote up the incident of the sloop carrying uniforms for Hessian soldiers. He then tore the page out of the ledger book and stuffed it into his pocket.

At eleven in the morning, Private Lucas Welch was alone in the kitchen peeling potatoes. His hands were wet and red and showed slight, bloody cuts. The private was definitely not in a good mood. "What d'ya want?" He hardly paused to look up when David entered the kitchen.

"I hear you're from Montauk," David began.

"What of it?" Private Welch continued to peel.

"I've spent many a good day there, fishing." David waited.

The private put down the peeler, rubbed his hands against his apron, and looked at David. He said nothing but held one hand out.

David put the folded paper in his hand. Lucas Welch squashed it into his pocket without a glance at it. "Right." He went back to his job.

"I remember you," David said, almost under his breath.

Lucas Welch, allowing a thin widening of his lips and a quick nod of his head, said, "Same here, mate." On his way back to his office, David felt a sense of victory. The brothers had not settled on a landing place for the battle. Aside from that he hadn't failed; he had helped the cause.

CHAPTER THIRTEEN

September 9, 1776

Long Island was abandoned. When General Washington decided in a council of war with his generals on August 29 that the battle in Brooklyn was unwinnable, he ordered his Massachusetts Marbleheaders to move his army of ninety-five hundred men in the middle of the night across the East River to Kips Bay in New York on anything that could float. Fishing dories, ferries, rowboats were taken from the night waters and pressed into service. Even rafts tied up to trees along the shore were conscripted into the makeshift flotilla. Crossing the troops in a dense fog, thick enough to obscure a man from seeing the hand in front of his face, the Marbleheaders were able to evacuate all of General Washington's army without a single casualty. The evacuation continued all through the night. Major Benjamin Tallmadge, leaving Brooklyn just before dawn in one of the last boats, noticed the fog lifting and saw a man, taller than any of the troops, still standing on the shore. He noted to himself George Washington was the very last man waiting to cross the river. Minutes after dawn, every single soldier was present and accounted for in Kips Bay. The *Phoenix*, of forty guns, and the *Rose*, of twenty guns, both British frigates anchored only two hundred yards off Kips Bay, never knew the retreat was in progress right under their noses.

The *Globe* gave us this news in columns across the front page. Were Ernest and Max wounded? Did they retreat with all the others? Papa had no word from either of my brothers. But the newspaper had it that the army was fighting the British up at Harlem Heights.

The talk in town was that the British would come here to the North Shore soon. But all of Long Island would be occupied. Papa was right. I asked Papa over and over, "What can we do?"

"Go to work every morning to the court and the schoolhouse. For the moment, there is nothing else to do."

I heard Papa leave the mansion in the wee hours to join his friends. I hoped they met with the whaleman, Caleb Brewster, and were making plans to sink British ships at anchor in Long Island Sound.

Days, I walked with Suzie to the schoolhouse to prepare for the children's return to school after the harvest. I used to love the start of the school year; the smell of the oil, the feel of the new horn books for the incoming children to practice their letters in, and even the breezes coming in through the windows—it all meant the start of a new school year. But this fall I dreaded the days ahead.

The wind blew a little quicker through the trees. Sycamore, elm, and dead maple leaves crunched under our feet as I walked with Suzie to Mr. Douglas's store. Winter was most assuredly waiting to descend on us.

In daylight when he had time, Papa met Eban at the shack, and they continued to clear out old, broken farm implements.

I had a horrible feeling Papa was getting the shack ready for us to live in. I didn't understand how the redcoats would dare take our home from us. How could Papa allow it? It wouldn't happen. I kept telling myself it wouldn't happen. I couldn't live in that dirty, oily shack one minute. It smelt of grease and dirt. It didn't have a true floor, just planks laid end to end with no effort of any kind to put them together and grass growing through the wood.

Mostly, life went on as it did before the battle in Brooklyn. Hannah scrubbed floors and baked her brittle cookies. We talked to each other only when we needed to. I thought of Max and Ernest all the time and prayed for Providence to care for them. Hannah missed my brothers, too. I sometimes saw her on her knees saying prayers for the boys instead of singing her Irish melodies while she scrubbed the floors. For once, I hoped her prayers would hasten to the heaven she often spoke of. When I walked along the roads and lanes, I heard people say "When the British come," not "If they come." Now, we knew.

CHAPTER FOURTEEN

September 17, 1776

Under the stone bridge with an arm full of bayberries Hannah needed to make beeswax candles, I stopped picking to listen to the sound of marching boots. Closer and closer they came with every passing second. I peered out from under the arch to watch British officers on horseback lead their foot soldiers in columns of four abreast across the bridge to the Northern Road. Five companies, eighty men to a company, passed—each man carrying a muzzle-loading, smooth bore Brown Bess rifle over his shoulder. Following in the procession, horses pulled gun carriages containing field pieces and boxes loaded with ammunition, baggage, and equipment.

When they were out of sight, I ran home through the woods. Breathless, I found Papa and Hannah standing in our front yard, facing an English officer in a dazzling red coat splendid with medals and ribbons, seated on a gleaming black horse.

"You are Philip Scott. You dwell in this house." The officer sounded curt, as though he were speaking to someone lower than himself in rank.

But Papa sounded calm and reasonable. "Yes, I own this house; the property on which you trespass is mine."

The British officer ignored Papa's words. He reached into his saddlebag and pulled out a paper, broke the red embossed seal, unscrolled it, and read: "By the command of our Sovereign King George III, you, Philip Scott, Judge of the County of Queens and Justice of the Peace in the town of Cow Neck, Long Island, New York Colony, are hereby ordered to gather your effects and remove with your family to take up habitation in the cottage bordering this property to the east three hundred yards."

The officer looked up from the paper. "Signed in absentia Colonel Daniel Braithwaite for His Majesty, King George III, on this Seventeenth day of September in the Year of Our Lord One Thousand Seventeen Hundred Seventy-six." The officer rolled up the document and put it back into the leather pouch hanging from his saddle.

"I am Colonel Daniel Braithwaite. I give you two hours until three o'clock to remove yourself with your family and your belongings to the aforesaid cottage."

"I know who you are. I see you found your way to York City the day we rescued you, when you were lost and out of vittles and water," Papa said out loud so all the colonel's troops and all our neighbors listening to every word standing in front of their homes could hear. The colonel flinched. His head snapped up. His mouth tightened and his eyes narrowed. He had not recognized Papa.

"Yes," Papa went on, "we all know who you are, Colonel. We have long memories in these parts."

"I'm sure you were properly thanked," the colonel said without looking up. "Now, to the business at hand. My officers and I will billet in your house. My soldiers will dwell with persons living on this lane and in this town. Remember: you have two hours to remove from your house into the cottage on the edge of your property."

"As I say, I have no wish to leave my house," Papa said.

As though Papa had not spoken, the colonel continued, "Again, I and my officers will dwell in this house. My men will billet with persons on this lane and in this town. Is that clear?"

The colonel stared steadily at Papa; Papa stared back. I saw the colonel turn away first. His gaze traveled out to our fields and the rows and rows of green gourds and ripening orange pumpkins waiting for harvest among spreading vines. I wondered if he was embarrassed at having to read an order from the king for removing our family from our home.

No. He was not embarrassed. When he turned back to Papa, his face was a mask of indifference. "Philip Scott, you are to keep your position as judge appointed by order of Governor Tryon, Governor of the Royal Colony of New York. You are to continue to serve in your appointed duties while it pleases His Majesty."

Papa picked up his musket. "Get off my land." Immediately, I saw redcoats' rifles aimed at Papa.

"Your land? You are just a peasant here." He spat out the word "peasant." "A nobody is what you are. This land is the king's land."

"The king can suck eggs," Papa said, loud enough to get a laugh from our neighbors. Colonel Braithwaite realized he was the butt of a joke, and he didn't like it. The neighbors uttered a full-throated, ear-splitting yell aimed directly at the colonel, which enraged him still further.

The colonel's troops stood ready to shoot Papa. "I'll strip you of your judgeship in a minute and throw you into the Sugar House jail in York City for the rest of your life should you or any of those hooligans try anything unpleasant."

My knees were shaking. Hannah held up a hand to her mouth. Her body was stiff as a board.

Now the colonel turned to the crowd of neighbors, "To you who live on this lane, I am Colonel Daniel Braithwaite. My troops will billet in your homes. You are required by your king to provide lodgings for his royal soldiers."

Papa kept his gun aimed at the colonel. An ominous quiet descended on our front grass while Brown Bess rifles kept steady aim at Papa. Yet Papa would not give in; he kept his musket aimed at the colonel. The sudden sound of boots shuffling closer across the grass made my mouth go dry and my stomach go upside down. "Papa, they have so many men, so many guns aimed at us." My voice shook. My legs wobbled. I had no breath, no saliva.

"Don't fret, Cassie." Papa kept his eyes on the line of guns facing us. "These redcoats put on a pretty show, but they have no grit."

"Papa, please." My papa turned toward me. In the instant, the colonel reached across his horse's mane and slapped its side. The horse wheeled around and galloped back to the waiting troops, spinning a cloud of dust in our faces. "Remember, two hours," the colonel shouted back at Papa, when he was out of range of Papa's musket.

CHAPTER FIFTEEN

Hannah, Papa, and I crossed the acre of grass to the miserable, dirty shack, carrying our clothes and pots and pans. When I walked through the door and saw its stained walls, pockmarked from farm debris, I felt sick. Papa's and Eban's efforts to clean it this summer hadn't erased the layers of dirt and oil and, least of all, the smell.

Papa pulled, pushed, hoisted, and heaved on one end, Hannah and I on the other, to shove the rusted parts of plows, hoes, and carriage wheels out of the shack and into an adjoining lean-to. It was the first time Hannah and I worked together since she came to us. I looked out of the spotted, filthy window to the hill next to the mansion where my mother lay at rest. The only thing that comforted me was that I could see her grave from here as well as from the mansion.

A blackened, nicked iron pot that had lain for a whole century under the runners of a sleigh sat on the plank floor. I nudged it with my foot. Black oil attached itself to my shoe. "Papa, who could have used this?" I asked.

He wiped his forehead with the back of a smudged hand. "Your grandmother, Mary Boonton Scott." He held the heavy iron pot in his two hands and looked into its depths. "She and my grandpa Nate Scott lived in this shack for two years before they built the house."

"It's mean and disgusting, Papa, just like this shack. I want to go home." The tears that had threatened all day long came down my cheeks in a torrent.

"This is home for now, Cassie. Stop crying. Go and help Hannah."

"I won't. I'm used to Scott Mansion. That's our home, not this horrible, smelly shack. I want to go home to our mansion. I hate this place. I want to go home."

I dried my tears on my apron and tossed my hair.

"There is no kitchen, Papa. At least, I have not found one, such as like at home." I knew I was being sulky and rude; I wanted Papa to know how miserable I felt in this oil-smelling, old shack, and so I stood with my hands on my hips and yelled. Still, he kept calm.

"There be a hearth. I left sticks from a broken chair last time I was here, enough for a fire to keep us today. Now, Go."

I swore I would never be easy about this dirty living place. It was too dreadful. Yet by nightfall we had washed the room down. Papa had laid a fire in the grate, and Hannah had plucked a chicken, plunging it into that same black iron pot with greens and rosemary and then filling it to the top with well water. Sitting on the dirty plank floor showing weeds growing up between the planks, I ate as though I were out in the fields all day working hard, and so did Papa and Hannah who sat on the one real seat Papa had found, which came out of a broken-down carriage, its stuffing torn apart and wood showing through it.

CHAPTER SIXTEEN

January 1777

*N*othing will make me happier than to squeeze the neck of that arrogant rooster. I jolted out of bed and over to the grate. Not even a burning ember. Cold ashes. Ice covered the split lip pitcher on top of the crude dresser Papa had pulled up from the shack wreckage on our first day in the awful place. Chopping the poker up and down into it got some water out of it to wash myself with. On tiptoe with my blankets around me, I stood looking through the eyelid windows. Ice covered the walk between the shack and the barn. Icicle knives hung from its eaves. Ice coated the bare branches of the trees.

Shivering, I pulled on my long underwear, my shift, and then my gown. I yanked my boots over my knees and grabbed my cloak off the hook, feeling grateful for its warm lamb's wool lining Mama had sewn into it. *If only my brothers, Ernest and Max, were home to take turns doing barn chores as they used to do.*

Late again. I was always late, always freezing, always hungry. *I hate this job. Why can't Hannah take a turn with it?*

The rooster strutted up and down the barnyard like a lord, his red comb and wattle shaking in anger at being kept waiting for his breakfast. I grabbed the bucket of feed and scattered handfuls in his direction. They made little holes in the snow, which kept the rooster busy plucking out the feed. The hens came around and pecked at the grain, keeping their distance from the rooster.

"Stand still, Jubie!" I stifled a sob. Inside the barn, it was warmer, but the cow was skittish. She resisted, swishing her tail back and forth in my face so fast the milk spilled on the barn floor. My fingers must have been cold to the cow's warm udder, so I warmed them on her thick, bristly hair. Jubie noticed. She stopped her impish behavior and stood calm and still. I was able to fill two pails with Jubie's and then Jamie's milk. Before Papa rode away in the fly to work, he would come to collect the milk, leaving one pail on the mansion porch for the cook to collect and bringing the other up to the shack for us.

But the worst of the morning was yet to be.

CHAPTER SEVENTEEN

"Hens aren't laying but scarce today, sir. Freezing cold affects 'em tolerable bad." I stood in a swirling mass of blowing snow and wind on the back porch of the mansion. The British cook stood behind the protection of the kitchen door of the mansion he held open an inch with his foot.

I held out three eggs in my mittened hands.

"What! That's all ye've got? What have you under that cloak in your pockets?" He emphasized *pockets* while looking down at me from a great height over a pair of burly arms folded across his behemoth chest.

"Oh, that's just the hot stones I warm my hands with in the cold. It's the weather, sir. It's taken a nasty turn, makes the hens broody." I made a quick curtsy, backing away.

"I'm not sure ye've not got a good few eggs in your pocket. 'Aven't you now?" The cook made a move toward me.

I stepped back. "No. Not at all, sir. If you care to look at the hens' perches, you'll see they're just brooding in this cold weather."

"Hmph! I'll be tellin' the colonel how scarce the eggs are gettin'. Here's a list of things we need. Give it to your father."

He was as ignorant as he was wide. I waited to show my contempt for the redcoat cook till I had cleared the mansion. I collected a good wad of spit in my mouth and spat it out at the exact place the cook stood to throw the waste into the pit every day. I prayed that the four eggs I'd saved would not break in my apron pockets or fall out before I got back to the shack. I saw last night's snow had drifted up against the side of the mansion as I passed by. It whitened the sandy, pebbled path between the sleeping soldiers' huts. At every step, I plunged farther and farther into deep drifts, slowing me down until I finally reached the shack door. Stamping my boots on the muddy plank floor, I felt in my apron pockets for the eggs: they were still warm and unbroken inside their clumps of straw.

Papa sat at the table reading *Rivington's Gazette* by the harsh morning light. Hannah stood at the hearth stirring gruel, which I hated with all my heart. Just boiled water with oats floating around in it. *We're eating like animals. Horrible! Well, today we would have eggs!* There was Hannah with her bright pink ribbon in her flaming red hair. So early in the morning too. Hardly light out yet! And just when I wanted Papa's full attention. "Papa, look. Eggs. Four of them!"

"Good on you, Cassie!" Papa looked up from his paper and smiled at me.

Hannah turned from the hearth, giving me the fisheye. "Did you steal those eggs, Cassie?"

"How could I steal them when they are Scott eggs?" I said as innocently as I could.

"Philip, this child will land us in the jail yet, the way she makes mischief against the soldiers."

I looked over at Papa. Sometimes, I did feel sorry for Papa. He had to weave a path between me and Hannah. It must be tiring for him and upsetting, too. I wished I could be different; I wished I could like Hannah for Papa's sake, but I just couldn't. He set down his newspaper and seemed to think a minute. He finally spoke.

"Well, we haven't had eggs in a month of Sundays, Hannah. Mayhap you could coddle them up or do something to them, could you, my dear?"

"Yes, I will, but I'll not eat them."

"Good, more for us," I said under my breath, which Papa heard and gave me a meaningful look.

But when the eggs slid out of the pan in a loose, trembling scramble, there were three pewter plates of eggs on the oilcloth-covered table. Hannah managed to eat her eggs with mouthwatering relish. Then she put her arm around Papa and smiled at him, leaning into his neck so that her masses of red hair fell over his face. Papa smiled back. *How disgusting.*

"I deserve credit for bringing these eggs, Papa! Why should Hannah get all the credit just for coddling the eggs?"

"You did good, Cassie." Papa was looking into Hannah's eyes, not even paying attention to me.

Hannah was. "Now, Cassie, it's best for you and Suzie to walk along the road this morning to the schoolhouse; the creek bank is full of ice. It's too dangerous," Hannah issued forth her instructions.

"I shall go my way and not let any ice bother me, nor will it bother my friend, Suzie."

"You see, Philip. The child pays scant attention to me."

"I reckon not," I said. "You're not my mother."

"Now, Philip, all I was trying to do was to protect her."

"Stop." Papa put his two hands up in the air. "Hannah, Cassie knows the creek and she knows the banks. She's been going that way all her life. So don't fret." Then to me, he said, "Cassie, you will watch out for ice on the creek bank. Won't you?" Papa lifted his coffee cup to his lips.

"Yes, I will, Papa." Papa was trying to make peace between Hannah and me. "Suzie's probably outside waiting for me. I shall go." I kissed him on the top of his head. I felt bad for Papa, so I closed the door gently behind me instead of giving it a good slam.

CHAPTER EIGHTEEN

Suzie's eyes opened wide. "What happened?"

"Hannah!"

"Yes. Hannah." I shook the branches of the birch tree until a shower of snow and cracking ice rained down over a mole hole, chasing the mole out of his warm lair across the frozen snow. "First, she asked me if I stole eggs from the British! Imagine! Our own eggs from our own hens. Then she told me not to walk along the creek because it snowed yesterday."

"That means we should walk along the creek for sure!" Suzie said. I laughed. We walked downhill to the creek. The air was quiet there, and there was less wind. We could hear each other talk and didn't see our breaths.

"I have to tell you something, Cassie. I'm going home today to our cabin. I have to leave Miss Hoary's house."

"Why? You like Miss Hoary."

"I do, but I don't like living with her. She doesn't know when to stop being the schoolteacher. She makes me go to bed at eight after she reads the Bible to me, and we have clove tea. I want to go home."

"Don't go home. Live with us till your papa comes home from the fighting. How awful to drink clove tea and go to bed at eight. Do come and live with us."

"No, Cassie. I can't do that. There isn't room, and besides, I miss my cabin. I want to go home and wait for my papa to come back. Besides, Old Eban next door says he'll look after me."

"Then shall I come with you when you tell Miss Hoary?" There was a cracking noise in the bushes. Both Suzie and I stopped in our tracks. A soldier wearing the hated red coat blazing with the emblems of a British officer stepped forward from the path in front of us.

"Good morning, ladies. I'm Captain Stonecroft. I see you do not salute an officer. It's required that you salute and step off the path if an officer walks toward you. However, I shall overlook the infraction seeing you were deep in conversation." He smiled. "Show me your passes, please."

I brushed snow from my cloak before I answered him. "I didn't bring it."

"I need to see your pass; would you be so good as to go back and get it?"

"No. I won't. I live here. These are my family's woods. That's Scott Mansion behind you. You know who I am."

"True. I do. But my colonel sent me out here to approve your passes, and that is what I shall do."

"Well, I don't have it with me, so I can't show it to you."

"Oh, Cassie, what's the use?" Suzie reached into her reticule and pulled out her pass.

"And you are going where, Miss . . . Mancks, is it?"

"To work. We work at the schoolhouse. We are aides to the teacher."

"Very well. Good day to you, Miss Mancks. You may go."

"I shall wait for my friend."

"Suit yourself. Now then, miss, you can come with me to see Colonel Braithwaite and explain to him why you do not carry your pass, or you can show me the pass and proceed on your way. Your choice."

I dropped my pass over his palm with as much scorn as I could muster. It made me angrier that he didn't seem to mind my contempt. He put the pass back in my hand with a polite smile.

"Remember, if you meet a British officer again on the path or on the road, you are to step out of the way and salute. It is for your own good I tell you this. Good day to you."

He walked away, and we saw him stand with his back to us among the trees.

"Cassie, why make such a fuss about the pass? Everyone has to show it."

"Well, I'm not everyone. I shall give them a hard time about it. I won't give them the satisfaction and make it easy for them."

"Wait. What do you think he's doing?" Suzie's face was full of concentration.

"He's making notes in his book about us, likely reporting us for not saluting him." I looked at Suzie. She looked at me. "I say, Suzie, let's give him a salute he won't forget. It will be for his own good."

"Aye. Let's." Suzie scooped up a fistful of snow.

The snowball, packed tight with pebbles, ice, and dirt; molded by Suzie; and hurled by me, smashed into the inch of bare skin at the back of the captain's neck, between his black helmet and his collar. Its edges fragmented into a hail of ice chunks, causing blood to flow freely down his neck.

"Got him right and proper, Cassie! Let's go," Suzie whispered.

"He'll never know who hit him. The woods are full of marksmen."

"He don't look to be too dumb," Suzie whispered. We took off running and didn't stop till we got to the schoolhouse.

There was Sarah Harkens blocking our way, standing in front of the schoolhouse door. "It's cold," I said. "Open the door, Sarah."

"I'm not cold, Cassie. I'm wearing the cloak my mama lined for me with lamb's wool."

Suzie wrapped her own thin cloak tighter around herself. "Stop being a mule, Sarah. Open the door. It's too cold out here," she said.

"I shall in a minute. I want you two to know I saw everything from the road. I saw you shape that ice ball, Suzie, and I saw you throw it, Cassie. The captain is flaming mad at you both. He knows you two did it."

"You told him," Suzie said.

"No. Suzie, I didn't."

"Who cares?" I said.

"Who cares? You two better care." Sarah smiled. It was a wicked, grim smile.

"The only way he could know is if you told him, Sarah. Come on, Cassie, let's go in. I'm freezing." Suzie pushed past Sarah's thick, soft fur cloak to turn the door handle, but Sarah was quicker. She leaned her back against the door handle.

"Shame your cloak is not lined with lamb's wool the way Cassie's and mine are, Suzie. You know, you really ought to have a warmer one. Come over this afternoon after school, and my mama will give you one of my old cloaks. Would you like that?"

"Would you like if I punch your face in?"

Sarah's chin lifted into the air. "Only ignorant people without good breeding would resort to violence, Suzie." Sarah opened the door and sniffed her way into the school room. Miss Hoary had lit the fire in the hearth, and the room was warm. The children were all in their places and quiet, practicing writing their letters. The older ones were reading their *Weekly Readers*. Miss Hoary looked up and smiled at us, even though we were late. I was thankful for the quiet and the warmth. We three sat and picked up the work that she had left for us to correct.

When would Sarah ever get tired of reminding Suzie she was a doorstep child, left at Mr. Mancks's log cabin as a baby early one summer morning? Mr. Mancks was the only father Suzie ever knew, and he was good to her. Suzie loved him as though he were her real father. Reminding Suzie her cloak was thin and offering one of her old ones was Sarah's way of telling Suzie that she didn't belong among us. She wasn't one of us; she was different.

Miss Hoary asked Sarah to work with the children on their arithmetic. Sarah walked up and down the room, calling out the different combinations, and the children waved their hands in the air when they had worked out the sums. Sarah was good at making a game of the numbers, and the children enjoyed singing out their answers. Someday, Sarah would be a good teacher. She knew how to make learning fun. And she loved to be boss for a few moments. But today was going to be a hard day. Even so, some days were harder than others.

CHAPTER NINETEEN

Somehow, the morning passed. Objective pronouns were learned by the older children. At noon, Miss Hoary set dishes of roasted oysters out and took pans of hot buttered biscuits off the grate for lunch. In the afternoon, I corrected the children's grammar, and Suzie read the beginning of *Gulliver's Travels* to the children. Sarah helped one child who couldn't write make her letters in her horn book. Every now and then, a gentle snore came from Miss Hoary's drooping head. Her quill lay limp in her hand. Toward dismissal, I looked out the window to see a steady fall of new snow beginning to stick to the ground.

Suzie and I plowed home through the snow, this time on the road. When we were too frozen to face the fierce wind any longer, we walked down the hill to the creek and huddled in the shelter of a large bush to catch our breaths.

"Cassie," Suzie whispered. "Look! Up the hill."

A tall woman dressed in a heavy, dark green woolen cloak and high boots, her copper hair shining against the sheen of the snow, stood on the crest of the hill. She turned her head left and right. She seemed to be waiting for someone.

"It's Hannah," I whispered. We pushed back into the bush. At the same moment, a British soldier steered a makeshift iceboat— a wide board attached to a piece of sailcloth, steered with a thick rope—down the creek across the ice, with the wind at his back. He aimed the contraption into a snowbank to stop it and stepped away.

Hannah strode down the hill, her hair streaming down her back. Her boots made a path through the rising snow down to the icy creek. She stopped in front of the soldier. He grasped her hands in his own. Hannah handed him a paper. They spoke another minute. He grasped her hands again and then jumped into his iceboat, pushed off with his feet, and tacked into the wind. Hannah looked after him for a moment and then climbed back up the hill to the shack.

"Now I know why she didn't want us to walk by the creek," I said. "She had spy business to attend to."

"Mayhap it isn't what it seems." Suzie recovered first.

"She gave him information about us to give to the colonel. What else could it be? Come on. Let's go up to the shack. I'm going to find out."

"I...can't, Cassie."

"Why not?"

"I told you this morning. I'm going home today."

"I forgot. Wait for me. I'll go to Hannah. I shall find out what she told him in that paper. And then I'll come with you and help you. It doesn't seem right for you to go into a cold cabin in the middle of a snowstorm."

"Eban will be there. I'm to knock on his door." Suzie walked a few steps. "I've got to go."

"Did you tell Miss Hoary?" I persisted.

"Yes, while you were outdoors playing with the children in the snow. I can't wait to get home. I miss my cabin so much, Cassie. Eban is going to watch out for me."

Suzie was already up the hill to the path, making her way through new-falling snow to her log cabin a milepost away down the Northern Road. "I'll come by," I shouted after her.

CHAPTER TWENTY

"Well, what are you in such a brown study about?"
Hannah looked up from a bowl of sticky bread dough. Over and over, she plunged her rough hands into the dough, kneading and shaping it. I stared at her hands. Large and red, they showed dark scabs like the hands of carpenters and smithies, so different from her face that glowed pink. She lifted the dough and set it onto a board on the wooden table. Hannah seemed proud of her hands. She splayed them out across the table, leaning forward to face me. We stared at each other. In that instant, I realized she knew we had seen her with the British soldier. Her pretense of being so busy with bread shaping was just to warn me off. She blew a sweaty curl off her forehead.

"Well, Cassie?" She kept kneading dough. Her knuckles were red with effort.

"I saw you down by the creek talking to the British soldier. You put a piece of paper in his hand."

"Your papa told you not to walk by the creek!"

"No. *You* did. Papa told me to be careful." She went back to shaping the dough into a loaf. "Aren't you going to explain?" I made my tone as belligerent as I could.

"No. There's nothing to explain, Cassie." The rhythm of her hands shaping the dough never stopped.

"I shall tell my father what I saw."

"Do that." Hannah lifted the loaf and laid it gently in the bread pan inside the old beehive oven she and Papa had cleaned out the day after we moved into the shack. It was the same oven my grandmama baked her pies and breads in. "There, now. This will be my best loaf yet. Your papa will be pleased." She turned her back to stir a stew bubbling in the iron pot on the hob.

"You are spying for the British."

"What?" Hannah laughed.

"This is how you pay Papa back after he rescued you from that dirty old inn down by the wharves in York City, where only sailors and watermen eat." I stood with my arms folded across my chest.

Turning, she looked at me, her eyes big green circles. "First of all, your papa ate there, and so did many other lawyers and judges. Second, your father did not rescue me. Mrs. Curry's Inn was a clean and respectable boarding house and tavern. Mind you, the sailors and shoremen who ate there were as decent and respectable as your own pa. Also, I never saw a rat scurry across the wharf outside Mrs. Curry's establishment like I see them now run through the grass down by the creek. You, fresh miss, don't know what you're talking about. Move, I need to get around this table and fix supper for my husband and your father."

Hannah busied herself lifting pewter plates down from the shelf above the mantle. Working around me, she let loose a torrent of words under her breath at the same time. "And me, the very last Irishwoman who'd wish an Englishman well! It's beyond my understandin' to be accused by this spit of a girl for spying for them lobsterbacks. It's a disgrace. I shan't put up with it." I saw her wipe a tear away with the hem of her apron. "I was happy there in the city where I earned my money. Why I'm here in this God-forgotten place where 'tis no pretty shops except for the one what sells pickles and flour and all these uppity women who don't have a kind word for a body, nor a cuppa. I don't have a single friend here like Molly Anderson, the Swede, who worked with me at Mrs. Curry's place. I miss her. I do. I'll tell Philip. That's flat!" On and on she muttered while she set pewter plates down hard on the table and stirred the stew with a vengeance.

Hannah was right about one thing; the women of the town did not like her. She had stopped asking Mrs. Fanshawe next door and Mrs. Comerford, who lived one more door along the lane, in for tea. I knew the reason for that. The town ladies were my mother's friends, and they did not welcome a woman from another country in her place. Hannah brought no beautiful china to dress up her table with and couldn't cook worth a soul. When she scrubbed the floor, or worked in the garden, she piled up her red hair like a washerwoman, and clumps of it fell down her neck. She sang the old Irish melodies so loud, she could be heard all the way to Mr. Douglas's store. Nothing had changed for Hannah since Independence Day when her pies got ruined.

The stew simmered in the iron pot. I had to admit it smelled good. The gravy was a dark brown; leeks and carrots floated around in its depths. I moved to stand near the hearth and warm my hands. Hannah reached over me to the mantle shelf and plucked some bay leaves from among the clusters of herbs. She stirred the dried bay leaves into the stew, something my mother used to do. "I'll go home, I will. I've got me passage," she muttered.

Just a bunch of meaningless words. I remembered that time after she first came to us when I overheard Papa tell her, "Your smile is like a benediction." *Would he say that now?* I wondered. He probably would because she always smiled and her eyes lit up when Papa came into the room. I had to admit it.

89

"Cassie, I mind you starin' at me, and I want you to stop."

"I'm waiting for my answer, Hannah."

"You'll have a good long wait then, won't you?"

"You spy for them." I flung the words at her.

"I'm no spy. There's your answer." Hannah shrugged, untied her apron, doubled it, and hung it over a hook on the wall. *She was too calm.*

"My eyes don't lie," I said. "I saw you put a paper in that British soldier's hand, and so did Suzie."

She sat down heavily on the chair. Her words came out slowly, "I'll tell you against me own better judgment! And then I want you out of my kitchen."

"It's not your kitchen. It belongs to my mother. You can't tell me to get out."

"Your mother never put a foot in this kitchen. She lived in the mansion. I live in the shack! Now if you want to know what I was doin' down there at the creek, here 'tis. The soldier I met down there is a young fellow from my own neighborhood in Dublin. He's twenty-one; he's had the bad luck to be captured in a bar on O'Connell Street, drug off, and dumped on an English ship bound for America. When he woke up with the king's coin in his hand, he knew it meant he would have to fight for the British. He didn't put the coin in his own hand. He was far from land. I told him the name of someone who could help him get back home."

"And what about the paper?"

"God's bones, but you are thick! I've told you."

"The paper?" I insisted.

"It was the name of someone who could help him escape."

"No, it wasn't. You gave away one of Papa's secrets to the redcoats in that paper. You told them about Papa's committee meetings. That soldier was your messenger to the colonel."

She turned her back to stare at the stew bubbling over the hearth. "I told them Brits nothing."

"I know what I saw."

"Forget what you saw, or you'll have us all wearing nooses 'round our necks." She stood up putting her face close to mine. "Sit you down, girl." Her face had gone white. I sat. "Now then, I'm no spy for the lobsterbacks. I hate them, every man jack of them. And what I told you is God's truth. Believe it or not. But you had better keep your gob shut about it. Do you understand me?" Hannah stood over me, her face a mask of malice.

"Yes." I gulped. "I understand you very well. I'm going out."

"And where would you be goin' at this hour? Your father will want to know."

"To Suzie's cabin."

"What do you mean? Has she left the schoolteacher's house?"

"Yes," I answered her while pulling on my snowshoes.

"Glory Be! Going from Miss Hoary's house, is she? She's a brave one."

"She has Eban to help her." I opened the door.

"Wait! You'll take some stew for her."

The last thing I wanted to do was to stay in Hannah's presence one more minute, but if it was about food for Suzie, I would wait. "Eban will be with her," I said.

"Then take stew for Eban, too. And bread." Hannah lopped off thick slices of yesterday's bread and ladled the simmering stew into a bowl, covered it with a sack, tied it with rope, and threw the clumps of bread on top. I made a snug place in my rucksack for the bowl and slipped the straps over my back. I pushed my way out the door into a blast of freezing air. My feet in their snowshoes sank into the soft snow.

Hannah's voice followed me out the door. She yelled outside to me, "Cassie, do not talk about what you saw. There's others to be hurt if you do."

I looked at her innocently. "But you told me you're not a spy. Who could be hurt?" When I looked back, Hannah was standing in the dimly lit doorway, getting wet and cold, watching me.

91

Winking campfires outside soldiers' huts gave the twilight an almost merry look. I stopped outside the mansion and saw through the french doors of the dining room a roaring fire and officers eating their supper. They didn't bother with a tablecloth; they ate with gusto and whatever spilled on our mahogany table stayed spilled. No effort was made to clean up. They threw logs on the already crackling fire. While our people froze, they warmed themselves by our fires with our wood, which they had forced us to give them. The people of Cow Neck were left shivering in the brutal cold of this winter. The officers in their scarlet coats and high polished boots were warm and fed, while our people were freezing and always hungry. While I watched, an officer pulled off his boot and hurled it across the room where it landed on top of my piano. I picked up a rock and aimed it at the head of the soldier who had thrown the boot. I had him in my sight. I would hit him right in the eye with it, right through the shattered glass into the midst of this contented, sloppy group of British officers.

"What d'ya think you're doing? Do you want to get us all killed?" Hannah grabbed my upraised arm and wrested the rock from my hand, throwing it into a pile of wood before I could gather myself. "Ye'd best get on your way if you're droppin' in on Susan."

"What do you care that it's our family home, our Scott Mansion, my mother's tea service, her china, her table, and my piano? What do you care about that?" I spat out at her.

"I do care. Now get if you're goin'."

CHAPTER TWENTY-ONE

An old Indian trod the snowy path in his wet moccasins. He walked with his head buried in his blanket, and he neither saw me nor answered my hail. I pushed my way along till I came to Old Eban's cottage and then on to the cobbled path outside Suzie's log cabin. The Mancks' cabin was lit like every other cottage, with one meager candle on the maple table to light the gloom. Suzie was unfolding blankets and settling straw near the doorway. There was no fire.

"Here's bread still fresh from yesterday and rabbit stew." I saw no reason to mention that Hannah had thought to send it.

"Supper for us? Oh, Cassie, do thank Hannah for me."

"In a pig's trotter, I will. Wait! I said that. Didn't I? How could I do that? How could I echo Hannah? What am I saying?"

"I thought it was funny," Suzie said.

A gust of wind and a blast of cold air shook the little candle in its dish. Eban, appearing like a mountain man wrapped in layers of squirrel skins and wearing his 'coon skin cap, his cheeks reddened and his eyes watering, stepped into the cabin, carrying a bundle of logs in the crook of one arm. The neck of a fat turkey hung lifelessly from his other hand, leaking a trail of blood.

"Eban, good on you!" At the sight of the turkey, Suzie was delighted. "We'll have supper for days."

"I was out Huntington way, and this here turkey just wandered across my path. Wasn't nothin' at all to end its days." Eban shook himself out of his heavy layers and sat down. Suzie ran to the cupboard and pulled down a deep bowl. The two of us slipped the bowl under the turkey to catch the blood.

"Eban, where did you find the wood?" I asked. He didn't answer me. His back was to me, as he dropped logs into the grate. He crinkled up a copy of the *Gazette* and threw it onto the pile. The newspaper flamed and soon sparked the logs into a burning fire that lit up the room such as we hadn't seen since the redcoats came. Eban knelt before the fire, warming his hands. His hair showed a golden yellow in the firelight. Suzie and I looked at each other. He must have used a flour-and-tallow mixture before he came out to make his hair so light. The only trouble was it didn't cover all his head. Over his forehead his hair was bright yellow, but around his ears and hanging down the back of his head and neck, Eban's hair was white as snow. I had to press my hand against my mouth to keep from laughing. Suzie did too at the same time. We could not laugh. We just couldn't.

Finally, Suzie broke the silence. "How shall we thank you, Eban?" she said loud, almost into Eban's ear.

"Ain't nothin'. Say, I'll have a bowl of that stew Cassie brought, if it's all right with you, Cassie, and yourself, Suzie." Suzie poured Hannah's stew into the pot hanging from the hob, and in a minute, Hannah's gravy bubbled merrily.

"It's fine, Eban. But, Eban, Cassie wants to know where you got the wood. I think it's better if you tell Cassie where you go to get wood these days." Suzie ladled out stew into pewter plates and put

Hannah's bread on the table. Eban looked straight ahead. He got up from his watch over the fire and turned toward me.

"I stole it off the mansion porch. It's your wood, Cassie."

"I'm glad you took it, Eban. Take it every day; the more you take, the less for them." Suzie handed me the salt saucer, and I set it in front of Eban.

"That's good of you, Cassie. I should have told you before." Eban looked properly solemn. "You best tell your pa what I'm up to though."

"My papa will say the same as me. The redcoats stole our wood from us. Least we can do is get some of it back," I said. "I hate them."

"I hate 'em too, Cassie. Prob'ly, I hate 'em more than you do. Don't you worry, we'll get our own back. They walk around in their fancy red coats, but we got the spirit of hate to warm us up. We're gonna win. Mark my words, Cassie. Now, it don't do no good to get hot about it, right before we eat Hannah's stew. Smells good, don't it, Suzie?"

Suzie sat down. Except for Eban's slurping, we were silent while we ate. Even I thought the stew was good. *Could it be that Hannah is finally learning how to cook?* We basked in the comfort of the fire. I sat back, feeling contented for the moment.

Eban finished up eating. He wiped his hands on his knickers and then reached into his pocket, gingerly pulling out a stained, still soggy envelope. With it came a shower of wood chips and even a few chunks of wood. "Cassie, this is sommat your pa should see."

"What is it?"

"'Tis a letter I found on the mansion porch while I was ferritin' out logs."

"Read it, Eban; you're close to the fire." Suzie paused scraping out the bottom of the bowl for the last of the stew.

"I cain't read. Y'all know that."

"Yes, you can read, Eban. I've seen you read. Just go slow, is all," Suzie said.

"Nah, there's some big, fancy words here, and I cain't figure 'em out. You best do it, Suzie. Here, I'll move over, and you kin sit here by the fire."

"I'll read it," I said, "since it's for Papa."

"It ain't for your papa. It's for the English colonel. I recognize the 'ficial seal. Prob'ly, somebody dropped it on the porch."

I changed places with Eban, took the paper from his grimy paw, and stood by the fire to read. "It's a message to Colonel Braithwaite from a Colonel William Jameson." The words went blurry on me. I felt myself drop down in a heap in the wooden chair. "Papa's in trouble!"

"What fer?" Eban leaned forward. Suzie sat down quick. The paper shook in my hands. I laid the paper in Suzie's hands. She read from the letter out loud.

Judge Philip Scott, a patriot, who we thought of as a hidden friend to our cause, has at intervals named certain individuals who he says, will work with us in our defense of the King and his colonies in America. However, it has come to our attention that the intelligence these informants give us is completely wrong most of the time, and that some of the secrets told to us about the Americans, such as locations of ammunition stores, which are empty when we get to them, and supply routes, which are in the wrong direction, have caused us much consternation. This man cannot be trusted. He has a lying character and we can place no more credence in the information he passes on to us.

"The British know that Papa plots against them." The revelation stunned me.

"Just don't lose this letter. Keep it hidden and not in your sleeve. Here, give over your cap." Eban ripped open the lining and stuck the letter inside my cap. Picking up a thin slice of wood off the straw-swirled floor, he sharpened it to a point with his knife and secured the cap's cut ends together. There was no way to tell the letter was inside.

"Thank ye, Eban." *There was no one like Eban*, I thought.

He lifted his layers of squirrel fur over his shoulders, put his 'coonskin cap back on his head, and picked up his gun. "Tell your pa to be careful, Cassie, real careful, 'cause them lobsterbacks are watchin' him."

My breath came fast and shallow. "I'm afraid, Eban. I worry about Papa. He goes out in the middle of the night to meet his friends, and they steal boats from Tories, who they know have robbed Patriots of their silver and their money, money that goes into British hands. It's too dangerous."

"Cassie, you're talkin' too much. Your pa will be all right; just tell him to be careful. Tell him I said so." He got up from his chair. "You fixed up pretty good now, Suzie?"

"Thank you, Eban. You'll come back tomorrow?"

"I'll be here waitin' for ye when ye return from school. You take good care, Suzie. Come, Cassie, I'll walk you home, if you please."

"No, thank you, Eban. I'll stay a bit with Suzie."

For such a large man, Eban was agile. He was out the Dutch door, as quiet and sneaky as a wolf stalking a 'possum. Suzie poured more tea for us.

"If they find out Papa's got that letter, they'll be coming 'round with guns drawn for Papa, Suzie."

"How will they find out? They won't." Suzie picked up her cup and sipped from it.

"No, they won't. Papa will burn it. But I'm scared for Papa."

"Did you have it out with Hannah what she was doing by the creek this afternoon?"

"Yes. We had a fight. She denies spying for the redcoats. I knew she would. She made up some story that the soldier on the ice boat was a young man she knew from Dublin. She says she wrote down the name of someone who could help him get away."

"Could it be true, Cassie?"

"I'm sure it's not. She made it up on the spot."

"Then you've got to tell your father she's a traitor to our cause."

"No. I can't. Papa will never believe me that Hannah spies for the British. I'm going to watch her and wait."

Suzie let out a deep sigh. "I'm afraid too, Cassie. I get more afraid every day for my father and for Max, and for Ernest, and for all the boys. I thought if I go home with all of Papa's and my things around me, I'll be less scared. But I'm home now, and I'm still scared. Papa could be captured or worse."

"My papa, too, and my brothers." Even as I said it, I trembled.

"What is to become of us if our fathers are captured?"

"Stop, Suzie. We can't think like that. Papa is smarter than all of the lobsterbacks. And your papa is too. You have to believe that if he's smart enough to lead the boys in battle, he's smart enough to keep himself alive."

"I know, you're right, but I can't get it out of my mind. In the middle of the night, I get so scared thinking about what could happen."

"I know. No matter what I say, I fear for Papa worse than I ever did before. I better go home and show this letter to Papa. See you tomorrow."

The last light I saw was the reflected glow of the candle on the snow as I stepped out into the dark night.

Fast-moving clouds appearing and reappearing in flashes of white cast tall, creeping shadows alongside me on the snowy path. I trudged along, the only noise the crunch of my snowshoes on the snow. Raw cold entered my bones, and I shivered inside my cloak. Soon, the gothic tower of the Presbyterian Church appeared through my smeared eyelashes. Stopping to rest, I leaned my poles against the stone wall of the cemetery, and then I saw an overhanging eave that I could stand under and worked my way into its shelter. A stockade fence had been built to conceal the first floor of the church except for a lone window cut into the wood and a thin, worn burlap hung over it. I peered into the church. Somewhere inside its depths, a single candle in a lantern shed a thin circle of light. It was hard to see inside, but I cleared the window with my palms, and soon I could make out sleeping soldiers sprawled on blankets on layers of straw scattered across the center aisle's marble floor. A huge desk and chair sat on the altar, where the baptismal font had been removed. I heard muted pawing and snorting.

Horses! Lodged in the church, probably behind the altar where there was a passage separated by a wall crossing from one side of the sacristy to the other. My fingers scraped against the cold, porous windowsill; I kept my face to the window to see whatever else I could of the British compound.

"Don't move!" Thwack! The cold steel of a musket barrel jammed into my back, and I was on the ground tasting snow and dirt. I twisted, tried to turn.

"Get up." Whoever he was gestured the way I should walk by squeezing the gun barrel further along my back where the cold steel pushed between my ribs.

"What are you doing here?" Now his breath came close to my ear.

"I was sheltering from the wind." My own breath came in short gasps.

"Likely. Don't turn. Keep both of your hands in front of you. Don't look at me."

But I did look, and for that I got another thwack, this time across my shoulders. I recognized him. He was the soldier in the iceboat who had taken a spy message from Hannah this very afternoon. So she had lied to me when she said he was hit over the head in a bar in Dublin and forced to become a British soldier. He had probably signed up on his own.

"In you go." He pushed me into a room where church vestments were hung. I stumbled over boxes and odd vestments flung over chairs. It took me a minute before my eyes got used to the gloom. In the distance, up the middle aisle behind the soldiers sleeping in rows, the vestibule doors were open. The town's firewood. Logs, hundreds and hundreds of them, possibly even thousands, lay piled up to the ceiling. A mountain of Cow Neck's wood to warm the hides of the redcoats! Even the pews had not been spared. Some lay split into half; others had been sawed into small enough pieces to fit a hearth. Sawdust covered the marble floor.

"What's this?" An officer walked a narrow path through sleeping bodies toward us, carrying a lantern. He spoke in a stern, low voice.

"Lookin' in the window, she was, sir," the soldier whispered to the officer. "Spyin', that's what she was doin'."

"Why, you're the Scott girl, the judge's daughter." He knew me and I knew him. How could I forget? He was Colonel Braithwaite, the same one who put us out of our mansion. He stared hard at me. And I stared straight ahead.

"Another damn spy. They're all over the place. Even the young 'uns they got workin' for 'em." I still felt the gun barrel beating into my back.

"That will do, Doggett; I'll ask if I need your help."

So this miserable redcoat's name was Doggett. "I was not spying." I was damned if I let him accuse me of spying.

"What *were* you doing?" the colonel asked. His voice had become soft as honey. He stepped forward, jutting his face close to mine. I felt his harsh breath and took a step back.

"I was sheltering from the wind. I was wiping my eyes."

"I see." He thought for a minute. "Your pass, please."

"I don't have it. I forgot it."

"Like father, like daughter, I see. Both liars."

I looked into his eyes, his mean, nasty eyes. "If we're liars, you're thieves. You stole our mansion, and you stole our people's wood."

The officer looked up at me, surprised at my boldness. "You'll keep a civil tongue, young woman, or you'll see the inside of my jail for the night. And feel a lashing to boot. Where were you coming from?" he said.

"I was visiting my friend." I tried to avoid his gaze, but he moved as I turned so as to face me directly again.

"Who would that be?"

"She lives past the milepost."

"Name?"

"It's none of your business who I visited."

"I know who she is, sir. Suzie Mancks. Her father's away fightin' with the Continental army," the soldier named Doggett piped up.

"I see. When and where did you first come across Miss Scott, Doggett?"

"Following this girl here. She went to that other one's cabin. And there was an old man, too, that I saw, sir. Went inside the Mancks girl's cabin carryin' a bloody turkey by the neck and some logs he was holding in his other arm."

"Who was he?"

"They call him Old Eban or just plain Eban around these parts."

I felt the gun shift on my back. The colonel caught sight of the gun.

"Put that gun down, Doggett."

"Yes, sir." Doggett pointed his rifle to the floor. I was much relieved.

"And?" The colonel's voice was harsh.

"The old man came out first but after a long time. I think they was eatin'. After a few minutes more, she did." He shoved his musket into my shoulder to indicate me.

"I just told you to put your gun down."

I shivered.

"Yes, sir." I felt the barrel leave my shoulder. Doggett continued as if the colonel hadn't just reprimanded him. "When she came to the church, she stopped and looked for a place to shelter, just like she said. She found that window, the only one you could see through, and she was gazin' into it. And that's when I came upon her and recognized her for the spy she is." Doggett finished up with a flourish.

"I was not spying. I was trying to keep dry."

"I'll stake my life on it, sir. She was spyin' on us."

"Be quiet," the colonel barked at Doggett. He took his time about speaking to me. "You must have had an important errand to come out on such a snowy, windy night. What was it?"

I remained silent.

"Better tell me. Otherwise, it could go harshly for you."

"I took food to my friend and to an old man named Eban, who lives next door to my friend."

"Is that all?"

"Yes."

"It sounds believable...but I can't help thinking about a certain letter that was lost this very day, and I'm wondering if your visit was tied into that."

"No, sir. My friends were hungry. I went there to give them food."

"All right. Let's try this: Now, your father travels all over the island, doesn't he, for his cases?"

"He's a judge. He goes where the assizes meet to try his cases." I saw the officer's eyes narrow, dark and mean. *I had to say something to help Papa.* I went on without thinking. "He goes all over, to York City, to Brooklyn, and even south to the Hempstead Plain, where he buys a cow sometimes. I believe he bought a cow from a farmer on the Hempstead Plain this week."

A flicker of interest lit up the colonel's eyes. "This week he bought a cow on the Hempstead Plain." The colonel stared at me. "That is what you said."

"Yes."

"You're right. He did go to the Hempstead Plain this week." The officer waited a few seconds. He stood across from me, folding and unfolding his hands across his chest. "Now, I'm looking for a lost letter. Most likely, a stolen letter. Know anything about that?"

"No."

"I believe you do. How do you know your father was on the Hempstead Plain this week?"

"He told me."

"Did he? And did he say he went there to the plain to spy on our camp there?"

"My papa would never do any such thing."

"I see he confides in you where and when he does his spy work for the Americans, doesn't he?"

"He doesn't spy."

"You've just told me your father went to buy a cow on the Hempstead Plain, which statement was in a certain letter posted to me but which seemed to have gone astray. I believe you have that letter in your possession. I want that letter. Give it over."

"What letter? I don't know what you're talking about. My papa hears cases on the Hempstead Plain often. He buys horses too, from a horse farmer there."

The soldier Doggett had picked up his rifle and aimed it at my chest.

The colonel gave him a withering look. "Do I look like I'm not in charge here, Doggett?"

Immediately, Doggett lowered his gun. I felt my eyes water. My nose began to run, and I began to sob out loud. "I don't know what you're talking about. I don't know anything about a letter. I want to go home," I managed to blurt out between my sobs and tears. "My papa waits for me." I hung my head so that my long, golden hair fell over my face, but not low enough to dislodge my cap. My shoulders shook from my sobs. "I want to go home. I'm so cold. I want to be with my family." I cried and cried and sobbed and sniffled, and then I drew deep breaths until I felt faint and sobbed some more. "Please, let me go to my family. I don't know about a letter." With that, I was reminded of Papa sitting home waiting for me, and I cried even louder, as loud as Hannah did on Independence Day, so long ago, after her pies were ruined.

Clearly, the colonel was exasperated. He might be believing me; mayhap he was on the verge of believing me. "Please, sir, let me go." I sniffled and sobbed out loud.

"You told me your father had been on the Hempstead Plain this week to buy a cow, a sentence that was in the letter. Let me have the letter and you can go home."

"But I don't know about any letter. You asked me where my papa travels to, and I told you some of the places he goes to judge his cases. When he's in those places, sometimes he buys a cow or a horse, sir." I wiped my eyes but could not control my tears.

"All right. Escort her home, Doggett, and get her pass. I don't care if it's on her person or in her home."

I cried louder. "No. No. Please, I need my pass. I shan't forget it again. I promise."

His face was still very close to mine. "I shall keep your pass until I see fit. Give it over. Just remember, you and your father: stay away from places where you don't belong. You will feel harsh penalties if you don't, my girl."

"I'm not your girl. I'm an American girl," I said through my tears.

"Get her out of here, Doggett. Tell Captain Stonecroft to see me tomorrow here at the church. Go. Now. This girl stinks up the place." He turned on his heel and walked away.

CHAPTER TWENTY-TWO

"G'wan now; get goin'." We were back in the woods. "I'm not thrilled escortin' ya home. Don't get on my bad side." Clearly, the soldier Doggett was not happy about following me home in the snow. At least his rifle wasn't jammed into my back. I knew the woods better than he did, and soon I was far ahead of him.

"Slow down, got to keep my eye on ya. Godforsaken place… hellhole for sure." He huffed and puffed. I could tell he was not used to country life; probably he'd never dug his way through a three-foot-high snowdrift.

"I can't hear you!" I yelled.

"Slow down," he yelled back.

Doggett caught up to me, mumbling to himself. I couldn't help smiling at his discomfort. "My snowshoe lace came untied," I said. "I have to fix it." When I bent down to pull the laces of my snowshoe together and tie it up David's opal ring flashed in the moonlight. Doggett saw the quick flash too.

Finally, the shack was in sight. He plodded along behind me in his soldier's boots. "All right, love. If you'll just take off that ring from your finger and hand it to me, ya can go inside and be together with your lovin' family, and I'll be on my way."

"I'll do no such thing. I will not hand my ring over to you."

"Ah, don't take on like that. Wouldn't you rather hand over your ring than have me go in and get your pass from your da? I'll trade. You keep your pass. I keep your ring. That's a good trade, ain't it? The colonel will get one of my special made passes. I'll put your name on it. I got a supply of 'em." He looked at my hand again. "Let's have the ring."

I didn't move. "Come on, miss. It's that cold out here. Let's have the ring." It was no use. The soldier Doggett slowly aimed his rifle at me. I took off David's ring and held it in my hand. "What are you going to do with it?" I asked him.

"I'll sell it. Thank you, miss."

"You English are lower than dirt!"

"I agree with that! But I ain't English. Tom Doggett is Irish and no lover of the English king. Best of the evenin' to ya, miss."

I watched him walk toward the road. He had put my ring on his pinky finger.

CHAPTER TWENTY-THREE

I struggled through deep snow to the door of the shack and stacked my snowshoes against the wall. In the kitchen, Papa sat, bent low over the table, reading *Rivington's Gazette,* his favorite newspaper. It was a Tory paper, but it was the most entertaining of all the newspapers in York City. I stood across from him, at the edge of the candle's light. He couldn't see my face very well. "Where's Hannah?" I asked. *How much did Papa know of our fight? Certainly, she told him we had a fight.*

"She went to bed early tonight. It's good you were there to help Suzie move back into the cottage, Cassie. Hannah admires you for that."

"She does?" *She didn't tell him about the fight.* I hoped Papa didn't see the look of surprise on my face.

"Yes. She told me over supper how anxious you were to go to Suzie's and help her move back. I thought you would like to know that Hannah praised you to me."

"I am pleased, Papa, but I didn't do that much. I just brought the food that Hannah cooked. It was delicious. Old Eban enjoyed Hannah's cooking, too. He watches over Suzie."

I ripped open my hat seam, took the envelope out, and handed it to him. "Papa, Eban picked this letter up off the mansion kitchen porch before dawn today while he was getting wood for himself and Suzie."

Papa opened the letter and read it. He looked up at me, standing over him. "They've got me there, haven't they?"

"Eban says the letter means you're being watched, and you should be careful."

"He's right. I shall." Papa got up to pour more tea for himself and a cup for me from the pot hanging from the hob. "Where's your ring, Cassie?"

"I'm not wearing it," I lied.

"You didn't lose it."

"No." I shook my head. At least that wasn't a lie.

Papa sat down and took a sip of hot tea. "I'm glad you're home, daughter. Sit. I haven't seen you all day." He looked across the table at me. He seemed to be taking my measure. "Besides, It's too late for you to be out." It was hard to keep things from Papa. "I stopped at the Presbyterian Church on my way home and leaned against the window to tie my snowshoe lace."

"I hope you didn't linger there."

I held the edge of the table to steady myself. "No, not at first. The redcoats have built a stockade around the church. Most of the windows are behind the stockade. But there was one window cut out of the wood. I looked into that window. A sentry found me looking and brought me inside where Colonel Braithwaite questioned me. About you, Papa."

I swallowed. Papa's face became stern and, more, angry. I went on talking. I had to get it all out in front. "I had read the letter at Suzie's, Papa, before Eban skewered it into my hat. I wanted to give you a reason for being on the Hempstead Plain this week." It took a few seconds to get it out. "That's why I told him you were on the Hempstead Plain buying a cow this week."

"What?" Papa's face turned red.

"I made a mistake. I shouldn't have said that, but I wanted to give you a good reason to be on the plain."

"You implicated yourself because you knew it was in the letter. He knew right away you read it." Papa shook his head.

"I didn't think." I sat on the edge of my chair, waiting.

Papa breathed an audible sigh. "Cassie, Cassie, what am I going to do with you?" He took a deep breath. "Well, there's nothing in this letter that would do me any harm. Hearing is not a criminal offense."

"The colonel threatened us, Papa. He said you and I are liars. He said we should stay out of places where we don't belong. It will go hard on each of us if he deals with us again."

Papa picked up the letter and threw it into the fire. "Do not go near that church again. Do you understand, Cassie?"

"Yes. I won't. But there is something else, Papa."

Papa dropped his head into his hands; his voice sounded muffled. "Is it something I want to hear, Cassie?"

"Yes, Papa. I found the wood. The town's wood. It's inside the church vestibule, hundreds and hundreds of logs, mayhap thousands. I saw them piled up in the vestibule with my own eyes."

"It strikes me it's not surprising the colonel thought you were spying, Cassie, and in possession of the letter."

I leaned over the table. "But I wasn't." My mouth went dry.

"Well, it was pretty strongly indicated to him that you were. Do you realize how close you came to being arrested, detained, and jailed? He could have tried you. You know the punishment for spying."

"Yes, Papa." I shivered. "All because I happened to look in the window?"

"You didn't happen to do it. You intended to see inside. That constitutes spying."

"But, Papa, we must get the wood back. It's the town's wood. The redcoats are hiding it from us to use for themselves." Papa put up his hands to stop me. But I wouldn't stop. "That's the reason they've built a stockade around the church, to protect the wood. But, Papa, I know where the opening is…"

"That's enough." Papa's voice was harsh.

"But we have to get the wood back. We must have a plan to get our wood back."

Papa shook his head. "No. *We* don't. Forget it. Put it out of your mind."

"Then there is a plan."

"This conversation is over. You have involved yourself in matters that don't concern you. Forget it."

"But…"

Papa put his hand up. "What did I just say?"

"I won't go near the church again as you asked, Papa." I stood in the doorway, "But, Papa, I'm sixteen years old. I feel I'm old enough to do something for my country. Boys, sixteen years old, go to war."

Papa's expression turned tender toward me. "It's how things are, Cassie. It's just how things are. Men go to war. Women and girls keep the fires burning at home. Now go to bed and stop scheming. Hear me?"

"It's not fair."

"It has nothing to do with fairness. It's about staying alive." There was no arguing with Papa. He was, after all, a judge.

"All right. I'll forget it. But from now on, Papa, I'm going to call you 'Father.' I feel I am an adult now."

Papa rubbed his chin. "Yes. All right, Cassie. It's fine."

"Well, being that I'm an adult, shouldn't I be a part of any plan to get back our wood?"

"Go to bed."

"I wasn't spying, Papa."

"Yes, you were, and you are fortunate you are alive to tell about it. Now, Cassie, it is late. You're tired. Good night, I'm very glad you're home."

"Good night, Father." For the first time in my life, I called my papa Father, but I did kiss him good night. He was a dear Papa, after all. I lay in bed, thinking and wondering what the plan was. There was a plan; I knew there was a plan. It suddenly came to me. The plan was to attack the church and get the town's wood back.

It was the secret paper Hannah handed the soldier Doggett. In it, she must have told him about the Patriot plan. That way the redcoats would be ready to defend the stolen firewood when we struck. Hannah! She was in it up to her neck. She was surely a British spy. Now I had proof.

But I had a secret too. I couldn't tell Papa the truth about my ring, I'd have to tell him about the deal I had made to keep my pass. And now I had lied to him.

CHAPTER TWENTY-FOUR

Tom Doggett bolted upright from his sleep. He felt for the Scott girl's ring on his pinky. Relieved, he fell back on his cot. He closed his eyes and fell to thinking of his family and his old life in Dublin with his mum and da and the little ones coming up behind him. Had he said a good-bye? Had he given his mother money that night? Had he kissed the little ones? He racked his brain. Some parts of the mystery of how he got to America would never become clear to him. He'd only left the steamy three-room flat to meet his mates in the neighborhood pub for an ale that night.

A blow on his head, the Irish sailor swabbing the deck told him, was how he got here. Likely thrown into a lorry and, still unconscious, dumped in the hold of the ship. The sailor talked as he pushed a dirty mop along the lower deck among sleeping soldiers' berths. Common practice, he said, for the English to drag an Irishman off and put the king's coin in his hand to let him know he was now a soldier in the British Army. Hadn't it happened to himself? the sailor asked. Sure enough, Tom had felt the king's coin clutched in his fist. He almost could feel it now as he lay in his cot. After that, he remembered climbing up to the rail of the ship, bending over and watching his vomit spray the ocean swells.

How he had hated the British for every minute of army time spent on this island in America.

But lately, something strange had happened to him. On sentry duty walking about the town in the early dawn, he noticed the sloping hills of this sleepy town were turning green. White buds appeared on the fruit trees. Blue water sparkled in the Sound. He began to question himself. What did he have back home in Dublin? He and his da were costermongers, selling their pies and tarts from their cart on the best spot approaching the Liffey in the morning. In the afternoons, they sold more meat pies on the opposite side of the river to Dubliners returning from work. His mum depended on their sales for money to buy supper to feed the little ones. He missed their cart; he and his da had painted it white with big black letters: TOM'S MEAT PIES AND TARTS. Sure, his da would be pushing the cart by this time.

I could stay here. *Why not stay here? Yes, why not?* The thought came to him, exploding like a musket shell in his brain. How? Simple. Offer to go over to the Patriot side of the war. Yes. He would talk to the father of the Scott girl, the judge. Hannah, yes, Hannah would help him. He was sure she would.

Wait a minute. Hannah was the Scott girl's stepmother. He felt the ring lying still on his pinky. He should not have taken that ring. Never. Why had he done it? He broke out into a cold sweat, thinking of Hannah's fury should she find out he had taken the girl's ring. Yet, so far, no one had approached him; the girl had not told her father. Hannah must not find out. *I'll give it back in the morning.*

Hannah Malloy, now Hannah Scott. It was a stroke of luck he'd met her. She had been cutting back bushes in the yard. He was sweaty from chopping wood when he had looked up. He couldn't believe it. A girl from his old neighborhood in Dublin was smiling at him here in America. He put his axe down. Each could hardly believe the other was someone from home. Here Hannah was, married to a judge and living well, that is, until his own regiment came and occupied the Scott Mansion, driving the family into a shack.

The day Tom Doggett met her, he had been desperate, near to deserting. He had been planning to swim across the Sound and then walk to York City and get work on a ship back to Ireland. He'd told Hannah everything that day. She was true to her promise to help him. It had taken her until midwinter to find someone to help him get back to Ireland. When she handed him the note on the creek, he had been delirious with gratitude. But for some reason, he didn't do anything about planning an escape. He had not sought out the Irishman who could have helped him. Now he knew why. It had taken all this time to become clear to him. He wanted to become an American. He twisted the ring on his finger. He would get the Scott girl's ring back to her. Yes, he would return the ring and then offer to help the Patriots.

When morning broke, he knew what he would say to the girl. He would say he took the ring to sell it for money to send back to Dublin to feed his little brothers and sisters, but he couldn't go through with it. He was sorry he took her ring. It was a good story; he wished there was some truth to it. Tom Doggett found a spot in the woods behind Fanshawe's barn, where he could look over to the shack and watch the Scott girl leave for her work at the schoolhouse. When she came out of the shack, he jumped out, nearly scaring her to death. "Will you stop, miss?" He held the ring out to her.

She backed up a few feet, showing him her fist. "You! Don't come any closer or I'll scream. I warn you." Now in the daylight, he could see just how pretty she was, with her long golden hair.

"I'm sorry, miss, truly I am. I thought I could sell the ring and send money back to my mum in Dublin, for food for the little ones.

But it was wrong of me to take it. Here 'tis." He hoped he looked sincerely repentant because he was. He held out the ring to her in his open palm. She looked at it but refused to touch his palm. He dropped the ring into her palm. She put the ring back on her finger; gave him a long, hard stare; and walked toward the road. Tom decided he would speak to the judge the first chance he got. He would spy for the Americans if they would have him. He would become more American than the Americans.

CHAPTER TWENTY-FIVE

At twilight, two men and a woman stood on the banks of Berry Cove. Shadows lengthened. A ribbon of crimson floated across the sky just before darkness settled in over Cow Neck.

"Why do you come to us?"

Tom Doggett had never stood up so straight since he had been with the sisters at St. Mary Magdalene normal school. His heart beat so loud he could hear it thunder in his chest. He found he had no saliva until he cleared his throat three times. "I want to pay them back for the way them Brits got me into the army. More, I'm an Irishman. I hate them British. I want to be an American. I like it here. I want to stay here. I want to help the cause."

Judge Scott nodded. He turned to Hannah. "What do you think, Hannah?"

"We can trust Tom Doggett, Philip."

The judge nodded his head up and down, considering Tom's words.

"Very well. If Hannah vouches for you, you must be sincere. Meet me in the meadow across from the Presbyterian Church at three o'clock Wednesday morning. I might have a job for you. Wear dark homespun."

Tom shook with relief. He now had a golden chance for opportunity in a new country. *You pulled it off, Tom!* Then he thought, *I got to stop thinkin' like that. I'm through pullin' things off.*

CHAPTER TWENTY-SIX

April 1777

Mrs. Comerford and Mrs. Fanshawe unloaded their wash baskets in the warm brilliance of the spring morning. The ladies spread their sheets on the grass to dry, fighting the wet edges flapping away from their hands in the strong east wind. Mrs. Fanshawe picked up rocks and dropped them on the edges of her sheets. Mrs. Comerford did the same. While the two ladies talked together, the sound of their voices carried in the wind over to me standing inside the thorny branches of the pyracantha bush. At first the ladies spoke out loud. "'Tis three fine days in a row, Olive Comerford. Except for the wind, why it's almost summerlike. Makes me jittery to have these warm days so early in the year." Mrs. Fanshawe made her way around the sheets to where Mrs. Comerford stood.

"That's so, Alice, real unnatural weather, to be sure. Did you read the column in *The Mercury* that General Washington is being considered a great leader by the Congress now that the word's gone out he won those battles in Princeton and Trenton, on Christmas

Eve? After the way he skedaddled out of Brooklyn last August, who would have thought it?"

I leaned away from the bush for a better hearing. The voices got low. I only heard Mrs. Fanshawe ask Mrs. Comerford would she walk with her this afternoon to the men's houses to tell them the time of the raid.

I jumped out from behind the bush. Immediately, the ladies stopped talking.

"Mornin', Mrs. Fanshawe, Mrs. Comerford. Is there a raid happening? I heard talk of a raid."

"How you heard, young lady, is 'cause you were hidin' behind that pyracantha bush." Mrs. Comerford always saw me in the worst light. "Go ask your pa, if you dare. I doubt your pa would want you meddlin' in his plans."

"I think Papa's best left be today, but I thank you for the advice."

But Mrs. Comerford wasn't finished. "I expect he's mad at you again, like he was when the British soldier brought you home that night. What was that all about?" Mrs. Comerford had a turned-down mouth, and I was sure it was because she had so many unpleasant things to say.

"I don't know what you're talking about, Mrs. Comerford. I'm sure I don't. What with all the gossip around these parts, I'm sure I don't know how we all get along. So many busybodies. Not you, of course, Mrs. Comerford," I said in my most honest tone of voice.

"You got a tart tongue, young lady. That girl, Suzie Mancks, she needs lookin' after with her pa gone. I see she's back at home in the cabin, ain't she? Her pa shouldn't have left her alone to go fightin'."

I knew Mrs. Comerford just said that to get some more news about Suzie. "Old Eban is helping Suzie," I said. "That's all I know. So if you'll just tell me when this raid is going to happen, I can probably help."

Mrs. Comerford folded her arms stiffly. "There is no raid. Anyway, what would you help with, young lady?"

I glanced over at Mrs. Fanshawe and saw a trace of a smile on her face, which made me bold. I tossed my hair over my shoulders. "Help with the getting of the wood back, Mrs. Comerford."

"And how do you know about any wood?" Mrs. Comerford stood with her hands on her hips.

"Same way you found out Suzie's back home, I reckon. Anyway, it's not hard to figure out. We have no wood left, except a few sticks for the kitchen grate, and that's disappearing fast what with the cooking. Nobody has any wood except the redcoats. They stole it all from us."

Mrs. Fanshawe cut in, in a quieter voice. "There is a raid, Cassie."

"Alice! We should not be speaking about it to this girl. I don't care if she is the judge's daughter."

Mrs. Fanshawe spoke in a low tone, but she was firm. "I believe we can take Cassie into our confidence, Olive. She is sixteen years old. You and I were married when we were sixteen. Why shouldn't she know? Mayhap she can help like she says. I believe she should know."

"You can do as you like, Alice. I'm leaving to do my candle making, but I don't hold with telling our plan to this slip of a girl who thinks the world exists for her and her alone. That's all I'll say." Mrs. Comerford walked across the grass with her head held stiffly up in the air.

Mrs. Fanshawe yelled after her, "Olive, remember our walk later. I shall call for you." Mrs. Comerford waved for an answer.

I always did like Mrs. Fanshawe. She had been Mama's best friend, and she had made hot dishes for Papa and me until Hannah came to us.

"Come and have tea with me, Cassie," Mrs. Fanshawe said. Once she had cleared away the British soldiers' sloppy breakfast crumbs and coffee cups, Mrs. Fanshawe and I sat down at her table with our steaming cups of tea, and I ate a fresh baked scone. Mrs. Fanshawe looked across the table at me. "You had to give up the mansion to them, but at least they don't live with you, like they do with us, Cassie."

"It's true, but I hate living in the shack," I said.

"It won't be forever. We have to believe. Let's talk about the raid on the Presbyterian Church. It is to get the town's wood back. Your father; Joe Comerford; my James; Zeke Thayer, father to young Nate; Old Eban; and Caleb Brewster will meet at the meadow across from the Presbyterian Church at three tomorrow morning." Mrs. Fanshawe took a sip of her tea.

"Tomorrow morning at three. Right." I sat up straight in my chair.

"Mr. Harkens will be awakened and told about the raid a few minutes before the men leave for the meadow."

"Mr. Harkens will be going?" My eyes widened.

"Yes. They decided to include him. They need him. He's big and powerful, and he wants his wood back. He has need for the comfort of a good fire too, even if he is Tory." Mrs. Fanshaw smiled at me. "He doesn't know a thing yet. They'll stop by for him on the way. He can't go running to Colonel Braithwaite or Captain Stonecroft if he don't know till the last minute." Mrs. Fanshawe stirred her tea. "Besides, it will be much better if he tells his British friends about the raid after it happens than before when they can't do a thing about it. Don't you think?" She smiled before she took another sip.

"I surely do, Mrs. Fanshawe, but I fear he'll tell the colonel Papa was involved in the raid."

"He won't. Not if he wants to keep your papa's boat to run up and down the Sound looking like he's on important business while he's only selling latches and keys and repairing damaged household treasures. Mr. Harkens would do just about any job for money," Mrs. Fanshawe said.

121

I nodded. It was true. I had even heard a woman paid him to wear her new shoes for a whole day just to break them in. It was worth it to Papa to keep Mr. Harkens busy on Papa's boat, since Patriots had sunk Mr. Harkens's boat. Papa felt bad about the sinking of Mr. Harkens's boat. He never said so, but I knew.

"Papa won't tell me anything about the raid. He told me to stay out of it."

"He's thinking of your safety, Cassie." Mrs. Fanshawe lifted her cup to her lips and blew ripples on her hot tea. "But I believe you can make a difference to us in our plan. I was watching when the sentry Doggett left you off at the shack that night. After he left, I plowed through the snow to your shack, stepped into that little place where you hang your snowshoes, and listened to every word you and your Papa spoke inside that drafty old shack. We need you, Cassie. We need you at the church at three tomorrow morning. You can lie on a blanket on the bottom of Mr. Fanshaw's farm wagon to get there before the others. Hide in the grass. Tell Caleb Brewster you know where the opening is in the stockade and then lead the men there."

I leaned over the table and spoke low. "I will, but they'll know I'm a girl and that will be an end to it."

"No. It won't. I'll help you," Mrs. Fanshawe whispered. She took a sip of her tea.

CHAPTER TWENTY-SEVEN

Wednesday, three in the morning

"Caleb! They've got swivel guns in the second-story windows and a stockade fence around the church!" Mr. Harkens's chest heaved. His voice quivered and quaked. He kept slipping on the wet grass.

"I know that. Be quiet, you nitwit!" Caleb Brewster's fearsome voice was low and commanding. Standing just feet from me as I lay in the high grasses on my belly, Caleb looked very tall and scary. He could send me home.

"Run back and tell the judge I just got here. Tell him to come," he ordered Mr. Harkens.

"They could shoot me, Caleb!"

"Stop shiverin' like a girl. Hurry. Get the judge." Mr. Harkens's back disappeared across the meadow.

Papa would be here in a minute. I stood up and stepped forward to face Caleb. My teeth chattered. "I know where there's an opening in the fence, back of the church."

He turned, swinging his lantern in front of my face.

"Who are you? Speak." His voice was tinged with fury. But I couldn't answer him for my fear.

"Answer me or I'll shoot you dead."

"I'm Henry Fromidge from up the Northern Road toward Huntington town." I gave him the name and the place I had chosen for my disguise. I had almost said my real name. Caleb Brewster looked at me long and steady, holding the lantern up to my face.

My words came out in a jumble. I made my voice as low as I could to sound like a boy's. "I was here the other night inside the church. I remember it. I could show you how to get in through an opening around back in the fence."

I felt my knees shaking in Mr. Fanshawe's overalls. What would happen when Papa came? Would he know me with my hair shoved up under Mr. Fanshawe's workman's cap and my body hidden under his rolled-up pants and his overlarge men's cloak. There wasn't much light in Caleb Brewster's lantern, just a wee candle inside it. He stared into my face. Finally, he lowered his lantern.

"You say you can lead us in there?"

"I've been here before. There's an opening in the fence in the back of the church. I know the way."

Papa came up to us. "Who's this?" My breath came in spurts. I was sure Papa could see it was me.

"I don't know him, Judge, but he says he could lead us round back."

They forgot about me for a minute while their glances traveled down from the big guns in the windows to the sharpened fence posts high enough to slice a man's stomach should he try to jump or climb over them.

"Somebody told them what we were up to. See the swivel guns up there, Judge. We got to spread out and go around back. This boy says he knows the way, says he was here the other day. He claims there's an opening in the fence. You recognize this fellow, Judge?"

"No. But I knew about the stockade. I sent a message to you in Connecticut. I see it didn't get there on time. You were probably halfway across the Sound. Mayhap this boy can help. The Brits would never expect us to get into a stockade."

"All right. We go 'round back. We're ready." Caleb looked over at me. "You sure you know the way in?" he turned and said directly to me.

"Yes."

"I'll get the men, Caleb."

"Right, Judge."

In that instant, Papa turned his gaze on me; he did not move. "Let me have that lantern a second, Caleb."

Papa moved to stand directly in front of me. He leaned his head close to my face and stared very hard at me. I tried to stay still and not blink. He handed the lantern back to Caleb Brewster. "I think this fellow will be able to lead us, Caleb." Papa disappeared behind the tall grasses of the meadow. He knew.

Caleb Brewster indicated we should walk low around to the back. I couldn't find the opening in the fence. He knew I was struggling to find it.

"Where is the opening?" he whispered. "You said you knew."

"It's beneath a set of eyelid windows in the back. I have to feel the fence with my hands." Caleb put the lantern on the ground and blew it out. Then he lifted me up and hurled me across the ditch. I landed on my back against the fence.

It took a minute until I got my breath back before I moved along. I walked, feeling the wood fence, looking up and remembering I had seen windows overhead, somewhere up there. I straightened up and looked up. Where was the door in the fence? Where was that spot?

My feet were catching the sharp stings of spiky pickets. I kept scraping my hands across the splintery wood of the fence. When it seemed like I could no longer stand the jabs of pain in my feet, I felt the spiny opening in the fence.

"Is that it?" Caleb hissed.

"Yes."

"Jump." I had to go back across the ditch. His arms were open. I leaned across the ditch. I looked down. Right under my feet were broken bottles and huge shards of glass.

"Come on. Jump! I'll catch you. I've got to get in there." Caleb was right; the opening was too small for two people.

I jumped but fell short. Caleb picked me up from the redoubt. I was scratched and bleeding. Branches and glass stuck to my back. Caleb brushed my back roughly until most of the glass was off me and then leaped across the ditch, reaching the jagged edges of the fence. Now he was standing among all the claptrap and waste facing the opening. Startled, I heard someone behind me; Eban came up out of nowhere and leaped across the ditch. I was sure he'd fall backward, but he caught hold of Caleb's shirt, and the two of them trying to keep a foothold, half falling back and forth, began pulling the pickets down with their bare hands, making the opening wider. In about a minute, they had widened it enough for two people to climb through. Eban jumped back across the ditch and handed me across. This time Caleb caught me, and I found the door of the church and opened it. The last I saw of Eban he was waving the other men into the church. I was in the same vestment room that I was in the other night. This time I trained my eyes on the interior, remembering where I had tripped over objects and vestments. I felt for the boxes and found them before I could trip over them. We were in the room behind the altar, which opened to a roofed but open-sided tunnel that ran alongside the nave, and the tunnel led straight back to the vestibule.

The vestibule doors would have to open both on the inside and on the outside to the graveyard. I watched Caleb looking into the nave. He must be guessing how many sleeping soldiers were huddled in blankets on the marble floors. A horse's low whinny came from somewhere close by. I listened to the sighs and snores of the men in sleep.

Caleb gestured for me to come to the front. I led the men out of the maze of open trunks, cases, and vestments strewn about, through the narrow, stonewalled tunnel, silent as a band of Indians in their moccasins. The soldiers under their blankets on the straw-covered floor slept undisturbed. We tiptoed along until the closed double doors of the vestibule appeared. Mr. Fanshawe rubbed cow balm over the doorknobs to keep noise down as Caleb turned them to open. The men spread soft woolen blankets on the marble floor. Mr. Fanshawe handed me the cow balm, and I greased the doorknobs of the outer doors. Caleb was able to open them noiselessly to the graveyard where Papa waited nearby with the wagon. But there was someone else standing behind a tree close by, seeming to be listening, someone I recognized: the soldier Doggett. He silently watched us. I flattened myself against the cold stone wall of the vestibule. After a few seconds, Doggett passed along and disappeared among the headstones. I must tell Papa. I must. But I can't run out there now.

Caleb whispered to me, "Stay here. You'll not get into trouble here."

Who does he think he is, telling me I'll not get into trouble? If it wasn't for me, he'd still be looking for the opening in the fence.

He moved to the line of men, spacing them out along the piles of wood. The piles grew less and less as the men worked.

After minutes went by, Mr. Harkens half-dropped a heavy log. He caught it before it hit the floor, but his elbow jutted out and hit me in the shoulder. The pain of it made me step backward, and my workmen's cap fell to the floor. My hair spilled down my back.

"What's this then?" Caleb whispered.

I dared not turn around to face him. I felt him looking at me. "I'm Cassie Scott, the judge's daughter," I whispered. I knew he would start to question me. To divert him, I whispered, "I saw somebody out there a minute ago."

"Who?" Caleb said, catching the next log.

127

"A British sentry," I answered.

"Don't fret" was all he said.

The pile continued to shrink. Caleb moved outside now and stood close to the stone wall of the graveyard, tossing logs over it almost faster than Mr. Comerford could catch them. Mr. Fanshawe came up and began to catch logs, and I saw Papa jump up into the wagon with Eban, both of them catching and sorting logs. It was almost over. There were just Caleb, Zeke Thayer, Mr. Harkens, and myself in the vestibule of the church now. Zeke Thayer was not happy to be left working with Mr. Harkens. The two men jostled each other as they pulled logs off the pile, trading insults under their breaths. Mr. Harkens seemed to grab Mr. Thayer's logs just before he could pass them over to him. It made for clumsy handling; I held my breath. Mr. Thayer handed a log roughly to Mr. Harkens; Mr. Harkens dropped it. The log thudded heavily onto the blanketed floor. I heard a noise loud enough to jolt the horses; they whinnied in fear and stamped their hooves.

"Scatter!" Caleb's voice was low and urgent behind me somewhere. I dropped the log I was holding and ran; I couldn't see for the gloom. All of us left inside pushed and shoved to get through the doors. We fought each other to get out into the air, clumsily falling over one another in the graveyard in front of the church. I tripped over broken tombstones and tree limbs and over ditches. Someone was pushing and pulling me along. Suddenly we were in the meadow. I heard birdsong. Dust from Mr. Fanshawe's wagon rose up in front of us as he gripped his horses' reins and sped away in the direction of town, the wagon throwing logs off its sides in his haste to get away. It was full daylight.

"Into the woods. Get down! Get down!" It was Caleb at my back pulling me along, but I could hardly run anymore. I got a stitch in my side, and I stumbled onto rocks. He pulled me up and dragged me forward; he kept pulling me until I felt I would drop. Then we were in the tall grasses, and I was sitting on the ground, panting.

I turned once and looked back, and I saw soldiers moving lazily in their night shirts out in the chill morning air, seeming to wonder what had happened.

"We made it. They've got off with the wood."

"Where's my papa?" My breath came in short spurts.

"He was in the wagon when Fanshawe got the horses moving." Caleb's voice sounded raggedy too. "It's all over." He smiled at me. "Well, I'll say one thing for the judge's daughter, you're not wanting in courage. Now, run home, Cassie Scott, quickly. Go."

"But what about the sentry hiding in the woods and watching us?"

Caleb closed one fist over the other and lifted both to his chin and seemed to think before he answered. He leaned forward toward me. "There are some things you don't know about because it's dangerous for you to know. Accept it. Will you? You did incredible work today. Now, go, Cassie Scott."

With Caleb's words of praise still ringing in my ears, I had to admit he was more likeable. I picked myself up and began to run away from the high grasses; I came out of the woods near the shack. I didn't meet anyone and was about to turn in from the road when the sentry, Doggett, strode out of a patch of woods up ahead. He walked fast and didn't see me as he crossed the path on his way to the British huts behind the mansion. His red coat was dirty and full of brambles. I was sure he was on his way to report Papa's and Caleb's parts in the raid. Doggett surely saw Papa loading logs onto Mr. Fanshawe's wagon. Mayhap Papa would listen to me even if Caleb hadn't. But then he might not: I so clearly disobeyed him. *But I have to tell someone; I have to.*

Inside, Hannah was kneeling by the fire, stirring a pan of gruel. She set it down before me, but I had no appetite. I rested my head on my elbows on the table. "Eat and go to bed, Cassie. You need to rest."

"I can't. I have to go to work."

"No, you don't. Mrs. Fanshawe went in your place."

It was easier to eat than to argue with Hannah. When I finished, I went to bed.

When I woke up, the smell of chicken stew wafted through the door of the tiny room. It was dark. *It couldn't be morning, could it? When did I go to bed? What day was it?* Kitchen sounds brought me to my feet. I heard a noise. I knew that noise. It was a chair being moved in front of the fire. We had a crackling fire again! Is Papa home? Is it night? I wore long men's knickers. How did I get them? Mrs. Fanshawe. The church. The wood. It must be night. Yes, we had got the town's wood back. I remembered.

Papa said I had never slept so long in my whole life. I had slept away all the hours since the raid on the church. I walked into the shack kitchen. Papa looked up from his newspaper. "Good evening, Cassie." He smiled at me. He wasn't mad at me. Hannah lifted a ladle of chicken stew over a hunk of bread and set the plate down in front of me.

I was starving. I ate like a field hand. Hannah and Father looked at each other. Hannah's lips seemed to curve a bit. Was she laughing at me? The kitchen was warm, and the fire in the grate gave us light and heat. I felt at peace.

CHAPTER TWENTY-EIGHT

December 10, 1777

Another winter was upon us. Suzie and I walked together to the schoolhouse before daylight and came home many afternoons in the dark. We had letters from Max and Ernest from Valley Forge where the Continental army wintered under the command of General Washington.

Papa left the letters on the kitchen table in the shack for me and Hannah to read. I found Hannah crying when I got up one freezing cold morning and walked into the shack kitchen. When she saw me, Hannah put the letter she had been reading down on the oilcloth and wiped her eyes.

"And there is nothing we can do about it," she said.

"About what?" I asked.

"About the way our boys suffer from cold and hunger away from the warmth of home," she said. For once, I didn't resent her saying "our boys." I picked up the letters and took them to the tiny room I slept in to read, a space I could never call a bedroom.

Max wrote how when the army staggered into the campground at Valley Forge, only about one in four soldiers had shoes. He wrote of bloody footprints in the snow. Drinking water was scarce. The soldiers were freezing, always nagged by hunger this winter of '77; "firecakes" kept them alive, Max wrote, made of flour and water, no taste and no nourishment in them. Some of the soldiers boiled grass for soup. Even though huts were being built, the cold was brutal inside and out. Wind whistled through their thin clothes, and many soldiers died from exposure to the cold. On reading Max's letter, I put my head down and cried just like Hannah did.

CHAPTER TWENTY-NINE

Summer of 1778

There endured in our town a sense of desperate calm. The redcoats made no more lists of supplies and food they needed from us; they simply took what they needed from our barns and kitchens. They raided our cellars for meats hanging from hooks and picked our shelves clean of jars of pickled corn, cucumbers, and beans. As summer progressed, they invaded our fields for corn, lettuce, tomatoes, and melons. They left a few scattered rows here and there untouched in the fields for us to eke out our summertime meals. Our cows continued to give them milk. And they thought nothing of stealing our butter, pies, and milk from springhouses along the lanes. They shot small game themselves until squirrel and pheasant were almost gone from our already thinned-out woods. Horses and saddles they fancied, the redcoats simply removed them from barns across town. Father said the British liked it here in America. "And why not?" he asked. "Who wouldn't like it here?"

I said, "Don't they miss their own country, Papa?"

"Your father asked that question rhetorically," Hannah said.

"What does that mean?" It must be one of her Irish words. Either that or she'd learned some high words from Papa.

Hannah turned from the mantle where she was putting up herbs to dry. "It means he don't need an answer, Cassie."

Has she been dipping into books too? I'll wager she has. There's nothing that woman wouldn't do to be in Papa's good graces.

As time went on and no redcoats bothered us in our shack, and we came and went without interference from either Colonel Braithwaite or Captain Stonecroft, I stopped worrying about the colonel's threat to place Father in the Sugar House jail in York City if he carried out schemes against King George. Mayhap the colonel chose not to punish the town for the raid on the church because he was enjoying the easy life he led here. Or more likely, was it that somehow news of Father's and Caleb's parts in the raid had gone unknown to him? As time went on, I began to feel more confident that Father would stay safe.

I had transplanted a young rose bush from the mansion's front yard to the side of the path in front of the shack. It showed buds, and I was happy about it. Yet every day underneath the calm, there lingered fear.

CHAPTER THIRTY

September 1778

Awhaleboat was needed to add to Caleb Brewster's fleet to sink British ships in Long Island Sound. The sun was warm on Judge Scott's back as he stood at the foot of Jesse Prouty's gently sloping hillside. Easing down to the Sound in soft grasses, the hill would be a perfect place from which to launch a whaleboat. The plan needed only Jesse's acceptance. Jesse was the perfect workman for the job, being a sawyer as well as a carpenter and a gravedigger.

"Will you do it, Jesse? Will you build the whaleboat in your barn?"

"Honored, Judge, to do it."

"Good on you, Jesse!"

"Only thing, and I hate to say it, but nobody's got money to buy my chairs since the war started. I'm fishing and hunting to survive like most people in town. But I'm in, and I'm sure Joe Comerford, my partner, will work with me."

"There's money enough to pay both of you."

"Done." The two shook hands. "I wish I could do it for nothin', Judge. I'd like to."

"Understood, Jesse."

There were no redcoats dwelling in this part of town. British soldiers billeted with rebel families in tidy, white-curtained cottages on higher ground uptown. Security was left to sullen sentries, who patrolled this low-lying land carelessly or not at all through the night. Jesse told Judge Scott of his practice of dropping rocks and broken branches along the paths used by sentries to further discourage them from patrolling the lonely route along the water. The results were good; after the redcoats thudded down the hill, tripping over all the obstacles in their path, "including broken glass," Jesse added, they generally avoided Jesse's property.

Most folks thought of Jesse as "eccentric" because he lived like a hermit near the water and away from the uptowners who bought his chairs. Before the war, almost every cottage uptown in Cow Neck had bought two chairs from Jesse to put on each side of their hearths. Uptown people thought Jesse's chairs were equal in quality and grace to those of Mr. Chippendale in Philadelphia, and they rushed to buy them the minute Jesse applied the last bit of finish. Now, British soldiers sat on them and used the rungs for mud stoppers.

Joe Comerford, Cow Neck's other sawyer, carpenter, and fellow gravedigger, agreed to work with Jesse. The operation was supposed to be a secret, known to no one outside of Caleb Brewster, Papa, and the builders themselves. But word got around to people who could help. Town Patriots dredged up the wreck of a half-sunk dory sticking up out of the mud at low tide; they took it apart, left it on the grassy banks back of the mill pond, and covered it in burlap to dry. A week later, they carted the planks, pegs, and ironware up the hill to Jesse's barn on a night when he had used precious English pence to buy hot peppers and chunks of bread to add to his mix of broken glass, logs, rocks and branches guarding his barn. After the curious sentry had fallen hard on his face, several Patriots waiting inside the barn heard the cheerful sounds of snorting, sneezing, and coughing; then mumbled cursing and at last boots stumbling away. Work on the whaleboat could go on uninterrupted.

CHAPTER THIRTY-ONE

Hercules Mulligan, bluff, hearty Irishman that he was, enjoyed a good stand in front of his men's clothing store on the Broad Way, across from the ruins of Trinity Church. Even today, a soft, sunny September day, there hung in the air the occasional whiff of charred wood to remind him of the devastation of that other day and night two years ago when Trinity burned. *But today is a beautiful day, and it deserves to be enjoyed*, Hercules reflected to himself as he traded greetings and smiles with British soldiers and everyday Americans, even the ones loyal to King George. Hercules didn't forget the ladies either and bowed especially as the pretty ones walked by his store.

The pigs waddling along in the dust up from Wall Street took no notice of the many wagons loaded with farmers' harvests traveling alongside of them or the carriages and messengers on horseback, who gave them plenty of room.

Hercules lit up a cigar and tasted the reassuring flavor of burning tobacco. He exhaled and took a sip from his coffee cup. The soft summer day with almost no breeze was perfect.

Hercules took a special pleasure in giving his blarney out to the British officers who strolled the streets, four abreast, as if they owned them. Privately, Hercules hated the redcoats for their arrogance and sense of entitlement. But in his shop "Hercules Haberdashery," they brought him good business. They needed boots, helmets, dress uniforms made from fine broadcloth, and gold braids for decoration for which they paid in solid British pounds, and not the almost worthless continental dollars. American belles wandering past Hercules's shop along the Broad Way were welcomed inside by a silver bowl of chocolates sitting on a table visible from outside the gold-framed, windowed doors. Hercules knew that the ongoing spirited, open flirting between the officers and the lasses was one reason his store revenues were climbing through the roof.

Hercules served rich Jamaican coffee to the officers. In chatting with them, they became quite comfortable and spoke freely. He listened carefully to their easy talk among themselves and congratulated himself on the good fortune that had brought the English officers together with American girls. Chocolates, Jamaican coffee, and pretty girls, he mused, were surefire ways to tempt the British officers to loosen up their lips. He had a lot to be grateful for, did Hercules. Not only was he a successful merchant catering for the British Army, but he was also able to pick up a steady stream of solid information to pass on to the people close to General Washington. Hercules was not alone in his pursuit of information. He was grateful to Cato, who worked side by side with him. Cato was more a friend and confidante to Hercules than he was a slave, and he worked for the Patriot cause. Cato enjoyed Hercules's trust. This very morning, Cato, pinning up the hem of a pair of pants for a redcoat officer chatting idly with another, overheard a valuable piece of information.

Smiling his thanks for the fitting, the officers moved on. Cato walked over to Hercules, who was in the act of concluding a satisfactory helmet and boot sale. Cato waited until the sale was complete.

He brushed the shoulders of Hercules's expensive, elegant morning coat with his dust remover and whispered the new intelligence into Hercules's ear.

Now, this lovely summer-like day when bright flowers still bloomed in gardens along the mud-spattered, gritty, pig-fouled, and crowded Broad Way, Hercules stood outside his store and waited for the runner who passed every day looking for crumbs of information to pass on to General Washington's spy network. This time he had a whole cake, thanks to Cato.

And while he waited, Hercules took time to smoke his cigar and empty a bag of bread crusts for the pigs who were now gathered outside his doors for their morning meal that Hercules fed them from his own hand. The first loaf of bread went to Caesar, the clear leader of the pigs, as only fitting to the leader; then Hercules fed big, round-bellied Alfie, second in command to Caesar. And Hercules acknowledged him by holding out a half-loaf for which Alfie gave a gracious grunt before he pushed away to breakfast on it. The other pigs stood together and politely waited to be fed from Hercules's hand. Hercules patted the pigs and eased them out of the narrow store entrance, as soon as they were fed, and then watched them waddle away behind Caesar and Alfie to stand in the shade of the Money Exchange.

Hercules was eager to tell his news. The French and the Americans had signed an Alliance. The French were getting ready to join the Americans in the war against England, and the English knew it. They were planning to intercept French ships at Newport. This news had to travel today. There was one man Hercules trusted who could carry this intelligence to Connecticut, there to be handed over to a Patriot messenger and delivered to the general personally. That man was Caleb Brewster, the whaleman.

Soon, a young Dutchman wearing buckskin stopped to admire uniforms in Hercules's window. English was his language, though his accent was Dutch. His name was Jan Deecke, and he worked for an import and export company dealing in Jamaican coffee.

Hercules looked up and down the wide dirt street before he spoke and then in a low whisper. "I need to give Caleb Brewster a piece of intelligence to take to Fairfield for General Washington. Where can I meet him?"

"Caleb's already in Fairfield." On hearing this, the day darkened for Hercules. The runner continued to look into the store window for a few seconds. "There be someone else," he said under his breath, "who will bring a new whaleboat to Fairfield tonight. He can take the information and pass it to Caleb."

The two men stood, looking straight ahead.

"Who would he be?" Caleb asked.

"I shall not say. But he works for us. He's never been caught." Sensing hesitation on Hercules's part, Jan Deecke said, "You'll have to trust me, Hercules."

Hercules passed the Dutchman his message. Jan Deecke slipped it into his boot while pretending to shake it free of a pebble.

"How will we know if it's got through?"

"Meet me at the Bull's Head tonight at ten. I shall report that all goes well or not."

Hercules threw the remains of his coffee into the dirt, where it made tiny circular puddles in the mud.

The pigs came trotting over for one last pet of his hand, but he darted into his shop and closed the door behind him while the pigs stood peering into the shop like little children with their noses pressed up against the store windows.

Morning passed in a blur of British pounds crossing Hercules's counter, followed by rich red British officers' uniforms pulled across in the other direction. Chatter snapped among the officers about which salon would provide the most entertainment and the best food for their delectation this evening. Hercules, accepting payment at his counter, was pleased to tell some of his highest-ranking customers wearing the most gold braid they would be very welcome at the salon Mrs. Richard Parvington would hold at her house at 12 John Street. She would serve them rum, engage them in fascinating conversation, and introduce them to lovely ladies and fine gentlemen loyal to His Majesty, King George III. The officers made their plans. Hercules smiled to himself. When he sat among his Sons of Liberty friends, he called these fine-looking officers "damn, stinkin' macaronis."

CHAPTER THIRTY-TWO

"Do you go to Mrs. Parvington's salon, 'Ercules?" Cato asked at the end of the day, with an arched eyebrow to show his sarcasm.

"No. I won't, but I'll meet you over at the Bull's Head around ten tonight for a beer and a plate of sloppy oysters. What do you say to that, Cato?"

Cato smiled. "I'll watch for you." The two men's eyes met in mutual understanding. The Bull's Head was Cato's neighborhood pub run by York City blacks and had a long history of serving a black crowd, although some white men were favored here. Hercules was one of them.

It was at the bar in the Bull's Head where the Great Negro Uprising of 1741 was hatched by two slaves—one, Caesar, and the other, Romulus—to burn the city down. The plan was doomed to failure. The authorities caught and hanged both conspirators. The Bull's Head was known for its subversive reputation, and even now, almost four decades later, information could be picked up at its bar. For the most part, its patrons were street sweepers, ostlers, farm workers, metal workers, and silver buffers—all of them with their ears to the ground for stray talk. If you were a known patron, sympathetic to the Patriot cause as well as the Abolitionist cause, as was Hercules, you were trusted, as was Jan Deecke.

Ten o'clock

Hercules and Cato stood at the bar of the Bulls Head Tavern.

"I'll have a flip," Hercules said to the bartender.

"Hercules, that stuff be powerful."

"Just one, Cato, to put me in good health and good spirits."

"'Ercules, they put wine and mix it with beer, then they t'row rum in dere. What? You crazy? You could get good and drunk."

"Here's to you, Cato!" He lifted his glass and downed the flip in three swallows. "That's good stuff, Cato. But I'll not have another." Though warm in the tavern, none complained, and the talk among the crowd of men on this fall night was pleasant.

"Good, you don't drink no more. Look who comes, 'Ercules. The Dutchman."

Hercules nodded. "I see him. He's making his way toward us."

The throng of sweaty men surrounding the bar made way for the Dutchman. He stopped to greet other Dutchmen, drank a beer with some of them, and then slowly meandered toward Hercules.

All three men leaned over the bar, speaking under the crowd's noise. "So," Hercules said, "how did the work go today?" The three men stood in a close circle.

Jan Deecke spoke low. "Good. I had to go to Staten Island to find the man."

"Who is he?" There was tension in Hercules's voice.

"I can't say more or give his name. He does hidden work for us. I gave him your message. He left late this afternoon to pick up a whaleboat at Cow Neck. His crew rowed it to Fairfield to be fitted out for a sail. He'll give your message to Caleb." A smile appeared on the faces of Hercules and Cato and even spread thinly across the Dutchman's somber mouth. "He should be reaching Fairfield just about now."

CHAPTER THIRTY-THREE

J esse Prouty's barn, earlier the same evening
"Shh!"

"What is it, man?" Jesse Prouty stopped polishing the hull of the newly constructed whaleboat. Outside Jesse's barn, a fresh wind had picked up, and the boat's timbers creaked in response.

"A branch dropped. Somebody could be out there." Joe Comerford held his polishing rag in the air.

"You're daft. Stop worryin'." Jesse kept rubbing the side of the boat. But both men stopped talking to listen. Silence again.

"Can't help it, mate." Joe's breath became fast and shallow. "If we're discovered..." Joe let the end of his sentence drop.

"Stop sweatin', Joe. Judge Scott got a new sentry. He's come to us from the Brits. We got word he's a good man, this fellow Doggett, come over to our side."

"I heard about him. Don't be too sure about Doggett. For all we know, he's working two sides of the street, a double agent. How do we know he's come over to us? How do we know he ain't a traitor?"

"Doggett never wanted to be in this war. He was clubbed in the head in a bar in Dublin and drug here to fight alongside the Brits. He's with us, not against us. Besides, Hannah Scott vouches for him"

"She's no bargain either, Jesse. I don't trust her; neither do a lot of other people in this town. How do you know she's not teaming up with him against us?"

"I know because Judge Scott vouches for Hannah."

"The judge is playin' a risky game. If he's caught, he'll be hanged, and our necks will be in nooses too."

"The judge's word is good enough for me, Joe." Jesse went back to polishing. Both men were silent again. Jesse ran his hand across the stern of the boat. "She sure looks good, don't she though, Joe?"

"She does. But by God, Jesse, this boat can make it plenty hot for us. I'm just not feelin' right about that soldier Doggett doin' sentry duty tonight, that's all."

"Forget Doggett. I tell ya he's all right. The best part of it is the way the hill slopes right down into the water outside the barn. It'll be real quick gettin' her launched."

A soft knock. "Trouble!" Joe Comerford's nerves had reached fever pitch.

"Douse the lantern. Shh!" Now Jesse Prouty's voice shook.

In the dark, the two men listened. Nothing now but the peculiar sounds of night. Paws scratching, branches cracking in the wind, and slithers through the grass.

"You bolted the door?" Joe whispered.

"'Course," Jesse whispered back. They listened. The knock came again, more insistent.

Tiptoeing to the barn doors, they carried hammers in their upraised hands. "Jesse, Joe?"

"It's Judge Scott. He's got someone with him." Joe poised his hand above the lock.

"Open the door." Judge Scott's low guttural voice sounded urgent. Jesse quickly oiled the metal bar on the inside of the barn doors and pried it backward through the twin braces that held it in place. As he did so, Judge Scott walked onto the sawdust-covered floor; David Van Essen followed.

"What's happening?" Jesse swallowed. His breath came fast. He was first to see the barrel of David's rifle aimed at his heart.

"Nothing, except I need the boat. Let's get her launched." David Van Essen stepped up, exposing his British Army officer's uniform to the glow of the candle.

"Wait a minute. You're Van Essen, the traitor." Joe moved to stand in front of the judge. "Van Essen. What's he doin' here, Judge?"

Judge Scott walked slowly over to Joe. "It's all right, Joe. It is. I don't see what else we can do except to let the whaleboat go."

"I say there is, Judge."

Judge Scott said calmly, "He's right here, aiming his rifle at us. He'll use it. He's already given his soul to the devil. He doesn't care."

Joe Comerford threw his polishing rag on the barn floor. "Do what you have to do then. I'll not be a part of it." He walked out of the barn, slamming the barn door shut behind him.

"I need that boat. Let's go." Red-coated David Van Essen moved to the stern. "Let's get her launched."

As if on signal, the barn doors opened wide. Eighteen burly rowers emerged from the woods and pushed the boat away from the barn onto the grass as Jesse closed the doors in practiced silence.

Silently, easily, the men slid the boat down the slope of the hill on the damp grass, where she cut into the water without a ripple. David Van Essen climbed into the prow of the newly launched whaleboat. The rowers took their places for lifting the oars from their locks. Easily, the boat slipped away from the banks of Berry

Creek and made the turn into the Sound. In a minute, she was out in the deep water and headed across to Connecticut.

Jesse and Judge Scott watched from the banks of Berry Creek. Off in the distance, the sentry Doggett watched them from a short distance away. Judge Scott waved. Doggett waved back and then turned and walked off.

Wordlessly, Jesse and the judge walked back to Jesse's barn. Finally, Jesse said, "I feel bad about Joe, Judge."

"I do too, Jesse. But it's better for Joe and for David if he thinks David is a traitor."

"Yeah, I guess you're right. Will I row you home, Judge? My canoe is tied up close by." In the hush of the morning air, the two men paddled along the creek, gently interrupting the glasslike surface of the water.

CHAPTER THIRTY-FOUR

Most mornings Papa and Hannah had their little talks over coffee before I came out to the kitchen. But this morning when I walked out to the shack kitchen, Papa was sitting down, holding his face in his hands. His boots lay on the floor; he had not begun his usual struggle to get them on yet.

"Are you sick, Papa?"

"No, Cassie."

"Why do you sit like that?"

"I am tired. That's all, and I have a long ride today into York City with Matthew Douglas."

"Papa, should you go into there? There are redcoats all over the place."

Hannah looked up from the fire. "Soon time for you to go to work, isn't it, Cassie?" I ignored her. *Something was going to happen. I needed to find out.* Papa bent down to pull mightily on his boots.

"I'll help," I said.

"I'll be fine, daughter." Papa stood up. Hannah helped him with his cloak.

"Why, Papa? Why do you go into the city with Mr. Douglas?"

"Just a piece of courtroom business, Cassie. Nothing more. I shall be home before dark. Depend on it." Papa kissed me on the cheek. He turned and gave a kiss to Hannah. I watched out the window as he hitched up Star and rode out onto the lane.

I shall tell him tonight about the sentry Tom Doggett who watched as the whaleboat left the barn. There was no doubt that Doggett was working hand in glove with Hannah to wreak havoc against our Patriot cause. *Yes, tonight I shall tell Papa.*

CHAPTER THIRTY-FIVE

All Hallows' Eve, 1778

Ghosts and goblins would haunt our island tonight. Papa was true to his word. He arrived at the shack just as evening fell. He, Hannah, and I were busy in the kitchen. We had a good fire every night now thanks to the raid on the Presbyterian Church. Since then, the British, even though they inspected every home for firewood, never found a single log. Though they looked in every shelf, under every bed, in every pantry, and outside, and under every woodpile, they never pulled up the floorboards in the cottage kitchens where most of the town's valuables along with the firewood were neatly stacked. Long poles were used to pull the logs along to an opening in the kitchen floor near the fire and then lifted up to remove logs as needed.

Tonight, in the tiny shack kitchen, I corrected sums and drank tea, grateful for the quiet and the fire and grateful for Papa's safe trip and his presence in the kitchen. Knowing he would stay home the next day to work on his cases, I felt at ease. I couldn't bring myself to tell him now of Doggett's spying on us;

tomorrow would do. The news would make him so unhappy, and he looked very comfortable, enjoying the warmth of his fire and the household sounds, shack or no shack. No harm could come to Papa at home, I was sure. The flickers of light and fire from the candle lamps and the noise of Papa's quill scratching on paper comforted me, too. Even Hannah, spoon in hand above the warm pot of chocolate, added to my contented feeling. A strong wind came up, and the candle flames flickered. Outside, the wind howled and whistled about the corners of the shack. But I felt protected with Papa in the house. Hannah stood with her back to us at the hearth, pouring the near boiling chocolate into pewter mugs.

I had not realized Papa had put down his quill and picked up his newspaper. I had one of those rare moments when I felt everything was just right.

All of a sudden, the door burst open in a gust of cold air. There had been no knock. Two British soldiers carrying Brown Bess rifles squeezed through the kitchen door. "Beggin' yese all pardons for enterin' without knockin'." The tallest one pulled his heels together smartly, cleared his throat, and continued, "Judge Philip Scott, you are under arrest, this thirty-first day of October in the year of our Lord, 1778, by order of his Royal Majesty, King George III." Having delivered himself of probably the longest speech he had ever made in his whole life, the redcoat advanced upon Papa. Candle fat sputtered on the table. Hannah's spoon sank into the tureen of chocolate. I dropped the child's sum book I was correcting onto the table, and my quill fell to the floor.

Papa bolted up from his chair. "What's the charge?"

"We don't know the charge, sir. All's we know is we are here to arrest you in the name of the King of England, your lawful sovereign. We've orders to bring you to Colonel Braithwaite. If you'll come peaceable like, it will go much easier for you, sir."

Papa strode toward him. "You've no right to enter these premises. Get out at once!"

"Afraid we can't do that, sir. Will you come peaceable like?" Though he stood his ground, the soldier's voice shook.

Quick enough, I reached for Papa's musket on the wall behind me and hurled it by the barrel to him. He caught it and got his hands around the barrel, but the silent redcoat was quicker. He managed to pull Papa's hands from the gun. The other soldier held his gun aimed at Papa's chest, but that didn't stop Papa. He struggled with both soldiers and came away with a Brown Bess at his side that he shoved across the table to Hannah, who threw herself against the table and managed to get her hands on the rifle. She ran with it across the room and aimed the gun at the other soldier, who had by now pinned Papa to his chair with a rope around his hands and looped around Papa's neck so that if Papa moved he would strangle himself. He then aimed his gun at Hannah, who already had aimed the gun at him. I lurched past him to the door, pushing the rifle away from him and making a grab for it. His finger was already on the trigger. Hannah was a second from death. She shot the gun off. At first the smoke was too dense to see, and the silence engulfed all of us. I heard her scream. As the smoke cleared, the silent redcoat smacked her hands away from the rifle. His eye was bloodied. I managed to open the door. The two redcoats now lifted Papa from his chair and hurried him to the door. I stuck my foot out in front of it, just after Hannah ran through to the outside, and the soldier went head over heels into the bushes. But he was up fast, barking at Papa, "Move. Move." I went after him, but he easily pushed me back inside, and I ended up just a step from the fire in the hearth. Worse, Papa was taken away without a word. He had been able to do nothing to save himself.

"Hannah," I screamed. My heart beat like thunder. "The fire!" The hem of my gown was on fire, creeping up through the petticoat. Hannah, holding her shoulder in pain, took a look at me and grabbed the nearest thing, the pot of water waiting to be hung up for tea on the hob. I felt the coldness of the water blot out the hot, hot fire. We both sat on the floor, trying to get up, but it was minutes before she or I could stand.

"What shall we do? Where will they take Papa?"

Hannah, her face blackened from gun oil and ashes, tied her bonnet and wrapped her cloak around her shoulders. "I'll run for Caleb."

"Where will they take him? What will they do to him? It's too late. They'll…"

"'Tisn't too late. Caleb will help us." Hannah left me standing in the open doorway. I heard her hitch up Star, and then she was gone into the night. Inside, with the door closed, the emptiness of the room and the sudden silence overwhelmed me. I shook with fear. Papa's newspaper lay scattered on the floor, and Hannah's chocolate had spilled and now burned over the grate. Pewter plates and cups lay askew mixed up with herbs from the kitchen garden and ashes from the grate. The fire in the hearth sparked and spat out burning embers. *Oh, Papa. They've got you. It has happened.* I put my head down on the table, clenching my fists. Hannah was gone a long time. When she didn't come back, I lay down on the cot near the fire. Soon, I gave in completely and sobbed. *Where is Papa right now? Please let him be warm and dry.*

CHAPTER THIRTY-SIX

Morning. I smelled coffee. I was cold. Something dreadful tugged at my heart.

"Get up, Cassie." Hannah stood over me. I hardly recognized her. Her hair was pulled back and tied up. She was dressed for the road with her heavy brown homespun gown almost hiding her old brown, muddy boots. I had been dreaming. In my dream, I felt the softness of the Persian rugs under my feet in our mansion's parlor. I was looking for my mother to tell her something very bad had happened. Her half-knitted scarf lay across the arm of our raspberry velvet sofa, the basket of wool alongside on the carpet. But I couldn't find Mama.

"Come, Cassie. Get up. We must talk." Hannah bustled over to the fire. The chickens, the cows, the dogs, and the horse—they all had to be fed. Why was she dressed in her cloak and boots? I felt a thud in my stomach, and I remembered the worst. Papa was detained by the British. I had slept all night on the cot. When I sat up, Hannah was pouring coffee.

I pressed my hands to my face. "Papa's gone. What will become of him?"

"Here." Hannah poured two cups of coffee and set them down. "Sit." She hovered over me, putting her hands on my shoulders and guiding me to the table. I pushed her hands away. She scraped the wooden chair out from under the table and waited while I sat. Sitting down opposite to me, she sipped from her cup of coffee and then leaned forward, folding her hands around her pewter cup. "Stop crying, Cassie. You don't have to go out to the barn today. I've done the chores. Stay here." She poured cream into my cup. "Cassie, I must go to your father."

"And I must go with you." I crossed my arms and held on to my shoulders. I felt the hot tears sting my eyes again.

"Not the two of us, Cassie. I have to go to Brooklyn alone to get your father back."

"I'm going too, Hannah." I saw her rucksack at the shack door.

"No, you can't come with me. I've got to go by myself." She went on, speaking fast. "Caleb told me that the British take prisoners from Long Island and put them in the hold of prison ships in Wallabout Bay in Brooklyn. Many men have died on these ships without food, light, and air. I must go there."

"I'm coming with you." I stood up to face Hannah, noticing for the first time I was as tall as she.

"No. You are not coming with me. You must stay here until Caleb tells you to leave." She slipped her shawl over her shoulders.

"I will not stay here. I shall go to my father. I'll follow you if I must." I rushed to put my cloak over my shoulders.

"Cassie, listen to me. I must first see my relatives in Brooklyn. I have an aunt and uncle who are loyal to the king. They can help us."

"I'm not surprised, and I'm sure you spy for them."

"No, Cassie. I do not." Hannah lifted her face, and I saw her eyes flashing black points of fire. "My uncle Livingston is Tory; I'm not. He will arrange for your papa's release from the prison ship."

"Why would he do that?"

"Out of love for me."

"He'd set a Patriot prisoner free out of love for you? I don't think so." I didn't bother to hide my disbelief.

"Yes. He will. My uncle came to me at Mrs. Curry's Inn when I got off the boat and asked me to come home with him and to live with him and Aunt Sally, but I wanted to be on my own in this new country of America. He understood. He said if ever I needed anything, anything at all, I should come to him. Now I need to get your papa off the prison ship. Caleb told me he will be on the *Jersey*, where prisoners are kept below deck all day, where the air is smelly and the food is wormy and bad. Caleb told me I have to do this alone. Do you understand, Cassie?"

"Caleb said that?" My stomach heaved. I didn't know whether to believe her or not. "How do I know you won't betray Papa to your uncle?"

"Give that up, Cassie! I love your father. I would never betray him." Hannah sat back in her chair. Her face was stone.

I looked at Hannah. *Is it possible she is speaking the truth? Shall I believe her?*

"I've got to go. You must take care of yourself until we come back." Hannah got up, drinking the last bit of coffee. She pulled her winter cloak around her shoulders and her plaid shawl over her neck and picked up her rucksack. With her hand on the door, she stopped and turned. "Cassie, my aunt and uncle live in the Heights of Brooklyn. Mail comes to them at the Blue Boar Inn. If you need to write to me, you can reach me there. Give your letter to Mr. Douglas at the store. He can bring it to me on one of his trips to Brooklyn. I hope to be back with your papa within a fortnight."

Forcing myself, I said, "I shall be grateful to you if you bring my father home." Hannah opened the door and was gone. In a minute, she was lost in the dust of the road.

Three weeks passed. No word from Hannah. I wrote a letter to her at the Blue Boar Inn and gave it to Mr. Douglas to give to her when he went to Brooklyn next to buy food for the store, but I never got an answer. Mr. Douglas made inquiries at the Blue Boar Inn and found out that Hannah had left the inn after visiting her relative.

The days became shorter and shorter. Nights I sat in front of the fire, thinking and wondering about Father. *Did Hannah get him off the prison ship? Where would they have gone? Had they tried to cross the Sound in the cold, angry dark and tried to put in somewhere on the way to Cow Neck? And the unthinkable, did my Papa die on the prison ship?*

CHAPTER THIRTY-SEVEN

Christmas Day, 1778

Still nothing from Hannah's quill had been received, either by me or anyone else, since the day she left. Early in the morning, Mrs. Fanshawe, Mr. Fanshawe, Suzie, Eban, and I walked to church. I didn't want to go, but the others would have me go, so I went, feeling bad. On the way, we met British soldiers walking to St. George's for Christmas services. We stepped aside on the path to let the soldiers pass. They didn't notice that we didn't salute.

Since the morning was cold, dreary, and colorless, everyone brightened at the warm, simple Christmas service at St. George's, pristine in its white wooden interior, untouched by the British because they worshipped there. I tried to cheer myself, but my heart was broken. I saw the town ladies had cut branches from pine trees and lined the altar with them. The gold vestments the vicar wore glowed in the candlelight amid the sparkle of the white altar cloth. Bowls of greens surrounded the cradle of the baby Jesus. If I had known Papa was safe, I would have enjoyed the pageant. It presented a welcome sight to all my neighbors, but for me there was only sadness. Ashamed I was that I admired the gold braid on the jackets of the handsome British soldiers and their reverence as they knelt with their hands folded. Some of them were my age, probably longing to be home with their families. After the service, I walked with Suzie, Eban, and the Fanshawes to their house, where Mr. Fanshawe poured rum for himself and Eban and a little bit for Mrs. Fanshawe, Suzie, and me. We ate delicious biscuits there, and I felt somewhat better.

If only Papa were here; if only he could have been with us. I missed him so. I didn't miss Hannah, but I did miss the noise she made bustling about the shack, singing in her booming voice, and her heavy boot steps in the kitchen. Now there was no noise in the shack except for the noise I made. It was probably the quietest time of my life, this Christmas, and the loneliest. Every day, I expected my father back home. And every day, he didn't come back.

CHAPTER THIRTY-EIGHT

March 1779

March was always a hard month on our island. I still had no word from Hannah or from Papa. But I was used to not hearing from them, and I barely cried about them. Last night, I had forgotten to bank the fire, and when I woke up before dawn, nothing but dead, cold embers greeted me.

Later, slipping and sliding along Berry Creek to the schoolhouse, Suzie and I battled a fierce nor'easter wind. I turned my face to Suzie. "Where is Eban? He didn't wave good-bye to you, the way he usually does." But my words were lost in swirls of wind choking them back and flattening my cloak against my body.

We came to a stop at Miss Hoary's cottage a bit further on by the banks of the creek. It was quiet there, standing against the cottage wall protected by bushes.

"What did you say back there, Cassie?"

"What happened to Eban this morning? He didn't wave good-bye to you."

"He went out Huntington way to sell his cow. Daisy's old and can't give milk anymore. If he can't sell her, he'll give her to a poor family for slaughter, rather than hand her over to the British."

Freezing and battered about by the wind, we arrived at the schoolhouse, late and hungry. Miss Hoary said nothing, only smiled at us. Inside it was warm and dry, and I felt better when I looked down at the fresh faces of the children. There was tea on the hob. *Mayhap things weren't all that bad, after all.* I poured myself a cup and sat down next to a child who was struggling with his reading. He was a dear child and smiled up at me after I helped him sound out his letters to make words. Lunch, followed by the dreaded arithmetic test, kept the children quiet and occupied till Miss Hoary raised her arm to signal the test was done.

As I opened the schoolhouse door to dismiss the children, a glorious blue sky with soft white clouds greeted us, and a light breeze crept in over the Sound. Suzie and I hurried to Jesse Prouty's grassy hillside on the chance there would be high waves out on the water against which the anchored British ships would heave and pitch right after a storm. It was always a good show to see British sailors tug on the ropes in the struggle to keep their keels even. But this day it was a disappointing show. Choppy, the water only heaved whitecaps close to the shore. Seagulls gathered in circles in the sky; wind swirls kept them soaring and swooping. We sat down on the warm, wet grass.

"Do you fancy our papas are well, Cassie?" Suzie said.

I looked down at a long blade of grass and didn't answer right away. "I've stopped wondering; it makes me too sad."

"I've got a letter from my grampa, Cassie. He wants me to come live with him and my grammy in York City until my papa comes home." Suzie looked out over the water.

I lifted my head, forgetting even the sadness of a moment ago. "Are you going?"

"Yes."

When I didn't say anything, Suzie said, "It will be very hard to leave here."

"Why must you leave? Do they say you have to leave?"

"I don't have to; I want to leave." Suzie hesitated, "I hate the way we have to live. I'm tired of being hungry. It's just going to be hard to leave Eban because he's looked after me so long, and Miss Hoary, and hard to leave you too, my best friend. I'm sad to go, but I want to go."

"But your gramps is Tory," I said.

"I don't care. He knows I'm a Patriot. My papa, his own son, fights for the Patriot cause. Gramps won't change Papa, and he won't change me. He just wants me to live a better life."

"I didn't think you would go live with a Tory family," I said. I shook my head and then picked up a yellow dandelion, twisted it, and then dropped the green stem of the dandelion. "You're going to York City to live with the enemy."

"Not the enemy. They are my grandparents. Yes, I'm going to go. They both want me to live with them. And I want to go." Suzie's face brightened. "Besides, in the city they have parties and balls and shops. Cassie, come with me. Gramps would be glad, I know he would be, if I brought my friend."

"No, Suzie. Papa will come home. I want to be here when he does."

"Think about it, please, Cassie. We could have so much fun."

"I'll stay here with the others. Besides, you might change your mind."

"I won't change my mind, Cassie. As soon as the roads are free of mud, Gramps will come for me." Suzie was looking far out over the water in the Sound. It just didn't seem possible that Suzie would go off to York City.

"I'll be lonely on the walk to school," I said finally.

"But you don't have to be lonely if you come with me."

A voice from the top of the hill came to us. "That's Sarah. Here she comes. She's singing the 'Madrigal of Spring.'"

Suzie jumped up. "I'm leaving. Tell me you'll think about coming with me to York City please, Cassie. I want you to come."

"No, Suzie. I don't want to go to the city."

"Do think about it, Cassie. Please. Here Sarah comes. I'm going."

But Sarah came loping up Jesse's hill before Suzie could run and she came to a stop in front of us. "I thought I'd find you here, Cassie! I stayed to help Miss Hoary put away the books. Isn't it heavenly out? I have news. Oh, Suzie, hello."

"Hi, Sarah" was all she said, standing apart from Sarah, as if she would start running any minute.

"What's the news?" I asked.

Sarah was thrilled to tell us. She licked her lips and began, "Well, Papa and Mama are having a recital and afternoon tea dance on Sunday next. I'm to sing. And guess what! You are invited, Cassie. I need you to play for me." Sarah said this as though I should be grateful for the honor.

"No, I don't think so, Sarah," I said, trying hard to refuse her in a nice way.

Sarah's face went red. "Why not? Why ever not?"

"I can't possibly play for you. I haven't played since the redcoats came. My piano is in the mansion in front of the french doors, where it gets all the dampness from outside. By now, it's out of tune and full of soldiers' boot marks."

"You can't mean you won't play for me, Cassie." Sarah's hands flew to her hips. She spoke harshly.

"I do mean it. I'm out of practice. I'm sorry. I shall see you in the morning, Sarah." Suddenly, the brightness went away from the day. "I want to go home right now. Good-bye, Sarah."

"But there's no one else to play for me, Cassie," she wailed.

"Sarah, I just told you I haven't practiced since we left the mansion to live in the shack."

"Cassie, you can practice on my pianoforte. Everyone's coming. The Fanshawes, the Comerfords, Mr. Douglas, and the Thayers. Mr. Ferguson will play his fiddle, and Miss Place will play flute. Miss Hoary will be there too. It will be such fun, Cassie. You've just got to play for me. Please, Cassie. Besides, the best news is that Captain Stonecroft said he will attend, too."

I started to walk away but turned at Sarah speaking the captain's name. "Do you mean that overstuffed jackass British officer who put us out of our mansion, standing at our front door with his gun pointed at us? Would I go to a party he attended? No, Sarah, I would not." I stood with my arms folded across my chest to show my contempt for the captain.

Suzie was already halfway down the hill. She turned and called back, "I'll see you tomorrow, Cassie." She did not say good-bye to Sarah.

"See you tomorrow, Sarah." I started down the hill.

"Wait, Cassie. Wait, please." Sarah kept up with me by taking two steps to my one. I was much taller than she. "Please, Cassie, say you'll come to play for my recital. Won't you, Cassie?"

"No. I won't, Sarah. I will not play for you. Not only that, I am mad at you because you didn't even ask Suzie to come, and she was standing right there. What kind of manners do you have anyway?" And then I thought, *Why not?* "There's one way I'll play for you, Sarah. Invite Suzie and Eban, too."

"I can't invite Suzie. She's an orphan. She was born out of wedlock, and Mr. Mancks found her on his doorstep. She's not the same as us."

I jolted to a stop and turned toward Sarah. "Sarah, you know that's an ugly rumor. But even if it were true, the best thing is Mr. Mancks loves Suzie, and she loves him as her father."

166

"All right. Mayhap it's a rumor about Suzie, but I've been hearing it all my life."

Sarah looked away down the hill. I couldn't tell if she was sorry she said what she did, or if she was just thinking of another way to get me to play for her. I started walking fast again.

"Cassie, I can't sing without you on the piano. I'll be too nervous. Please, Cassie, play for me on Sunday afternoon."

I turned around and stopped to look right into Sarah's eyes. "I told you, if you invite Suzie and Eban, I'll do it."

"Eban! But, Cassie, he's the town handyman. He's an old wreck, and he's a bit teched in the head, people say."

"Damn and blast, Sarah! What if he is the town handyman?"

"Cassie, you love to play the piano, and you love to dance. Remember how you and that turncoat David Van Essen danced at the Liberty Feast? Captain Stonecroft said he will come; mayhap he'll dance with you."

"Are you deaf? I wouldn't dance with him if he dropped to his knees and begged me. And why would your parents invite the British captain? Both of us know why, and so does everybody else in town know your father is loyal to King George. That's why Colonel Braithwaite hasn't seized your house. That's why you invited that odious Captain Stonecroft, his second in command."

Sarah's face reddened. Her hands went straight to her hips. She was so mad at me spit beads tumbled out of her mouth as she spoke. "We can't help that the captain is friendly to us. My father is a true Patriot, but he needs to make money so my mama can keep a good home."

"What's a Patriot doing selling his wares to the British?" I asked sweetly.

"There's not a thing wrong with it, Cassie."

"Your father is making money off the British, which makes him a sympathizer, a lobsterback."

Sarah took a step closer to me, facing me. "Is that so? Well, you know what, Cassie? You think my papa is a king's man? What about your boyfriend?" I stepped back. Sarah stood nose to nose with me.

"He's not my boyfriend anymore," I said.

"That's good because my father saw him in the First American Loyalist Regiment on Staten Island the other day. And, Cassie, he was wearing the red coat." It was Sarah's turn to speak sweetly and my turn to sputter.

"It doesn't surprise me, Sarah, not one bit. He said he would." There was nothing else to say.

"Anyway, I have something for you. Here." Sarah pulled a crushed, battered hat with a wide, floppy brim out of her pocket. It was pinned with all kinds of lures and metal hooks. She dropped it into my palm.

I lifted it to my cheek. "David's fishing hat."

"He gave the hat to my papa. He asks that you hold it for him till he comes home. He thinks you will take care of it for him."

"He does, does he? Well, he'll have another think coming. This is what I think of his hat." I hurled the hat away from me. "There."

"Oh, Cassie, I'm sorry, really I am. I just wanted to make you feel bad 'cause you won't play for me." Sarah looked contrite. "I wish I hadn't showed you his hat. Please play for me on Sunday next."

"No. I shall not." A long, deep sigh came out of me. I thought of the good hot food Sarah's mother would make. *The hams; the roasted turkeys; the smooth, buttery potatoes; the sweet desserts; the wonderful pies; and the cobblers. All the kinds of foods we didn't have since the war started. Suzie and Eban were hungry too.* I heard the words come out of my mouth.

"I told you. Invite Suzie and Eban; I'll play for you."

Sarah stayed quiet a minute. "You'll come over my house to practice after school this week every day?"

"Yes," I muttered.

While Sarah struggled with her thoughts, I began pushing the bushes aside. "All right, I'll invite them. What are you doing, Cassie?"

"I'm looking for David's hat."

"It's not in the bushes. It's sticking out from behind that rock. Do you see it?"

I picked up David's hat and shook it out. "Yes. I'll stop by tomorrow after school."

"Wait, Cassie, please stop walking ahead of me." Sarah's breath came in spurts. I kept walking fast. "Can I come in for a little while? It's turning very cold again, and the sun's going down. Shall I share a cup of tea with you?"

"I have work to do at home, Sarah. Remember, invite Suzie and Eban. Here's your turnoff; I'll see you tomorrow." I watched Sarah walk along the path to her house. She looked down.

I had reached my door. I shut the door behind me and then walked to the window to watch Sarah trudge on home.

I sat down in the rocking chair with a cup of sassafras tea. My mind was full of troubled thoughts. I was sorry I was mean to Sarah. *Will Suzie change her mind and not go to her gramps if she comes to the recital? Mrs. Harkens's good food would help with that. After all, I'm only going to the recital for Mrs. Harkens's delicious food. What kind of Patriot am I? I don't care. I'll eat well and so will Eban and Suzie. We're all hungry for good food too. So I refuse to feel bad.* We were all thinner than we were last year. I only wished I had one of Hannah's brittle biscuits to go with my hated sassafras tea. I wished I had kept some potatoes for myself when I brought a supply of them over to the mansion this morning for the redcoats. Should I go with Suzie to York City to live with her gramps and her grandma? I would eat well there. No, I shouldn't. I fell asleep in the rocking chair.

CHAPTER THIRTY-NINE

April 1779

S carlet. It was the stain of scarlet so out of place, and the rows of gold braid and medals gleaming from the English officer's jacket that so shocked me here among my American friends and neighbors. Captain Stonecroft stood in the entrance to the Harkens's observatory. His shiny black boots reflected off the black-and-white floor tiles. He smiled and greeted Mr. Harkens, that shameful Tory, and bowed deeply to Mrs. Harkens, who smiled widely back at him. In regal fashion he made his way among the crowd, smiling at the ladies and nodding to the men. Yet he was not paid back with the same return of good spirits by most of the guests who simply stared at him. Still, he was received civilly; no one threw a tomato at him which might have been because they hadn't been planted yet. The captain stopped at Suzie's and Eban's circle; he bowed to Suzie, and put his hand out in the air to Eban, reminding me of a dead fish the longer it hung motionless in the air. After some seconds, the captain withdrew his hand, gave a slight nod, and moved to stand on Suzie's right. Eban squared his shoulders and folded his hands in front of him so tight that his veins stuck out purple. The room took on its festive noise, and the moment passed.

Afternoons practicing with Sarah had turned into evenings when Mr. Ferguson, Miss Place, and I played for Sarah in the empty observatory. Today, the observatory had been turned into a ballroom. Chairs were stacked against the walls. The room filled up quickly. Folks stood around the wooden platform Mr. Harkens had built for us musicians. Sarah's pianoforte had been hoisted up on the platform by Jesse Prouty, Joe Comerford, Mr. Harkens, and Mr. Fanshawe. People smiled up at us, which made my fingers very shaky. I desperately hoped I would be able to play along with the others without mistakes. A soft light shone down on the women's gowns, gowns rarely taken out of their linen wrappings since the start of the war, some not seen since our first Independence Day. Silks and taffetas in jewel colors, some lively printed calico ones— all worn by the ladies with pride for the recital and tea dance today.

Mr. Ferguson held his bow and fiddle up to his chin, and Miss Place held her flute. My fingers hovered over the keys. The pianoforte had the main space on the platform. Mr. Ferguson gave us the order of music: first, the quadrille, and then the minuet. A lively polka would end the dancing part of the afternoon.

When Mr. Ferguson struck a chord on his fiddle and sawed away, my fingers found the notes, and my bench shook with the stomps and stamps of ladies' heels and men's boots. I looked out over the dancers. Captain Stonecroft and Suzie dancing together? The two of them! They looked so interested in each other. I had a sinking feeling in my stomach; I felt hurt for my brother Max. But I had no time to think about any thing but the music. I kept up, pounding away as noisily as I could, hoping any sour notes would be lost in the raucous music.

Captain Stonecroft and Suzie stayed talking on the dance floor, looking into each other's eyes after the dance had finished. There appeared quite a few lifted eyebrows among the guests, and heads turned to watch the couple. Elbows nudged other elbows. I was relieved when Mr. Ferguson lifted his bow into the air, and we played the minuet, the dance music from Europe. The stately steps were performed in perfect symmetry by the couples on the harlequin-tiled floor. Suzie and I had exchanged gowns. I wore the yellow gown she had made for Independence Day, and Suzie borrowed my mama's blue gown with rosettes I had worn that day so we would each have something different to wear. My masses of blond hair in the new style against the deep yellow of the gown looked very becoming, I was told. And Suzie's dark hair against the sky blue of my mama's gown got looks from more than a few people standing with their glasses of wine, watching the dancers.

Of all things to happen, a string came loose on Mr. Ferguson's fiddle. He left with one of the servants to tighten the string, and the room erupted in a storm of laughter and talking. Sarah came to me, walking purposefully. Ramrod straight and angry, she wasted no time. "Well, would you look at that, Cassie? Can you believe your lying eyes? Why that scamp Suzie has captured all of Captain Stonecroft's attention. And she just an orphan. She has no heritage, I declare! Look at the airs she gives herself. I'm going over to rescue the captain."

Overhearing Sarah, Mrs. Fanshawe turned to her. "Nonsense, Sarah," Mrs. Fanshawe said. "You'll do no such thing. The captain is simply talking to a pretty girl. Look, she's coming over here. He is too. Now, behave yourself; the world doesn't revolve around you."

I couldn't resist. "Why do you want to rescue him anyway, Sarah? He is the enemy."

"He's mighty handsome, Cassie, and he could turn coat, you know. He would make an excellent American."

"What a dreamer you are, Sarah!" I laughed. But I was a dreamer too. I reminded myself of my daydreams about Caleb Brewster. I hadn't forgotten him, his broad shoulders and dark hair and his way of managing the raid on the Presbyterian Church. And Caleb was on our side, not a flaming redcoat like Captain Stonecroft who I imagined spent more time in front of the glass then he did in the front line of his troops. By that time they were facing us; Suzie, all flushed in the face, and the captain smiling down at us. Now, Sarah's mother, Mrs. Harkens, had joined our little circle. She fanned herself with her lace and black silk fan. On her head, atop a beehive of ringlets, rested a stuffed red bird with a diamond beak, peering out over the crowd.

"Hello, Miss Scott, Mrs. Fanshawe." The captain was gracious, as well he ought to be, in the enemy camp as he was. "You look lovely tonight, Miss Harkens."

"Thank you, Captain." Sarah was clearly happy to be singled out for a compliment. She was all set to speak, but Mrs. Harkens strode into the conversation.

"Hello, Captain, dear. Sarah, hold still; one of your curls is out of order." While Mrs. Harkens fixed Sarah's curl, Sarah smoothed away the little wrinkles in her shimmery green satin dress. She did look pretty today, I had to grant. Would the captain ask Sarah to dance? I hoped so. She so ardently wanted to dance with him.

The captain smiled at me. "Excellent playing, Miss Scott." Captain Stonecroft bowed. Everyone curtsied, except for me and Mrs. Fanshawe.

Though he spoke to us all, the captain looked down at Suzie again. He couldn't seem to take his eyes from her. "I notice Mr. Ferguson is resuming his fiddle and the flutist is seated. I take it there will be more dancing?"

"Oh, most assuredly, yes. What will you like, sir?" Sarah's curls bobbed up and down, so eager was her answer.

"Well, I like the waltz especially," the captain said.

"I'll just go and arrange it," Sarah said. She walked boldly across the floor, holding my hand to follow her. "I just know the captain will want to dance the waltz with me, Cassie," she said.

I turned back to hear the captain say "Do you know the waltz, Miss Mancks?"

"Yes, yes, I do." Suzie had been gazing around the room, biting her lower lip, worried that some people might go back to calling her Tory because here she was talking and dancing with the British captain. I could tell she was of two minds about it.

Mr. Ferguson refused to play the waltz once he knew Captain Stonecroft had requested it. Miss Place argued it was beautiful music and we should honor the captain's request. Mr. Ferguson gave in. Confidently, Sarah made her way across the room to the captain's side to claim her dance.

"Sarah, Sarah, wait! I think the captain will dance with Suzie," I yelled. But she didn't stop. The music started and the dancers took the floor. When she saw the captain and Suzie walk out, the captain guiding Suzie by a hand on her elbow, Sarah stood stock still — heartbroken. The captain had just bowed to Suzie and she to him. Mr. and Mrs. Harkens made formal bows, and the red bird bowed, too, on top of her nest of hair. Mr. and Mrs. Thayer, as well as the Fanshawes and the Comerfords, made their bows to each other, and the music played. The captain was a good dancer; Suzie seemed enchanted dancing with him.

There Sarah was, standing alone next to a potted fern. I walked over to stand next to her. The corners of her mouth were turned down. I didn't know what to say to her. The captain was an elegant dancer. Delight was written all over Suzie's face as she danced with him. Mr. Ferguson on the fiddle and Miss Place on the flute made wonderful sounds.

I said in a whisper, "It is a lovely party, Sarah. Let's go sit down and have a glass of lemon water."

Sarah stood rooted in place, her body rigid as a stone statue. She didn't answer me. Finally, she spoke, almost to herself. "I can do the waltz," she said. "Why wouldn't he ask me to dance?"

"You mean the captain? I wish he had," I said.

"Thank you, Cassie." Sarah's feelings were hurt, and I could not blame her.

"Of course, he shall ask for a dance, Sarah." Passing by with Mr. Harkens in tow, the two having left the dance floor, Mrs. Harkens heard us. She leaned across me to put an arm around Sarah. In so doing, her bird fell backward from its nest and toppled head over heels so that its tiny yellow feet stuck up through Mrs. Harkens's hair nest and its head bobbed up and down in the air. With an assist from that lady, it was right side up again. Plainly suffering shock from such a humbling indignity, the poor bird's eyes popped wide open, and it fell forward, beak first, its feet now upended against her beehive of hair. Mrs. Harkens noticed nothing of this latest tragedy. Sarah put her handkerchief to her eyes.

"Don't fret, my dear." Mrs. Harkens patted Sarah's back and guided her to a less crowded spot in the observatory. The red bird's flesh swayed this way and that in a most energetic fashion. I didn't look on at Sarah and her mother's progress any longer. The music ended. A barrage of clapping burst forth from the audience.

Mr. Ferguson shouted out to me from the impromptu stage: "Come up here, Cassie, and take your bow." I was happy to be included, even though I hadn't played the waltz. Atop the stage, a fresh burst of clapping set me smiling. I curtsied.

There was a request asking for the American song: "Johnny has gone for a soldier," reminding us of the day our boys left for Brooklyn. It was a song everyone knew. Our musicians played it with much feeling, and we all sang it with expression. The song brought tears to the eyes of those who had fathers, sons, brothers, and sweethearts in the war. The captain and Mr. Harkens stood off in a corner not singing but talking in low voices.

"Better to get back to the program. Polka time!" Mr. Ferguson set the beat, and it was fast. The rousing polka gave me a chance to bang away at the piano again, and the dancers two-stepped across the floor like swirling tops. Sarah accepted a dance from George

Tredwell, who had served a year in the Continental army and was now a clerk in Mr. Douglas's store. The two seemed to be stepping on each other's feet and bumping into each other. I saw from the frown on her face Sarah was not happy dancing with George. He was such a clutterbug! He didn't know a single dance step. I noticed Nate Thayer was dancing too, with Miss Hoary. That was sweet, to dance with his old teacher.

As soon as the captain heard the music, he excused himself from Mr. Harkens and hurried over to Suzie, grabbed her hands, and took the floor. My mama's blue gown flew around her as she danced, and I was reminded of Mama so much at that moment and also of Max. I couldn't help picturing my brother and how he would feel if he saw Suzie enjoying herself so much with the English captain. On that July 10, the day of our independence, so long behind us, how happy Max and Suzie had been to talk about their marriage plans, how pleased Max was with Suzie, and how she had smiled at him. Mayhap it was a good thing that Suzie would soon leave Cow Neck, even though she was my best friend.

The captain bowed to Suzie and led her by the elbow to a chair next to Eban. He set an empty seat next to Suzie's, and I saw Suzie lay her glove down to save the chair when he headed for the table. He scooped up two plates of food along with silverware and was soon back, handing Suzie a napkin and a plate of food, and he hesitated to sit down without at least offering Eban the other plate. Mrs. Fanshawe, who happened to be standing next to me, saw his hesitation. She said to me, "You know, Cassie, these English can't stand to look impolite, even when they've been snubbed."

I watched as Suzie took the plate from Captain Stonecroft's hands and put it into Eban's hands. "Thank you, Captain," she said.

Eban stood up, holding the plate of food away from himself. He cleared his throat. "I do not accept food from a British officer like you with your braids, medals, and your polished boots. Go home to your England. You're not welcome here." Now, he tilted the plate of food onto the front of the Captain's jacket.

For a moment, the only sound was Captain Stonecroft wiping sauce and turkey from the front of his jacket. Everyone stopped talking. The musicians stopped playing. Eban sat down again and stared straight ahead.

"Eban, how could you! The captain is our guest. You have been most insolent and disrespectful. Apologize at once." Mrs. Harkens came striding over; her bird perched upright again, its black, beady eyes scolding Eban.

The captain recovered. "No. That is not necessary, madam. The old man is entitled to his feelings. I wonder if I could trouble you for some sort of..."

"Here. Let me help you, Captain. Just take off your jacket, and we can remove all this stuff." Mrs. Harkens was beside herself with apologies. "So sorry, Captain. Eban, you are a fool of the first order."

Suzie sat stone-faced and still next to Eban.

"Eban, you should eat now. Please." I stood above him. He took the plate from me and immediately started eating in huge gulps. Suzie looked up at me, trying to smile.

The room stayed quiet out of a sense of unease for the scene Eban had made. There wasn't a person here who did not feel the same way as Eban, but it was hard to watch the English captain looking embarrassed, especially in front of Suzie, the girl he was quite openly fond of.

Mr. Ferguson and Miss Place played softly while folks ate. Soon the level of talk increased. People began to laugh again. Captain Stonecroft had walked out of the room with Mrs. Harkens and now had come back. What magic did Mrs. Harkens use to clean the captain's jacket, I wondered, for it was, although a deeper red, unstained.

Mr. Ferguson and Miss Place stopped playing eventually to get plates for themselves. Folks again headed for the dining room table after servants took away the remains of the supper and replaced it with fresh baked breads, scones, jams, jellies, cakes, cobblers, pies, and urns of hot coffee.

I ate dessert with the Fanshawes. We three kept sideways glances fixed on the captain and Suzie, now chatting quite amiably in their seats, while Eban still stared straight ahead, sitting alone next to Suzie's vacant seat.

"I must go and get Eban. He needs more company," Mrs. Fanshawe opined. Another chair was brought while Mrs. Fanshawe brought an unrepentant Eban back to sit with us.

"Will you take dessert, Eban?" Mrs. Fanshawe got up and asked. Then, to me, she whispered, "No one was speaking to him over there. I shall get him dessert." Mrs. Fanshawe brought two slices of lemon cake on a pewter saucer to Eban, who ate them with gusto. When she sat down next to me, she said quietly, "Eban looks a bit wan and tired to me, a bit peaky."

I was immensely grateful that Mrs. Fanshawe was paying attention to Eban. We had made room for him in our circle, and he seemed to smile. "Shall I tell you something?" I whispered to Mrs. Fanshawe.

"Please do, Cassie."

I spoke very low, almost into her ear so as not to be overheard. "I only came here today for the food and for Eban and Suzie to eat well, too. I told Sarah I wouldn't play for her unless she invited Eban and Suzie."

Mrs. Fanshawe smiled at me and whispered back, "I imagine we're all here for the food. But the evening does give us a chance to dress up again. We shan't be sorry for it. It looks as though Captain Stonecroft is enchanted with Suzie. Very sweet, it is. Tomorrow, he'll be our enemy again. I'm sure he'll be over to hitch up our horse for his morning ride to town."

As she spoke, the captain steered Suzie to a less crowded part of the observatory, near the archway where a window beckoned to them.

"Sarah has eyes for him, but he sees only Suzie," I said. "Anyway, it's wonderful food here. I do feel sorry for Sarah that he's not asking for a dance."

Mrs. Fanshawe smiled at me. "Let's just enjoy the food and forget about the three of them." That was one of the reasons I liked Mrs. Fanshawe; she always made me feel better.

Miss Hoary came by, and Mr. Fanshawe brought a chair for her next to Eban. Miss Hoary held two crystal goblets of sherry and offered one to Eban. He looked up, and his whole face became enlivened. The two began talking. Eban's hair glistened a soft yellow in the candle light, although some loose coffee grounds from the coffee that he had used to get a reddish glow to his hair still clung to a few strands. I was glad he was here. All the people for whom he worked fixing things through the years had greeted him fondly. I was sure everyone forgave him for his misdeed. Both Miss Hoary and Eban sat quietly and happily together and talked in soft tones while Suzie and the captain stood by themselves at the window, looking into each other's eyes, seeming to forget there was anybody else in the room.

After a while, Mr. Ferguson motioned Sarah to the piano; in a formal voice, he said, "We will now listen to Miss Sarah Harkens sing the 'Madrigal of Spring' accompanied on the pianoforte by Miss Cassandra Scott."

Sarah stepped to the piano, her gown gleaming and shining in the light given off by the candle chandelier. I played the introduction to the song, and Sarah gave the old medieval lyrics a beautiful rendering. When she finished, everyone stood up and clapped for her. There were shouts of "Brava." Sarah curtsied prettily. Generously, Sarah motioned me to stand up and take a bow next to her.

The end was near. Twilight came over the Harkens's house. The captain stood, grasped Susan's hand in both of his, smiled down at her, bowed, and said some soft words to her, then began to take his leave. There were smiles when it was observed by all that he stopped at the table to pocket two or three scones in his napkin. Next, he turned to say his good-byes to Mrs. Harkens, who seemed a little bit out of countenance to be taken leave of so abruptly. "Won't you stay for the coffee, Captain? It was so generous of you to provide it for us, real Jamaican coffee. We are so pleased."

"I was happy to do it, Mrs. Harkens, but now duty calls."

"Sarah, the captain is making his farewell." Alarm sounded in Mrs. Harkens's voice. Implied was a warning, *Come quick before he gets away.* Sarah and I still stood on stage, basking in the warmth of Sarah's reception and, surprisingly, appreciation for my playing, too. We left the makeshift stage and walked over to Mrs. Harkens and the captain.

Sarah curtsied. "Thank you for coming, Captain. We enjoyed your visit."

Captain Stonecroft shook her hand, gazed into Sarah's eyes, and held her hand for a moment. "Good-bye, Miss Harkens. Your singing was quite wonderful. I hope you come to England some day and sing for His Majesty."

He's right about Sarah's singing. Not that Sarah would be asked to sing for the English king, but then again, why not in time to come? She is good enough. The captain shook hands all around and left.

Suzie's eyes were shining. "Did you see me dancing with the captain?"

"Yes. I did see." I kept my mouth shut about Max.

Suzie must have realized how I felt. "It were nothing, Cassie. You know how I love to dance."

Sarah's eyes were shining too. "The captain is charming, isn't he, girls?"

"I don't know about that. He was nice to dance with, though." Suzie studied her fingernails.

"You saw how the captain held my hand right before he left, Suzie?" Sarah asked.

"I did, Sarah. The captain is very gracious."

Sarah gave Suzie a long look. She smiled, but it was a little sad smile, as though she had just realized it was Suzie the captain had eyes for after all.

"Mind," I said, "he didn't hold my hand and he didn't ask me to dance." Not that I was in any way jealous.

"That's because you threw that ice ball at him, Cassie." Now that the evening was coming to a close, Sarah had forgotten her manners.

"You didn't tell him, did you, Sarah?" I said.

"No. I hardly had his attention long enough to mention anything to him. And why would I tell him how you two hit him in the back of the neck with that ice ball? What do you take me for?" Sarah was offended. Her nose flew up into the air.

Suzie was so pleased with herself she put out her hand to Sarah. "Thank you for inviting Eban and me, Sarah."

"Aye, thank ye, Sarah," Eban said. He gave Sarah a bow from his waist, causing his coonskin hat to fall off his head. There was a scramble for it on the floor. Mrs. Harkens was first to bend over to pick up Eban's hat, but she was unsuccessful. Mr. Thayer, rushing to pick up the hat, bumped heads with Mr. Ferguson, who scrambled for Eban's hat, only to have his hand pushed away by Mr. Harkens's big grab. He held the hat up triumphantly, coming away with it, but also with the red bird that had decorated Mrs. Harkens's hair. Its claws were now digging into Mr. Harkens's scalp. Eban put his hat back on. Mr. Harkens plucked the bird out of his hair and, not knowing what to do with it, stuck it back into Mrs. Harkens's plumage. She turned it right side up, gave it an about-face, and made the bird stare out of the back of her head.

The red bird was now staring off into space. No one laughed, although there were hands clamped over mouths. It would have hurt Eban to hear them laugh. He would have thought they laughed at him. He coughed, and his face reddened. He sat down again in the chair. "Eban looks sick," I told Suzie in a low tone.

"Yes, I know. He got home the day after he found a family to take his cow, and he seemed all right, but he hasn't had any energy since."

"Mayhap he's tired. That's all," I said. "Look, he's gone and found Miss Hoary's cloak."

"I'll walk you home, Eileen." He tried to lift Miss Hoary's cloak over her shoulders, but he couldn't. He started and stopped; he seemed to waver back and forth. I helped Miss Hoary with her cloak.

"Eban, we must go. It's almost dark," Suzie said. "Thank you again, Sarah. We can all walk home with you, Eban, and then walk Miss Hoary home." Eban sat down hard in his chair, struggling to put his squirrel-tail fur cloak over his shoulders. Suzie helped him. "We must go; you can walk, can't you, Eban? Suzie's voice was colored with fear. Eban tried to get up, and with Suzie's help, he did get to his feet, though he was unsteady. As he stood, he tried to smile at Suzie.

Sarah, still smiling from the captain's praise, woke up from her reverie. She had not seen Eban's struggle to stand. She put her arm on mine. "Thank you, Cassie, for accompanying me." She gave me a bright smile. The evening had not gone well for her. I was glad the captain had said a very sweet good-bye to her.

Sitting in the rocking chair later on, it came to me that the three of us were unhappy at the end of the night. Sarah didn't get to dance with the captain. And that was the purpose of the recital, to show Sarah off to the British captain. Instead, it was Suzie, lonely and missing Max, whom the captain chose. I never stopped wishing David were here; he had betrayed me and his country. I could never forgive him for it, but I missed him. I missed him more and more.

And now Eban was sick. Miss Hoary, Suzie, and I walked him home. He shivered and clung to Suzie's and Miss Hoary's hands. When we got to Eban's cabin, Miss Hoary told Suzie and me that she would stay awhile with Eban and that we should go on our way. She would prepare hot broth for him and keep him company. I waved good-bye to Suzie at her cabin and walked home, let myself in, and here I was, dropped into the rocking chair. *It had been a night out of time at the recital.*

After a while, I lit the candle lamp and made tea. I picked up David's fishing hat, fingering all the colorful lures. I was there for every lure he'd made and stuck into his hat. No wonder Suzie wanted to dance and flirt. It's hard on a body to miss someone you know is coming home to you, as Max was coming home to Suzie. It's even harder to miss someone who is not coming home to you, as David was not coming home to me.

I sipped my tea. There were good things about the evening too. I had almost forgotten how much fun it was to play the pianoforte. And it was good to taste things I hadn't eaten in years, especially the sweets: raspberry pudding, lemon pie, and apple cobbler, and glasses of cold cider. I had thanked Mrs. Harkens, and I really meant it. She had worked hard to give enjoyment to all of us, her neighbors, and to provide wonderful food. I had loved playing with Mr. Ferguson and Miss Place. It was different with Mr. Harkens. I left him with a smile I didn't feel and a handshake. *And Eban, I must visit him tomorrow. He'll be all right. He's indestructible.*

CHAPTER FORTY

May 1779

"How is Eban?" I asked Suzie. We were walking home from the schoolhouse and over to Jesse's hillside to sit in the sun and look down at the water, something we did every day now in the warm weather.

"He's still sick. He sits in his rocker with a blanket, near the windows, and stares out. He won't eat."

"That doesn't sound like Eban."

"Even Miss Hoary can't get him to take much food when she stops in after school. They talk about old times, about when he was a boy and she was a girl and there were only a few cottages in the town."

"You don't want to leave Eban?" I said.

"It's true. He's a good friend to me; I shall miss him. But it's not the only reason. Cassie, there's another, and you may as well know it. You remember Sarah's recital?"

"How could I forget? I still remember every bit of it. It was fun; it was like Cow Neck used to be. And you liked dancing with the British captain, didn't you, Suzie?"

"Yes." Suzie brushed a grasshopper from her gown. "I did like it." She looked up at the cloudless blue sky and then down at the grass.

"What's the matter then?"

"I feel sad. Soon it will be time to go. My gramps will come for me, now that the roads are all dried up and the rains are gone."

"You don't want to go?"

"Yes, Cassie, I do. I want to go. It's just hard, that's all."

"Have you told Eban you're going?"

"I shall when he feels better."

"You don't seem at all happy about going," I said.

"There's something else, Cassie. I'm fond of Captain Stonecroft."

"Oh, Suzie." I had convinced myself that it was just the fun of dancing with the captain that Suzie had enjoyed so much, but now I could see she was entranced by him.

"Cassie, if you come with me to York City, I will forget him. Please change your mind and come with me. In the city, there are parties and shops with hats and ribbons, calico gowns and taffeta gowns, and coffee shops. I could forget the captain in the bustle and hustle of the city. We could walk along the river and take French lessons. And remember, Cassie, how you love French hairstyles and fashions."

"I don't care anything about French lessons now or fashions. I want Papa to come home. And I want the war to be over and my brothers to come home."

"But I didn't tell you the best news. The captain is quite fond of me, Cassie. He said so. But I really do want to marry Max. Just think about moving to York City. You will have your own room in a nice house. In the city, people eat Gloucester cheese from England, Scottish salmon, black tea from Ceylon, not that bitter sassafras tea we drink. There's even a new coffee house. There's talk about it in *Rivington's Gazette*. Look." She fished around in her book bag until she came up with the newspaper.

Suddenly, I didn't want to stay with my friend anymore that day. "I'll see you at school tomorrow, Suzie."

"Wait. Do you see?" She pushed the paper into my hands. *'Mrs. Treville supplies music, fire, and candles at the new London Coffee House in Broad Street.'*

"High people are found there. High people, Cassie! Do come. You must come. Gramps will be delighted. There's theater. We shall go to the Theater Royal in John Street." Suzie paused for breath.

"I'll stay here, Suzie." I glanced at the paper and handed it back. "Bye."

Suzie called after me as I walked away, "Cassie, I hope you don't think harsh of me because I am fond of the captain and I'm going away."

"I don't think harsh of you. I wish you good luck in York City. 'Bye, Suzie."

CHAPTER FORTY-ONE

May 30, 1779

Late at night, a chunk of metal from some ancient piece of farm equipment, dislodged by wind, knocked against the door. I was still up in the kitchen. But then two rough, harsh knocks followed and then Suzie's voice, shrill and panicky. "Open the door, Cassie. Open the door."

"What is it?" What's the matter?" Suzie's cloak hung off her shoulders. Her boot tops were wet with mud from running. I closed the door. She stood in the kitchen, gasping for breath.

"Eban. I stayed in his cabin overnight." She took a shallow breath. "He was coughing badly. His head sank back on the pillow. I ran to get water." She stopped for breath. "When I got back to his cot, his eyes were open. I don't think he was breathing. Please come."

Running through the night in the chill to Eban's cabin, I thought, *I've never seen a dead person. How will I know?* Suzie was there before me. The door was open. She stood next to the bed, holding the lantern. Shadows from the lantern flickered over Eban's face. He stared out of open eyes.

"Eban? Eban?" Suzie cried out. "Eban!"

I listened to his chest. There was no breathing movement. His chest was flat and still. "It's no use, Suzie. I think he is dead," I said.

We prayed the Lord's Prayer over Eban, left the room, and walked across the grass to Suzie's cabin. Suzie sank down in a kitchen chair, and I made tea for both of us. We sat at the table, but no words came. Suzie cried a lot. At dawn, she and I walked to Jesse Prouty's cottage and told him of Eban's death. All morning long that day at school, we heard Jesse Prouty and Joe Comerford hammer pegs into wood planks to join together Eban's pine box in the meadow across from the schoolhouse.

CHAPTER FORTY-TWO

May 31, 1779

It was a dismal dawn, not even a slit of rose to lighten the sky. A thickness hung in the air, prompting all souls trudging uphill with bent heads behind Eban's pine box to pull our cloaks closer to us. I walked with Suzie; the Fanshawes walked on either side of Miss Hoary, each holding one of her hands. The Comerfords, Mrs. Harkens, and Sarah trailed after. A long line of town people walked slowly behind us. The last time I had seen Eban and Miss Hoary, they were talking together, drinking glasses of sherry in the soft candlelight of Sarah's observatory.

Suzie held her handkerchief up to her face. It was all I could do to keep from crying too. "Old Eban was good to me, Cassie; I'll never have a better friend."

"You still have me," I said, knowing that she would be going off in her grandfather Mancks's carriage at the end of Eban's burial.

"I shall come back as soon as the war is over. I don't want to go, anymore, Cassie. I shall miss everyone so much." Susan's answer was muffled in her cloak.

"I think you have to find out what city living is. Then mayhap you will come back."

"You're right, Cassie. I shall come back someday. I know I will. I still love Max too." At that, I wondered.

The ceremony took ten minutes. Jesse Prouty and James Comerford had not only doweled Eban's coffin together but also dug a rectangular hole six feet deep that would receive him. Since Eban did not attend any of the town churches, and Papa had been captured, Mr. Brooks of the Quaker Tradition gave a blessing over Eban's casket. The two sawyers lowered the ropes that held the pine box into the grave.

The sun rose as Suzie and I walked to her cabin from Eban's funeral. "We might never see each other again, Suzie," I said.

"Of course, we shall. We'll be sisters when Max and I marry. You're being much too dramatic, Cassie!" Suzie smiled as she said it. It was the first smile I'd seen since Eban died.

"Yes, I guess so. But I shall not marry, I do not think."

"Now, why do you say such a thing? Why do you say you won't marry?" Suzie stared at me.

"Who is here for me? David will never come back after the war."

"Bosh on that! He will come back for you."

"Mayhap he will, but I could never marry him now, after his time spent in the British Army. And worse, the town would never accept him. He'll be a pariah if he comes back."

"The town will accept him in time," Susie said, but I sensed that she had already left our town in her mind and was not truly paying attention to what she was saying to me.

For a moment, I felt harsh toward Suzie. She was leaving and I was staying. She was going off to wear silks and dance with handsome English soldiers. She would meet high people who would bend and listen to her light chatter in their candle-chandeliered salons while I was committed to my shack and Miss Hoary's schoolroom. "I wonder," I said, turning toward Suzie on the path, feeling as mean inside me as the inside of a wild boar's stomach, "do you think the country will go easy on people like David who turned coat and worked for the British?"

Suzie kicked a stone. "I do, Cassie. I really do. Besides, he didn't have his heart into it. Look! There's Gramp's carriage. He waits for me."

We had come to the end of the path. The carriage horses grazed on grass outside the log cabin door. Susan's rucksack sat aside the coachman's seat. Suzie's gramps leaned out the window, looking for Suzie. Behind his head in the shiny black carriage, a red velvet lining caught the shaft of a sunbeam. Suzie clambered up the step and disappeared into its warmth. She waved to me out the window. "Cassie, I'll write. You write too." I waved back and watched until the coach moved out of sight; then I turned and walked to the schoolhouse.

Miss Hoary had arrived before me and was seated at her desk in the schoolhouse, her face held in her hands. She did not look up at me. I boiled water in the pot hanging from the hob, took a cup of tea to her, and then leaned over and put a hand on her back. When she did raise her head, she gave me a thin smile. Her eyes were red; she had been crying. She looked forlorn; I sat across from her and held her hand. We just sat that way, Miss Hoary and I, for a minute or so; then I walked away and put the horn books out on the desks. The children would soon be coming through the door. I hoped the hot tea would restore her. *Was Miss Hoary the sweetheart people talked of that Eban loved in his youth? I believed she was.*

CHAPTER FORTY-THREE

June 18, 1779

The letter from Suzie postmarked Whitehall Street arrived in Cow Neck on my doorstep as I got home from school. I waited until supper to read it outside in the soft grass outside the shack.

Dear Cassie,

It is a long time that I have been gone from Cow Neck, but I think about the town and you and all the others almost every day, and I miss you all too. Life in York City is very pleasant, and I am enjoying a great deal of social activities. Every day, I go to a coffee shop and talk to my new friends from the great families on Beekman Place, who my grandparents have introduced me to. They are nice girls; I have many friends among them, but they can't compare to my friends in Cow Neck. I miss you and wish you would join me here, but I know the children would miss you so much if you left Cow Neck. I miss Miss Hoary. Please remember me to them all. Even Sarah.

Nights we go to the salons and speak with the English soldiers who love our customs here. They also go to the theater on John Street as we do, and we often see the same people at cotillions and balls. I am so very popular at these dances, Cassie. You wouldn't believe it. Last week a British general, whose name I cannot remember, asked me to dance several times, and I am sure I could have fallen in love with him had I not been spoken for. I miss Max. I am forgetting the captain since he is nowhere in this busy city. But it is fun to dance. I do wish we could see each other as we used to do. Good-bye, Cassie. Please write to me. Love, Suzie.

I put the letter on the table next to the candle. The letter was pure Suzie. I wished I could see her, too. There were no other letters from Suzie, nothing from Father or Hannah. Max's last letter from back in February, lay on the table next to Suzie's. In that letter written while wintering at Morristown with the troops, Max wrote *"The winter is harsh; it is freezing cold here. We boys have not got enough to eat, though Mrs. Washington and her friends cook for us often. Blankets, there are practically none. Many times the fellows must put paper in the soles of their boots to cover up holes. Some, there are, whose boots are worn down to only their uppers. There is much blood on the snow up here."* Since then I had been praying hard for my brothers and for Papa, and even for Hannah.

The days wore on. The British soldiers greeted me on the lanes and wished me a good day. I was sure they felt sorry for me, living alone. I reckon they thought I didn't have anyone to talk to. But I did. Mrs. Fanshawe had asked me to come to supper every night. I was glad to have a place to go, but I did not stay nights with the Fanshawes, even though they wanted me to. I could not. I knew there were some Tories about who would set my shack aflame if it were empty. I called it "my shack" now. It was all I had. I had not heard anything from Ernest. I did wish he would write, and

I missed Suzie so much since her grandpa had taken her to York City. Sarah worked alongside me in school, and we walked and talked together much more since Suzie left. I thought Sarah would like to be friends, but she was just not Suzie.

CHAPTER FORTY-FOUR

June 20, 1779

Today was my birthday. I turned nineteen years old. Between eleven and noon, I saw three people walk through the path between the soldiers' huts. I had thought no one would remember me today, but I was delightfully wrong.

"Chocolate coffee, Cassie! For your birthday, and lemon cake." Mrs. Fanshawe led Miss Hoary and Sarah into the shack. Miss Hoary handed me a quill dipped in gold ink.

"And a locket, Cassie. I hope you like it." Sarah smiled.

"I do like it! I like everything," I said. Mrs. Fanshawe spooned the delicious chocolate into the pot of coffee she carried and then poured the mixture into the last of Mama's china cups taken from the mansion. Soon the kitchen was filling up with the fragrance of lemon icing and hot chocolate coffee. Sarah cut pieces of the cake she baked and laid the slices on pewter plates.

"I'm the luckiest girl in the world to have such good friends. It's a lovely June twentieth!" I felt so overwhelmed with gladness I almost cried.

"Let's eat Sarah's cake," Mrs. Fanshawe said.

We spoke of Eban fondly and of Suzie's leaving. No one spoke of my father and Hannah for which I was relieved because I didn't want to cry in front of them. Sarah told us that her parents would leave for England soon. They had made up their minds. "I shall not go with Mama and Papa," she said. "I love this country, and I shall stay." Still, her eyes watered as she spoke.

Mrs. Fanshawe laid her fork down. "Sarah, you will miss them. Might it better to go than to stay and be alone here?"

"I've lived here all my life, Mrs. Fanshawe. I know I'll miss Mama and Papa awful bad, but I want to stay. Mama says she will return to see me. I will go to England to visit them and see if I could get used to living in England. But not now. I want to be here for the day the British leave our island."

"I'll stay too, and you, Cassie, what shall you do?" Miss Hoary and Sarah stared hard at me.

"Did you think I would leave?" I asked them.

"Suzie left. We thought you might go, too. You could join Suzie at her grandpa's house in York City, where living is much better than here." Sarah spoke slowly as though she almost didn't want to hear my answer.

"I shall stay here with you all."

"I knew so," Mrs. Fanshawe said. We four held hands around the table. "We'll be one for all and all for one," Mrs. Fanshawe said.

"We shall. Good." Sarah smiled at me again. Since Suzie left, Sarah had become much friendlier to me. I began to think of her as a friend. She called for me every day and walked to school with me, chatting and smiling all the way. I wondered what had happened to the old Sarah. I liked this new Sarah much better. For one thing, she was a committed Cow Necker.

"I must go and help Mama pack." Sarah got up from the table. "But I am so glad that you all will be with me after my parents leave."

196

"I shall walk you home, Sarah," Miss Hoary said.

After Sarah and Miss Hoary left, Mrs. Fanshawe lingered. She wrapped up the leftover cake. "Caleb Brewster wants to meet with you, Cassie."

"What does he want with me?" Suddenly, my stomach got all jittery. "I haven't seen him since the night we got back our wood." But I had thought of Caleb many times.

"Tonight at David Van Essen's cottage, he'll be in his boat by the creek."

"What time?" My heart beat faster.

"Eight thirty."

CHAPTER FORTY-FIVE

Evening

I could think of nothing else but meeting with Caleb. For the rest of the day, I busied myself with all kinds of made-up tasks and brushed my hair until it shone. At eight o'clock, I could wait no longer. The sun began to sink below the horizon. Twilight settled over the water. The leaves of the Aspens trembled. Winds stiffened the breezes across Berry Cove out to the Long Island Sound. Streaking gulls caught pockets of air, floated motionless, darted, swooped, soared, and streaked away to their nighttime lairs. Only the bats remained, flitting among the bushes. On the water, fireflies popped, winked, and disappeared. A swarm of gnats engulfed me so that I had to stop rowing and clear my face. Caleb Brewster's rowboat rested in the shelter of bushes, its prow pushed up against the banks. Almost invisible to me in the twilight, Caleb sat in the rower's seat, concentrating on his whittling, as the darkness increased.

"There you are." Caleb reached out and pulled my boat sidewise up the bank adjacent to his own. We sat across from each other, each in our rower's seat. Caleb set his whittling aside and laid his knife on the wet floor, then crossed one arm under the other over his chest. I saw the power of those arms and shivered. *Would I not like to be held in those arms?* Darkness settled over the creek, but I could still see his face in the moonlight and his dark hair.

"Here sits a brave girl," he greeted me.

"Woman. I'm eighteen now."

"Oh, when did that happen?"

"Today." I felt grown up telling Caleb my advanced age, but he didn't seem to take note, for he puffed on his pipe a while before he spoke.

"Did you celebrate?"

"Sarah Harkens made lemon cake. Miss Hoary and Mrs. Fanshawe came. They all brought me presents." I waited a second. "What did you want to see me about?"

Caleb hesitated. "I have news of your father and Hannah, Cassie." Caleb looked down for a moment. "Cassie, your father has been off the prison ship for some time. He and Hannah have traveled to Connecticut."

"To Connecticut? Why?"

"Your father can't come home. It is too dangerous. If he does, he'll be recaptured, tried in an English court, and found guilty of treason to the Crown. You know what that means, don't you?"

"Yes." I forced myself to answer, but I choked before I could say it, "It means death by hanging."

"Here." He took off his bandana from around his neck and handed it to me. "Here, wipe your tears." He waited while I tried to stop crying. "I'm sorry, but it has to be this way. Don't be afraid, Cassie. Your father and Hannah will come home when the war is won."

I shook my head. I couldn't speak.

"I have other news. I hesitate to tell you, but I must."

"What?" I breathed.

"Ernest was wounded at Stony Point when the redcoats over-took the fort May twenty-ninth. I have word that he is being taken care of at a Patriot farmer's home in New Windsor."

I put my face in my hands. "How badly is he hurt?"

"I've not received any more information other than what I've told you."

"I want to see him," I said.

"There is a way, a plan. Listen to me, Cassie." Caleb leaned forward. We've abandoned Stony Point and left it to the British. General Washington wants it back. There is a must-have report waiting for us there. It's in the possession of a British Army officer. We have a plan to get the report. If you are willing, Cassie, this plan will involve you."

"What could I do?"

"You will go into the British camp at Stony Point and get the report containing the intelligence. Then you'll take it to General Washington in New Windsor."

"How would I get this report?"

"Once you are inside the camp, you'll give the guards your pass. They will point out the officer you should see. In this officer's tent, you will come into possession of the report."

"And my brother?"

"You will go to him after you've given your information to the general."

I stayed silent.

It was hard to watch Caleb's face show disappointment in the sliver of moonlight. He went on as though he hadn't noticed I hadn't spoken. "Here's the plan. Listen. You are Dolly Ashton, daughter of Lev Ashton, a butcher in Stony Point. Your pass is signed by General Clinton, Commander of the British forces in America. His seal has been affixed to it, which verifies your iden-tity and your purpose in the British camp. Don't ask how your pass was achieved."

"Why not?"

"Because I can't tell you. Now, your story is that you are there to take orders for sides of beef that your father, Lev Ashton, will deliver to the quartermaster. Your sister, Patsy, usually takes the orders for beef, but she is down with sickness. All true. Except for Patsy who will relinquish her own role for the day so as to remain free from suspicion and British revenge."

I shook my head. "I'm afraid."

Caleb looked at me for a long moment. "You're afraid?" His next words seemed to be choked out of his mouth, as if it was painful to him to have to say them at all. "What happened to that brave girl who led us into the church bulging with British soldiers, to get our wood back?"

"I'm not brave anymore, Caleb."

"Yes, you are. You're perfect for this job. You're above suspicion. We need someone above suspicion, someone who would never be taken for a spy. You're young; you're unknown at Stony Point. You will be believed. You're just right for this mission. Will you do this work for your country, Cassie?"

"No." I couldn't look at Caleb.

Caleb sat back and heaved a deep sigh. "All right, Cassie. I must not have understood what this war has done to you. I should have, but I did not. I fear I've been a bumbler." It was completely calm on the water. Neither of us spoke for a time. But I couldn't let him think he was to blame in any way for my cowardice.

"No. It's not you. I've been afraid since Papa was taken. Suzie's gone. Max is gone. David is a traitor. And now Ernest is wounded. I can't stand it anymore. I can't, Caleb."

"I understand now, Cassie." Caleb reached across his boat and took my hands in his. "It's tough to take. Isn't it?" Caleb let go of my hands. He picked up his oars and leaned forward, his elbows bent, ready to row.

I hated to see him go. "Caleb, could I sit next to you in your boat for a little while?"

"Yes. Yes. Come aboard." He helped me across and moved over, and I sat next to him. Caleb put his arm around me. "It's a damned long war. You've been brave, Cassie."

"Yes. I was, but I'm not now." I felt comforted in the shelter of Caleb's arm. We both were quiet and listened to the crickets chirp.

Finally, Caleb said, "I must go, my dear girl. Cassie, you stay safe and well. The Fanshawes will look after you. I shall make it my business to make sure you stay safe. Come, I'll help you across to your boat."

But I stayed sitting. "Caleb, I shall go. I shall go to Stony Point. I shall."

He looked at me full in the face. "No."

"Yes. I'm not scared now, Caleb, now that I'm with you. I want so much to see my brother, Ernest. Sitting next to you, I'm not afraid. I can do it. I've always wanted to do something for my country."

"Cassie, you've already done much for your country."

"I shall go to Stony Point."

Caleb continued to hold his arm around me. "It is something you must do alone, Cassie."

"I believe I can, if I think of you and all the others who are fighting so hard for our liberty."

"I think that you can. I believe you. I know you for the brave girl you are."

"Woman," I said.

"Woman," Caleb repeated. I saw a trace of a smile on his face in the thin moonlight. "Yes, a brave woman. I will meet up with you again soon in York City. I'll have Mrs. Fanshawe give you your instructions. Keep up being brave, Cassie."

CHAPTER FORTY-SIX

"Papa is not coming home." I sat across the table from Mrs. Fanshawe in her kitchen the next morning, drinking tea and eating a scone. "But I believe you already know that." I looked at her sidewise.

"Yes, I do know, Cassie. I belong to your father's circle, same as Caleb."

"I can't say I didn't wonder if you were with them. But now I know."

"Now you belong in the circle, Cassie. We're proud of you. Be proud to be part of us. On Thursday, the day after tomorrow, you will take the ferry, which leaves Cow Neck on the high tide at nine o'clock in the morning. The boat docks at Coenties Slip in York City at about one o'clock depending on the winds and tide. Walk a few steps to Wall Street. There you will find the Tontine Coffee Shop, which fronts *Rivington's Gazette* newspaper office. Once inside the shop, there is a hallway that connects the restaurant with three rooms, numbered one, two, and three. Open the door of room two with the key in this purse." She held up a brown leather bag the size of the palm of my hand. "Caleb's plan of action is also inside." She put her index finger on top of its surface and kept it there while she spoke. "You need to study the paper inside this leather bag, Cassie. Memorize the details of the plan. Read it again and again." I picked up the purse.

"At one o'clock leave the room and walk back along the hallway into the restaurant. Caleb will be sitting just inside, at a table facing the kitchen."

The leather bag felt warm and soft in my hands. Across its top, a slim drawstring made from the same leather pulled the bag tightly closed. Mrs. Fanshawe filled my teacup with hot tea. "Read the paper at home, Cassie, in the quiet. Know it by heart."

"I shall." Somehow, holding the leather bag made Caleb's plan real to me. *I felt the crippling fear rise up; I could die on top of Stony Point.*

Mrs. Fanshawe laced her fingers together and rested her chin over them. Leaning on her upraised arms, she looked at me steadily. "You'll do fine, Cassie. Caleb has seen to it you will be closely guarded," she said, as though she had read my thought. "He will be in the Tontine, but he won't be able to stay with you for very long. The British leave no stone unturned looking for him. He has sunk two more ships in the Sound." She paused. "They want him strung up high."

"I'll be on the ferry for York City Thursday morning." I tried to sound resolved.

Mrs. Fanshawe hugged me tight. "Until freedom, Cassie," she said.

"Until freedom," I said. I gave Mrs. Fanshawe a hug and left the comfort of her cottage.

CHAPTER FORTY-SEVEN

June 22, 1779

York City! I stepped out the door of the smoky, tobacco-smelling parlor floor of the Tontine coffee house and gulped deep breaths of fresh air. I had found the room and dropped my mobcap, apron, and reticule on a chair. It was good to sit in a cool room after the hot ferry ride, but the street called to me. I bathed my face in cool water from a pitcher on top of a chest of drawers and shook out my hair before I put my mobcap back on my head, hating to wear it but feeling safer with it covering my head, knowing I was in a place where I knew no one. I wanted to be out mingling with the morning crowds on Wall Street for the first time in my life by myself, completely on my own. I had two and a half hours before I would have to be back at the coffee shop to meet Caleb, and though I hadn't let him know, I had my own plan, and it didn't include resting in a locked room.

The wind was blowing up cool from the water. Crowds of people rushed past me on Wall Street down to the water. Workmen in thin shirts and overalls carried leather bags full of tools. I bought a tankard of cream tea from a girl who balanced the tray on her head. Women in cloaks and bonnets hurried to the fishing boats. Crates of fresh vegetables from Long Island and Jersey farms littered tables on the edges of the moving crowd. I was pushed along and at times lost my footing. Smells of fish mingled with the smell of fresh baked bread. It was the noisiest, most exhilarating time!

At the foot of Wall Street, a dense forest of tall-masted ships rocked slowly in the water. Brigantines, ships of the line, frigates, barks, sloops, whalers, schooners, fishing dories, and even old wooden rowboats all jostled against each other, straining to keep their hulls upright and their mooring lines free.

"Fish here, fish here," deckhands yelled down to the crowds on the pier, all the while hauling barrels of gleaming, wriggling, silver-backed fish out onto the slippery decks, their scales glinting purple and green in the sunlight. Wrapped up in old newspapers, the fish were hurled down from the decks to the waiting throngs. As piles of flounder, bluefish, oysters, clams, and eels grew smaller, new barrels of fresh fish were dumped from ships' holds onto the slippery decks. On the pier money changers pushed away worthless Continental dollars with wet, smelly hands in favor of British pounds sterling. Over the whole wide, noisy spectacle, a brilliant, blue, cloudless sky reigned.

In the midst of the bustle and hubbub, I found myself pushed by the crowds into a niche next to a statue of the English king. I held my reticule closer. Caleb had cautioned me to be careful not to attract unwanted attention from thieves who he said were legion on Wall Street.

A certain boat flying the Dutch colors, a sloop, with a polished hull and brightly colored sails waving gently in the breeze, caught my eye. Two men stood on her bridge slightly off balance while they spoke. One, who I took to be the captain, was dressed in a blue jacket with gold buttons and the other could be Caleb Brewster himself, dressed as a merchant in a buff jacket and rich man's pants, wearing shiny black boots, and without his beard. Could it really be Caleb without his beard and dressed like a gentleman? He leaned forward, his massive head full of black curls almost butting into the face of the ship's captain. It *was* Caleb; I knew that intense look he gave the Dutch captain. I had felt his dark eyes on me twice, once as he asked who I might be outside the Presbyterian Church and one more time as I sat in his boat with his arm around me two nights ago, the night of my birthday.

Blossom, in two-feet high gold letters painted on the stern, was the name of the boat. Suddenly, I stopped listening to the noise of the yelling crowd and fishermen's cries. *This boat will take me to Stony Point.* I couldn't get my breath; I was all over scared. I would leave New York, and I would become Betsy Asher. I couldn't do it.

Caleb shook hands with the captain. He would pass this niche. My whole body shook. He scrambled down from the bridge. I trained my eyes on the pier where he would alight; I yelled out, "Caleb, Caleb." I had to tell him I couldn't go on the boat. I couldn't do this. I couldn't go to Stony Point. But the crowds were thick, and he passed by and was swallowed up in an instant. He hadn't seen me: *I must stop shaking. I must.* I breathed again and again, deeply. My fear, when it came up, had the power to overwhelm me. How could I tell him? I must do it. I must go and get the report and give it to General Washington. I will. I will. Now I was glad Caleb could not see me in my weakness; my knees were shaking, and my breath came in gasps.

I looked to see if I still had the British pounds Mrs. Fanshawe gave me for the trip; I saw they were still there and left the shelter of the niche, wishing that the Sons of Liberty would tear down this statue of the English king and make it into bullets as they had done with the one on Bowling Green in '76.

My plan was to go to a dry-goods store on the Broad Way Caleb had told me about, where I could buy ribbons and combs. I must go to that shop since I hadn't had any new ribbons or jeweled combs since the war started. Even though no one in Cow Neck had violated the nonimportation clause by buying goods from England, this was York City! Perhaps the fripperies came from Holland.

Uphill from the water at the foot of Wall Street, I walked against the crowds to the Broad Way and saw City Tavern, the restaurant and dance place I'd read about in the *Gazette*, splendid in sunlight. Known all over for the best food in the city, it was also used for assemblies where British officers danced with American young ladies. I wondered had Suzie been there yet. There were fewer people out walking on the Broad Way. As I went along, I saw the ruins of the once proud Trinity Church standing in its charred ruins among the gravestones; the great fire of September 1776 had taken its toll. Some people claimed the redcoats had burned the Church down. But Papa didn't blame the British for setting the fire. He told me it was the presence of all those wooden houses leaning up against each other chockablock that caused some spark of fire to ignite not only Trinity but almost the whole of the toe of York City.

The graveyard among the ruins was tempting. Wild flowers grew, and mountain pinks trailed along the grass. The sun shone mildly on my back, and on impulse, I walked into the serene place. The inscriptions on tombstones were old, from the early seventeen hundreds. Inside the cemetery, the noise from hawkers of food and drinks went away; I heard only birdsong.

Here and there, sheep nibbled on the grass. I sat down on an overturned slab of stone, took off my bonnet, and fixed my reticule behind my head for a pillow. It was warm and quiet, and I was so tired all of a sudden. How long I slept, I didn't know, but I woke up to find myself staring into the black, soulful, unblinking eyes of a lamb chewing grass not a foot from my face. The lamb's warm, grassy breath hovered near my head. I sat up, hoping to entice the little thing closer so I could pet it, but it spooked and ran off a few feet and stood gazing at me. I pulled a handful of choice grass and held it out for the lamb. It came closer, looked at me, and nibbled the grass from my hand. "There now, isn't that better than the dirty stuff you were chewing?"

I spoke gently, but now the ewe strode over and nudged her lamb away from me. The lamb didn't move fast enough, and its mother butted its behind so that it leapt in a scatter of hooves and landed on top of another fallen tombstone. It stood trembling, trying to stand firm on all four hooves. I laughed.

"You haven't much of a way with lambs, Miss Scott!"

Startled, I looked up into the face of Captain Frank Stonecroft. "I apologize. I thought you saw me," he said.

"No. I didn't," I said in the coldest tone I could manage.

"I need to speak to you, Miss Scott." He sat down on an overturned tombstone across from me.

"How did you know I was here?" I folded my arms as stiff as I could across my chest. "Did you follow me?" I looked into his eyes. "Yes, you did, didn't you?"

The captain had the grace to look ashamed. "I was on the same ferry as you, but I sat between barrels of pickles next to the horses. I'm sent by Colonel Braithwaite to the city to find the reason you travel today. The colonel knew of your travel arrangements and so..."

"You followed me," I interrupted. "What could be so important to your Colonel about my trip to the city?"

"Miss Scott, I'm trying to be pleasant. What is your purpose in the city today?"

"It's none of your business, nor his."

"If you refuse to say, I must take you back with me."

I scoffed at him. "How do you plan to do that, Captain?"

"By force, Miss Scott. My colonel wishes to know why you have come to the city today. I hope I don't have to resort to force to find out."

"It's of no significance to your colonel what I do."

"Yet he wishes to know."

"Well, he won't find out. Your colonel dwells in our mansion and takes everything away from us, my mother's porcelain china, our horse, our saddle, our cows milk, and our chickens. He's even got my pianoforte! He will not know the purpose of my trip to the city. And that is that."

"All I need to do is find out your mission today."

"I shan't tell you."

The captain took out of his jacket a set of leather hand restraints, the likes of which I had seen as a piece of evidence during a case of Papa's some time ago. They did not scare me. "What will you do? March me down to the ferry in those things?"

"If I have to, Miss Scott. I don't want to."

"I'll scream all the way down to the water!" The captain and I faced each other. I could see the captain picturing himself dragging a yelling, outraged girl, kicking and screaming down to the boats and hating every step she took.

He said softly, "I don't want to march you back to the ferry, Miss Scott. Someday this war will be over, and we will all be peaceable subjects of our King George as we used to be. This anger you have will fade. We in England shall live in peace with our brothers and sisters in America."

I spat on the grass. "That's what I think of your king's peace!"

"Really, Miss Scott, you act like my twelve-year-old sister in London! Look, just tell me why you're here, and I'll leave you be."

"If you must know," I lied while I looked straight into the captain's eyes. "I'm to visit my friend Susan who lives here now and to buy ribbons in the Notions store."

Captain Stonecroft looked directly into my eyes. "Miss Scott, this will be very bad for you if you lie. My colonel does not forgive, and there's the noose always lurking."

"He'll have to look hard in Cow Neck for a tree to hang it from, won't he, since your troops cut our trees down to keep yourselves warm? You remember, don't you, Captain?" I didn't bring up about the raid on the Presbyterian Church from where we got most of our wood back.

The captain at this point just wanted to be rid of me. He pondered, "So you've come for ribbons and to visit your friend. Is that your story?"

"Yes. That's my story."

He rubbed his hand across his face and nodded. "Of course, you must have your ribbons and your visit with your friend. I shall inform the colonel of the innocent nature of your travel. I am glad that your errands are so benevolent. As long as you know the penalty for lying to the crown," he broke off.

I didn't answer. It turned out the captain was not finished, after all; he sat down next to me on the broken tombstone. "The sun is so pleasantly warm today, is it not?" He pulled a long green blade of grass out from the soil and began to knead it between his fingers. Staring down at it, he said, "We have many ruins like this one in England. Sometimes, when the sun shines after some days of rain, churches give teas in their churchyards, and people sit as we are, on the tombstones, and eat their cakes and teas. I've seen rainbows from graveyards." He paused. "This place, Miss Scott, it makes me think of home."

I almost liked him at that moment. I reckoned he wanted to be with his family in London, just as much as I wanted to be with my mine. But my heart hardened as I thought of the way my father was captured and put on that horrible prison ship. The captain smiled, stood up, dusted off his uniform, and bowed. "Good day, Miss Scott. Enjoy your day in the city. By the way, your friend Susan, would she be the same young lady named Susan with whom I danced at Miss Sarah Harkens's recital?"

"Yes."

"I would so like to call on her, but I don't know where she dwells. It seems she lives no more in Cow Neck. I've scoured the town looking for her. It is a great puzzle for I came face-to-face with her at a salon a fortnight ago here in York City. Alas, I didn't ask where she lives. If you would be so kind as to give her my regards...and ask her if I may call?"

"I do not know if she will be at home for guests, Captain."

"But if she is?" The captain's face was alight with hope.

"Yes. I shall."

"If it is all right, I can knock on your cottage door tomorrow?"

"I shall do my best, Captain." I put my mobcap back on, which I hoped was a signal I would be leaving immediately.

I smiled, rather grimly, and made my way out of Trinity's precincts. When I looked back, the captain was standing at the corner next to the church ruins.

CHAPTER FORTY-EIGHT

"John Laboyteaux, Tailor," the gold lettering on a green painted wooden board sign said. "Scotch Plaids, Linens, Ribbons, Green Baize, Black Silk Gloves." I walked into the cool, shady interior of the shop. "I would like a yard of the pink ribbon on the top shelf, please."

The merchant used his rake to pull down the bolt of ribbon. He measured the material along the wooden tabletop that served to measure its length. It was just the right shade of pink, which would make my golden hair glow in the sunshine. "One pound even, miss."

Indignation rose in my throat. "What! A pound!"

"Yes, miss."

"Why, that's absurd. Ribbons don't cost that much."

"Well...this one does, miss. Will you be wantin' it?"

While I pondered, he waited, holding the scissors in his right hand, ready to cut off a yard from the bolt of delicate ribbon. I really wanted it. I tried to square my chin and look firm.

"Unless you can sell it cheaper, I shall not." I stood firm and unsmiling.

"No, I can't do that, miss."

I walked out and stood in front of the store window. The clerk had left the ribbon lying along the wooden tabletop. It would heighten the blush in my cheeks, and it went so well with my long hair. I took a deep breath and walked back into the shop, emerging a few minutes later onto the sunlit street one English pound lighter and a yard of pink ribbon richer.

Susan's grandfather lived on Beekman Place. Great houses lined the street. Soon I came to number 82, a huge mansion, its front door gilded with a shiny brass knocker. As I waited, watching, there was movement of the heavy drapes in a parlor window. Someone in there saw me. The door opened.

"Suzie!"

"Cassie, it's you." Suzie opened the door wider, waved me up the stoop. I stepped into the most beautiful house I had ever seen in my whole life. Suzie walked me through the spacious rooms. Raspberry-colored velvet couches rested on Persian rugs in the parlor. Where the rugs ended, the dining room floor was shined to a fare-thee-well and the mahogany table gleamed. A bowl of fresh flowers occupied the center of the table, and a candle chandelier holding hundreds of candles hung from the ceiling. When Suzie illuminated it, gorgeous light shone on the polished mahogany table and chairs and spread through the floor-to-ceiling windows. Down the slope, the blue waters of the river floated, calm and serene in the sun. Small boats sailed by, turning the scene into a picture painted by an artist. I could see the river in one direction and, by turning around, the street of rich homes opposite Suzie's grandfather's house.

"It's so good to see you, Cassie! I've missed you so much."

"I missed you too," I said.

"Come upstairs to my room. No one else is home right now, and cook is off today. What are you doing in the city? Why didn't you write that you were coming? Can you stay? We'll go to a coffee shop after I've shown you the rooms." This came out all in a breath; I had forgotten Suzie's habit of talking in a great rush. I was so glad to see her again.

"I've come on the ferry; I wanted ribbons to wear in my hair with my taffeta gown, and I read an advertisement about the tailor, John Laboyteaux, at Beekman Slip, so here I am." It was more pretense with a bit of truth into the mixture, but I couldn't say more, or Suzie would ask questions. I was so used to talking with Suzie, it was hard not to tell her everything.

"I would have gone with you! I buy buckles for my shoes there and ribbons all the time. Anyway, I've so much to tell you, Cassie!"

"Tell me. It's so rich looking here."

"Yes, my grandfather is very rich. He is so good to me, and he misses my papa very much."

"I know. I miss my papa, too, and my brothers." Suzie hardly heard me, so interested was she in what she was saying.

"Cassie, there are so many balls, cotillions, and recitals here! Look at all these gowns my gramps bought for me!" She flung open her closet door; I faced a rack of jewel-colored, sashed, and ribboned gowns that nearly took my breath away. "I must tell you I have been having the most agreeable time here in York City. Every night I go to a reception or a play or a salon, where gentlemen and ladies chat and listen to music. Even British officers come, and they have lovely manners. Actually, there is someone who comes to these salons from Cow Neck."

"Who?" I asked, hoping it wasn't the captain.

But it was. "The British officer, Captain Stonecroft. Remember? We threw the ice ball at him. I danced with him at Sarah's party?

And I did like him very much. You remember, don't you, Cassie, at Sarah's recital?"

"Yes. I do remember him," I said and felt, all of a sudden, a blow so hard in my stomach I had to sit down on the satin-covered bed. *But Max? What about Max?*

Suzie kept right on talking. "I hadn't seen him for so very long, and then one evening, he walked into Mrs. Parvington's parlor, and we found ourselves in conversation among a roomful of people. We had a very nice chat; it was such fun seeing him. But I haven't seen Captain Stonecroft since. I do find myself thinking of him at times. I fancy a dance with him, the way we did at Sarah's party." She must have noticed the disbelief on my face for she did not look at me. And then she bolted upright. "I haven't forgotten Max, Cassie. I love Max. You know that. But I love to dance; you used to like to dance too, Cassie. I wish I could be more like you. I wish I didn't like this life so much, but I do, and I have so much fun here. It's all silly fun, smiling and dancing, chatting with the handsome officers. It means nothing." Suzie smiled at me; it was a wan, sad sort of smile.

"I saw him just a little while ago."

"You saw him, Cassie, today?"

"Yes. He asked me to ask you if he could call on you."

Suzie's eyes lit up. I looked down, thinking of how Max was far off fighting for us all, probably longing for Suzie and home. As if Suzie read my mind, she began again, serious and sober. "Oh, I don't care, Cassie. He can call if he likes. It's nothing to me. I want to have a bit of fun, that's all. Come on, let's go for a walk, shall we? And get a coffee?"

"I can't stay. I must catch the afternoon ferry back. I wanted to see you and say hello. And I wanted to give you Max's letters. I walked by your cabin and found them sticking out the door."

Suzie looked down at the carpet. "I couldn't face telling Max I was leaving Cow Neck. He would have been sorry to hear I would be leaving my friends." I put the letters in Suzie's arms. She lifted them to her cheek. Tears came to her eyes. "Oh, Cassie, I miss Max so much."

"I know; I miss him too," I said.

"Can't you catch a later ferry? That would be so good, Cassie."

"No, I should go, Suzie." I looked out the windows again at the water and the grassy lawn and made ready to go. I got up from the chair and walked to the bedroom door.

Suzie followed me. "Wait, Cassie, please. I want you to know I do love Max. You believe me, don't you?"

"I know you love Max, Suzie. You just showed me. I've got to go or I shall be late for the ferry."

"I'll walk you down to the wharf, shall I?"

I gripped the doorknob. "No. It's getting on to one o'clock. I don't want to miss the ferry. I'll have to run. Good-bye, Suzie."

"Bye, Cassie. Remember me to everybody."

"I shall. Bye." I was almost to the Tontine Coffee Shop before I remembered. The captain was waiting at the edge of Trinity. I gave him Suzie's permission to call, and her address. *War is like that*, I thought.

CHAPTER FORTY-NINE

Caleb Brewster had chosen a table without any hanging lanterns overhead. He sat in the dark part of the coffee shop, facing the kitchen where servants rushed past him in and out of the swinging door carrying food trays. His back was to me and the other patrons. He looked up and sidewise and then quickly looked down as I approached the table. "Sit down. Sit down," he said sharply under his breath, reached across the small table, and shoved out a chair for me to sit on. My back rested against the wall.

"You look different without the beard," I whispered, leaning across the table.

"It's these fancy rags. Not used to 'em." Caleb spoke so low I could hardly hear. He did look odd wearing gentlemen's knickers and morning coat over his ruffled shirt, and he looked younger without the beard, but I kept these things to myself.

"I walked to the water this morning," I said.

"Sought out the boat, did you?" He was now holding the side of his face with his left hand and whispering through his fingers. I looked up to see a redcoat with his hand on his sword hilt standing close to our table. He looked down at Caleb as though he was struggling to place him. After a moment, the soldier gave up and walked slowly to a table filled with redcoats.

"No." I spoke low. "I wanted to see the wharf." He looked up, nodding his head from side to side.

Seated at a table to the front of the shop, the troubled redcoat waited until the servant appeared through the swinging doors and stood up to yell at him, "I'm waiting for roasted beef ten minutes already. Why is it I don't have it?"

"Hold your horses; it's coming," the servant shot back as he disappeared into the kitchen.

I felt better to see the English soldier tear into his piece of meat when it finally came. He wasn't interested in Caleb at all. It did not take long for the whole table of redcoats to finish up and leave. I felt free again to talk to Caleb. "I saw you talking to the captain on the bridge of the Dutch boat. I hardly recognized you," I said.

"Redcoats expect me with a beard. It's why I shaved it off. Anyone walk behind you, follow you here?" He, too, spoke more naturally, now that the redcoats had left. Still, Caleb was not at ease, every now and then looking around at diners still present in the shop.

"Captain Stonecroft found me in Trinity Churchyard."

"What did he want?"

"Wanted to know what I was doing in the city. I told him about some ribbon I needed to buy in York City and that I was going to visit Suzie."

Caleb didn't look up from his plate of mutton. "You must have charmed him, I'm thinking."

I felt the red coming into my cheeks, but then he might not have meant to flatter me, so I ignored his words. "I reckon so, but he warned me about doing espionage against the king."

He took a sip of his coffee and leaned across the table. His face came closer to mine. "Are you sure you're willing to take on this job at Stony Point? Tell me the truth, Cassandra. Are you wavering? It isn't too late to tell me."

I took a deep breath. "I'm sure, and I don't like to be called Cassandra."

"You're a brick, Cassie. You know that? A real brick. Someone I know I can depend on."

I felt very pleased to think Caleb approved of me. I couldn't really voice my troubled feelings for him because I was too shy; yes, I was. Cassie Scott, scared to tell him I liked him a lot, but if I couldn't tell him of my feelings for him, I could confide my weakness. "Fear attacks me and then it leaves me. I'm getting used to fear. It comes and goes," I said.

This time Caleb put down his cup. "That's the way it is with fear, Cassie. I have it too. But know this, someone will be watching over you. You'll have cover the whole time you're in the British fort."

"Who?"

"Can't say. You'll not be in danger there. Let's go over the plan."

I spoke very low. He had to lean further toward me to hear. He nodded his head a few times to show he knew I got it right. "The ship's name is *Blossom*. She's docked facing Sweeney's restaurant. She sails under the Dutch colors at one thirty this afternoon."

"Good." He looked down at the repeater on his wrist. "Which time is now one o'clock."

"Yes," I said. "Are you leaving?"

"In a minute. Go ahead." He poured the last of the coffee into our two cups while I rattled off the plan. I took the cup from his hands, feeling a shock when our fingers touched. Caleb lifted his own cup to drink. His fingers around the cup looked thick and stubby, and his broadcloth sleeves were having a hard time easing around his burly arms.

I took a sip of coffee; my mouth was very dry. "I'm Dolly Ashton, daughter of Lev Ashton, dairy farmer from New Windsor. I'm here in the British camp to take orders for sides of beef for the troops. My sister Patsy comes every month on this errand, but Patsy is sick today. I'm taking her place. Patsy has told me I'm to see the quartermaster. I ask for the quartermaster's tent, go there, and hand him the order forms. He'll fill them out and sign them and hand them back to me. Shall I go on?"

"So far, so good." Caleb nodded.

"The quartermaster, who is not one of us, is in possession of a report that we need. It's been arranged that at some point, he will leave the tent. The report will be lying on top of the pile of documents on his desk. I will know it. It's a list describing British troop strength, quantity of guns and powder, amount of field pieces, and how our troops loaded with guns and ammunition can approach the summit quickly, quietly, and with the least amount of effort." I paused. Caleb eyed me closely while I spoke. "I pick up the report. I put it in the leather purse given to me by Mrs. Fanshawe. I leave and follow the path down to the water. Wait for the king's ferry to take me upriver to New Windsor, where I will find General Washington's headquarters in the Thomas Ellison house that can be seen from the ferry. I give the report only to General Washington."

"Good. Then what?"

"I walk to Lev Ashton's dairy farm. His acreage begins next to the Ellison house, almost on the water. I'll find Ernest there, healing from the wound he got at Stony Point from the first battle." I felt my eyes getting misty. "I shall be so glad to see him." This would not do; I wiped my eyes. "The family will keep me overnight, and the next morning, *Blossom* will pick me up and take me down to York City."

Caleb raised his cup of coffee in a toast to me. He took a long time before he spoke. "Cassie, don't forget who you are, a Patriot. I saw only raw courage from you at the Presbyterian Church." Caleb put his big paw over my hand. "You will succeed."

221

I nodded. "Yes, I will, Caleb."

"Yes, you will." He turned his head. "Look across the room, will you? Do you see a stout fellow sitting right next to the door wearing a yellow scarf around his neck?"

"Yes, I see him. Who is he?"

"Hercules Mulligan. He owns a men's outfitting shop near here. He's with us. He's one of the Sons of Liberty." Caleb's face was alight with energy and enthusiasm. I glimpsed for the first time that Caleb's world was much wider than mine, that he had many secrets and many connections. In the same instant, I realized he loved the excitement and danger of spy business.

"Hand me that leather bag Mrs. Fanshawe gave you."

I took the little purse from my reticule and passed it in my palm to him across the table, and I then waited while in one operation he pulled the ends apart and put my pass and the order forms I would take to Stony Point inside. He sealed the purse and slid it to me under cover of a saucer of biscuits. "Your pass is signed by General Clinton, Commander of the British forces in America. No one will question it. I must go, Cassie."

"Where do you go?" I whispered.

He hesitated and then framed his words in soft-speak. "To sink some ships, of course." He grinned at me. "Some leviathans of the British stripe residing in our Long Island Sound." He kept looking at me. "By the way, you look pretty today."

I felt my heart jump. Surely, he must have noticed my hair; I had brushed it until it shone this morning and again in the tiny room at the back of the Tontine, where I had slipped the pink ribbon in it.

"I'm going to ease my way to the door. I'll walk out to the street with my head down, and you'll see Hercules get up and leave betimes. Wait a few minutes and then go. By the way, you'll never see me again in these fancy rags. I'll be back in my woodsman's clothes afore the night's out, girl."

"Woman," I said, smiling up at him for the last time.

"And a grand one at that." Caleb held my hand in his for a long moment. "Until freedom, Cassie." He was gone and out the door. The man with the yellow scarf around his neck, Hercules, sauntered out the door a minute later. I got up from the table and walked to the door, pretending not to notice a Hessian unit of ten soldiers being accommodated for their dinners. Once seated, they looked up and stared at me over their bowls of stew as if they'd never before seen an American girl. I tossed my hair, glad again that I brushed it so that it lay smooth as silk on my shoulders. But it didn't help with my fear of what I had to accomplish at Stony Point.

The American girl is about to enter the enemy camp to gather specific intelligence; I must stop shaking. I am about to take my life in my hands as a spy, and I do not want to think about that. I want to think about ribbons for my golden hair. But at the same time the terrible fear creeps up, rises and falls in my stomach.

CHAPTER FIFTY

The sloop, *Blossom*, made its way up the Harlem River along grassy banks on which children played and fished. The Dutch captain, a tall, old, white-haired man whose name was Paulus Detrick, called down to me on the slippery deck and invited me up to the bridge, where it was dry and sunny and much more pleasant. After we left Spuyten Dyvil where the Harlem joined the North River, the river grew wider and no more children played and fished along its green slopes. All along the shores were high cliffs and palisades with maples and sycamores marching down to the water's edge. The sloop took a course in the deep channel of the river. We followed in the wake of a frigate, her twenty-eight pounders pointed back at our bow. Behind us, a huge man-of-war carrying sixty-four pounders aimed at our little sloop's stern caused looks of horror to appear on some of the Dutch sailors' faces down on the deck and on my face too.

Home in our Long Island Sound, I had seen British men-of-war. Anchored in calm waters, on a sunny day, they looked serene, almost majestic parts of the seascape. But today, under sail, pushed along by a stiff wind and a heavy chop to the water, the man-of-war bore down on us, dwarfing the sloop, seeming at times to almost ram into us. The British ship was frighteningly close.

"They are not interested in us," Captain Detrick told me. "They are interested in bigger fish. I put you down soon at Stony Point."

It could not be soon enough, even though I knew I would have to make a harsh climb when I got there.

There it was. Stony Point was still some miles away high up over the river, jutting out to almost meet the opposite shelf of land Caleb told me was called Verplanck's Point. That night in Cow Neck when I had met Caleb at the bend in Berry Creek seemed long ago. I felt the fear attacking me again, in my stomach, climbing up into my bones and prickling my skin. I felt it in my mouth. My breath was fast and shallow. How was I to do this job? To distract myself, I repeated the plan over and over. I'm Dolly Ashton. My sister Patsy is sick…*Could I possibly go home? I want to go home. No, I can't. I'm on this Dutch ship, and I've got to do this job. York City is a faded distance behind me; I can't go back.*

Too soon the Captain motioned I should follow him down to the deck. We both sat in the tender, and we were lowered to the water. The oarsman rowed us to shore. I put my mobcap on and picked up my reticule. In only minutes, the captain held my arm and walked me down to the muddy bank. He bowed to me right before he took his place in the tender and was soon rowed back to the *Blossom.* I watched the brave little sloop ford the river and sail into the distance. I was alone except for the noise of birdsong.

From where I stood under the shelf of Stony Point, I could not see the top. I began to climb. Soldiers' boots and animals' hoofprints had made a muddy hash out of the path. At first the path climbed gently. The air was cool. But soon the hill became steep, and I began to sweat. I pulled off my cap and tore off my apron. I doubled my apron on the hard ground before I sat down on it. I had to sit more often as the path grew steeper.

Climbing, climbing. All of a sudden, the path opened up to a flat piece of land. A small graveyard had been fashioned with clumps of stones piled atop one another to form a low wall enclosing a clutch of tombstones. Dirt piled high to form graves, crudely carved wooden crosses incised with soldiers' names were stuck into the mounds of earth. Wildflowers resting on the graves were fresh, recently picked. I began to read the names aloud to myself: "Josiah Hawksworth, James Faunton, Patrick Hingle, Thomas Dennison, John Mueller, Andrew Curlin, Isaac Morrison, Elias Smith, Ernest Scott." Ernest Scott. Not my Ernest. My Ernest was recovering at Ashton's farm in New Windsor, I knew it was true; Caleb told me. I dropped to the ground. I read the letters again: Ernest Scott. My Ernest. No. No. No. Another Ernest. But deep in my heart of hearts, I knew. This grave held my brother.

I sat on the ground next to Ernest's grave and patted the mound of dirt on top. Sobbing into my hands, I cried for my dear brother. I don't know how long it was before I smoothed down the dirt around his cross. Ernest was dead. There were yellow flowers around his cross. After a while I put my hand on the cross, felt its rough wood, and patted the dirt down smoothly around his cross. But it did no good. Ernest lay dead under the dirt and flowers. It did no good at all to cry. But I couldn't stop. I sat on the ground, my head bent, my hand around the flimsy cross, and cried.

After a while, my tears stopped, and I sat quietly next to Ernest's grave. I noticed a thin leather-bound book lying nearby, its pages riffling in the breeze. The flyleaf read Private Elias Smith, the name scrawled on the inside page. A folded paper fell out; I saw it was a letter, unfinished.

"My dear mother," I read out of the blurred pages. *"It is cold here in the camp at night, even in July. Stony Point is not named after a mountain, but it is high enough for fierce winds that blow right through our thin covers. There are rumors of an approaching*

army. We don't know how soon, but we shall be ready to trounce them. I play my fiddle every night and my friends sing. My friend Ernest is especially eager to learn the fiddle, and he is a good learner too. I have not taken up tobacco, you will be glad to hear, though some of the fellows do."

The letter trailed off, a letter that died with Elias Smith. He and Ernest must have fought side by side and been good friends. I wiped the thin book with the hem of my gown and tucked it back into the mounded soil of Elias Smith's grave. I sat for a while longer and prayed in this forlorn little graveyard. I prayed out loud, "Dear brother and dear friend of my brother, I shall never forget you. I'll come this way again." *They didn't die alone,* I kept saying to myself over and over. It was some comfort. I kissed the cross above Ernest's grave and walked on.

CHAPTER FIFTY-ONE

"Who goes?" Two redcoats carrying Brown Bess rifles, flashing steel bayonets attached, stood guard at the entrance to the fort. Tents of different sizes lined the perimeter and in the middle ground. Nearby, smithies bent over open forges, shoeing horses' hooves, leather aprons tied to their waists. Across the way, fat from roasting beef spit out from fires built in the open air.

"I'm Dolly Ashton. My father is Levi Ashton of New Windsor. He owns and works a dairy farm there." My words were so well practiced they tumbled out of my mouth.

"Papers?"

"I come here under a flag of peace." The soldiers didn't look convinced. One held his rifle pointed at my chest while the other examined my papers. He examined my pass for what seemed a long time. Even though it carried the signature of the British general, Sir Henry Clinton, who had taken command of the British forces in 1778 after General Howe resigned in 1777, it didn't seem to satisfy these soldiers. I held my breath until the one soldier handed it back to me. How that signature got there was a marvel to me, but

Caleb told me I would be safe with my pass, and so I felt safe. Still, I prayed they didn't notice my trembling hands as I put the pass back into my reticule.

"What's your purpose here?" the taller of the two soldiers addressed me.

"My father supplies your troops with beef once a month. I come with order forms today."

"We have someone who comes every month here, and you are not she."

"My sister, Patsy, usually takes the orders, but she is ill with a stomachache." I answered, adding, "My father sends me instead."

"Patsy Ashton is ill?" His voice changed to concern. "How does she heal?" The soldier pointing the rifle lowered it to the ground.

"She is feeling much better, but she needs to rest," I said, feeling very much untruthful.

"That's a benefice!" He cleared his throat, became businesslike again. "Give over your order forms."

"Yes, sir." I handed him the order forms. He looked them over carefully. *Were he and Patsy Ashton sweethearts?* But I had no more time to wonder. At least, it distracted me from my fear.

"I believe I need to look for the quartermaster's tent," I said, after a moment.

He handed me back my forms. "Proceed along the path. The quartermaster's tent is the largest you come to. Mind, you bring your sister my good wishes, Paul Buchanan's good wishes."

"Yes, sir, I shall." He handed me back my order forms and motioned me inside the stockade. The noise of sawing, hammering, polishing, and beating steel in that center space rattled any calm I might have felt. The soldier pointed out the path to the Quartermaster's tent.

Uniformed officers threaded their way through the throng of laboring soldiers. I kept to the perimeter of the space. All the tents looked large to me. Here and there a break in the fence revealed the steep drop to the river. From the ship a distance away, Stony Point hadn't looked so high. Overcome with tears for Ernest, I had not noticed the river falling away from me. Now, from the top, looking down, I stared at the river, a tiny ribbon far, far below. A long, oblong tent, its flap smacking back and forth in the breeze, presented itself. Stacks and stacks of Brown Bess rifles, steel bayonets attached, shone in the bright sunlight. I peered into the tent when a hand clapped my shoulder.

"Cassie!"

I jumped. David Van Essen stood before me, wearing the red coat.

"Get inside." He held open the tent flap.

I stood in the opening. "You are the quartermaster?"

"Yes. Go inside." He closed the tent flap behind him. "Sit down." He cleared a space on the chair among the stacks of papers and other supplies. "Quickly, what do you do here?"

"Traitor!" I hissed.

"Don't waste my time. Answer me."

"I came here to see my brother Ernest at Levi Ashton's farm. His daughter, Patsy, was ill. I offered to do a favor for him to take these forms to the quartermaster." The lies were getting easier to tell. "I would not have done so if I knew you were the quartermaster." That part was true.

All David said was "Patsy is ill? That is too bad. Give the forms to me." David's quill scratched out the numbers on the forms. He did not look at me. "How does Ernest keep?"

"My brother lies dead in a rough grave halfway up this hill."

As if I had slapped him, David sat back in a heap. "I did not know he died."

I leaned forward. "I want to know what happened to him."

David shook his head and did not speak for a while. "I can only tell you he was shot when the British captured Stony Point."

"And where were you when Ernest was shot?"

"I was in another fort at the time. When I arrived, I read the casualties list and found out Ernest was injured."

"…taking care to be far away from the actual fighting, I'm sure," I said, not masking the contempt I felt for David.

David flinched. He looked over at me. "Ernest was shot in the shoulder. I heard he was healing at Ashton's farm. That is all I know."

"Did you at least try to see him?"

"No. As a Loyalist soldier, I could not. I'm told it wasn't much of a battle. The Americans were outnumbered by Clinton's army. There was nothing for the Continentals to do but flee. Most of them made it." David dipped his quill in the inkwell. "I shall finish writing up these orders." He did not look up again.

"When did my brother die? His grave and all the others' graves were dug recently. There are fresh flowers on his grave." I felt myself beginning to sob. I willed myself to stop.

"I don't know when he died. He was injured on the day of the battle, September twentieth last year. I've told you everything I know, Cassie." There was something in the way David avoided looking at me directly. This was not the David I knew, barely speaking to me. A revelation hit me. Could I be wrong about David? I looked at him. His eyes were wet, too. He was sad.

Caleb had told me the quartermaster was not one of us? But could he be one of us? "David, are you spying for the Americans?" I whispered.

His face assumed a stone-hardness that I'd never seen before; he did not look at me directly. "I told you the day of your Liberty Feast on Shepherd's Hill, the day of your so-called independency, I do not believe in the rebel cause, and I remain loyal to my king. I owed my allegiance to King George then, and I do to this day and shall forever. I renounced any loyalty to the American cause. Do you understand?"

"Perfectly."

"Good." He stood up. "I'll arrange for an escort out of the fort." He strode across the tented room and slapped open the flap.

Yes. It was clear to me now what a silly, foolish girl I had been. I wasted no time but went right to the pile of papers on his desk. No document lay atop the pile carrying the raised seal of the English King. I sat back in disbelief. The tent flap slipped aside noiselessly. A redcoat came through dropping a document on the pile. It carried the King's seal. He was gone before I could look up.

Troop Strength, Armaments, Defenses on Little Gibraltar
Stony Point nicknamed Little Gibraltar
Troop Strength
1 of 2 detachments of 71st Regiment
Grenadier Company
Detachment of Royal Artillery
750 troops
ARMAMENTS
15 field pieces
2 brass cannon
4 mortars
4 small howitzers
DEFENSES
Fleches—earthen-cannon positions

This was what I was sent to get. I shoved the paper inside the leather purse and sealed the leather together with the sharp buckle Mrs. Fanshawe had given me. I jammed it into my apron pocket as David strode through the tent flap; he didn't even have the decency to hold it open for me. "There will be someone waiting for you at the bottom of the hill to guide you to the ferry. He'll put you at the ferry landing. Good-bye, Cassie."

I brushed past him, turned back to face him. "I shall not say good-bye, being that my brother died at the hands of your army."

I had no doubts now, no regrets. David had rejected me and the land of his birth. I had cried over his loss, but in that moment, I hated him.

CHAPTER FIFTY-TWO

The horse grazed the thin grass next to the riverbank. The rider wore the red coat of the British Army and the black helmet. He sat in the saddle and looked down at me just coming off the path. He led his horse over to me and jumped down to the ground. "Time to leave, miss . . ."

I backed away. "I will not. I'm here for the ferry." My words had no meaning for him. He crossed in front of his horse, lifted me up, and threw me over the horse's back. I had no choice but to scramble to right myself and sit forward in the saddle.

"Never you mind, miss. Ferry's out of service today. Sorry for the rough ride. But we have to get you out of here. You're in good hands. You mustn't worry." he breathed harshly on my neck. We jounced along the banks of the river until a road came into sight.

"Where are you taking me? I demand you put me down now," I yelled back to him.

"No need for fear. I'm taking you to New Windsor." His voice was ragged with the gallop of the horse.

"Who *are* you?" I twisted my neck, trying to see his face.

"Samuel Smith, miss, a Patriot."

"But you're wearing the red coat."

"Took it off a dead Brit. Coat makes it easier to get around in the woods among the enemy." I hardly heard him for the trees rushing past me and the wind in my face. After some miles, Samuel Smith slowed his horse to a trot. "Here you are, Miss, New Windsor. Much luck to you." He helped me down from the horse, waved to me, and rode away in a gallop.

A man in knickers and homespun shirt stood on a flat bottom boat, wide enough to carry cattle. He poled close to the bank. "I'm Jack. I'll take you across." That's all he said. I stood on the shore. There was nothing to do but to believe him and pray. I stepped off the bank onto the raft. The man named Jack said nothing else to me, nor I to him. As we gained the ground on the other side of the river, he pointed to a yellow house. "Colonel Thomas Ellison House, just there," and I was off the raft on firm ground, thanking Providence for my deliverance. But who provided for me?

CHAPTER FIFTY-THREE

New Windsor, four in the afternoon

"May I make application to speak to General Washington?" It was cool in this room with its thick stone walls. Lit candle sticks rested on each of the four tables at which young Continental army officers sat reading or writing, quills in hand. I was very aware of the mood of quiet study and how I looked so out of place with my mud-spattered, stained gown and tangled hair. But so far, the aide hadn't noticed me. He had not looked up even though my shadow interrupted the shaft of sunlight falling across his handwriting. I asked again and curtsied. Finally, he did look up, and his mouth tightened in a line of irritation.

"Your business?" The officer stared at the bits of wood and grass and berry spots that clung to my cloak. He made no effort to hide his distaste, recoiling in his seat as he looked up and saw me.

"I have information for the general."

He shoved a writing tablet toward me. "Write it down. I'll see he gets it."

"I have to hand this information to the general myself."

"He's not here. You can leave it with me, and it will reach him. Write it down." I did not pick up the offered tablet or the quill. He went back to his work.

"Please, I do need to speak to General Washington. Can you tell me where he is?"

The aide stood up. "I cannot. You'll have to tell me your information or write it down."

There was no more talk to be had from him. I walked toward the door, conscious of how the other young aides were looking pointedly at my disheveled self.

Outside there was a well. I lowered the bucket, filled it half full to bathe my face and hands. I filled the dipper with water and had a big, long drink. I wiped my hands on the hem of my gown and brushed off the grit. Trying to wrestle my damp, unruly hair under my mobcap became a struggle. Curls stuck out. Giving up, I tied the bonnet to my apron. Some distance from the fieldstone house, I found a camp chair under a tree and sat down, training my eyes on the door. If the general came through, I would see him.

But once I was sitting down, in my mind I saw again the mound of earth, Ernest's name cut into the crude cross, and the wildflowers. I tried to thank Providence that Ernest had a friend, the soldier who would rest in the next grave forever. I wept quietly.

"Hello?" A tall fellow wearing homespun approached me, carrying a rucksack. "Is something ailin' you?" He was young, about Ernest's age, twenty-one or so. He had sandy hair and a face framed in freckles.

"No." I looked up, wiping my eyes.

"Do you want some water?" The fellow sat down on the grass.

"No." I looked away.

"Well, something is wrong, ain't it?" he persisted.

"I came to see General Washington. He is not here."

"Jonah Higbie knows where he is."

"Who's that?"

"That's me. I'm from North Carolina. I came up here to join this man's army. I'm just waitin' till I get in. What's your name, and where do you hail from?"

"I'm Cassie Scott from Cow Neck, New York."

"You live down there near York City?" His face was a study in wonder.

"No. I live on another island, Long Island."

"Say! I bet you been there to York City, ain't I right? Sure ya have. It's a real sparky place, ain't it? You want to see the general? He went to Newburgh. I think he'll be back soon. He's lookin' to set up headquarters there in a while."

"Where is Newburgh? Is there a ferry?"

"Nah. Them redcoats took the ferry out of service just a coupla days ago. I got a boat. I could row ya there."

"I thank you for the offer of a boat ride, but I'll walk. Can you tell me how much of a walk it is to Newburgh?"

"Don't know. I ain't never walked it. I got my boat down there, ready to row." Jonah Higbie tilted his head toward the river, stepped back a foot or two, and held his rucksack out. "Look, I'm gonna open up my rucksack and see what all I got to eat. You look hungry. I got a couple of apples. How 'bout we go down by the water under a tree to eat 'em?" He pummeled his rucksack. "Yup, and I got a couple of hardtack biscuits. Come on, Cassie Scott."

I was very hungry by now. It was nearly four o'clock. I'd eaten nothing since the bread and meat I ate on the ferry to York City. Jonah Higbie walked ahead, and as he walked, he talked. "Like I said, I ain't a soldier, Cassie. I'm a kind of handy man around here. They ain't nothin' I cain't fix. But I want to join up soon's I can in this man's army."

We had traveled around to the back of the fieldstone house. Jonah Higbie squatted down in the shade under a weeping willow tree, yards from the back of the house. From here we could see the sparkling North River lapping at the grass. I dropped down and sat with my back against the tree, feeling fresh breezes fluttering through the branches. I could hear the murmur of voices from the house.

"Ain't it nice here, Cassie?" He spoke so low I hardly heard him. Jonah Higbie reached into his rucksack again, pulled out hardtack biscuits and apples, and handed me a biscuit. "Don't go smackin' your lips and chompin' out loud on the biscuit, or they'll hear us in the house. This here space is supposed to be for the officers to rest in."

"There's bugs in this biscuit." I held it as far away from me as I could.

"Just pull 'em out. They all be dead now."

"Oh, no. I couldn't."

"The water's cold. Try some from out this flask." I noticed Jonah Higbie's hand was dirty; I didn't want to sip from his flask. But I closed my eyes and took the dirty pewter flask from him. The water was cool and delicious going down my throat. If I was going to eat, it was going to be this biscuit. I opened my eyes and pulled out two dead insects from the hardtack without gagging. I was famished. I swallowed every bite.

"Well, current is runnin' upriver now but due to change soon. If you want to go to Newburgh, it's a good time to go. I don't rightly know if the general is comin' back here to New Windsor this very afternoon. Mayhap tonight. Mayhap tomorrow. Better get goin'."

He was on his feet, already walking fast down to the river. I scrambled up and hurried after him.

"Thank you. I can't pay much."

"Don't make no difference to me," he said.

I was out of breath. "Where is your boat? Isn't it tied up to a dock?"

Jonah Higbie didn't answer me. "Come on! Come on!" He gestured I should follow fast. "Behind these bushes. Here we are. Hop in. Be quick about it."

I hopped into the rowboat. There was an inch or so of water on the floor. Fish hooks lined the bottom of the boat. Jonah Higbie rowed like a demon out into the North River. We traveled fast. He didn't speak for a few minutes. When he did, I felt uneasy at his words.

"What you want to see the general about? You got a message for the general, Cassie, have you? What's your hurry to get to see him?"

"I need to speak to him," I said.

"Something written down?"

"Why do you ask?" I said to put him off. Suddenly, I was a bit afraid, out on the water with this person, Jonah Higbie.

"Just talkin'. There's a lot of people with messages for the general. I been noticin' that." Jonah Higbie stayed quiet. I kept quiet too and looked out, pretending I was enjoying passing the houses on either side of the river. He rowed in silence for a long time; I noticed Jonah Higbie was rowing slower. He was struggling now against the current. The tide had changed and was running against us. His face was red from the effort.

He kept rowing as he spoke. "I been takin' messages myself, Cassie. Things I hear when I'm out and about, to people I know would be interested in 'em. They pay me good for 'em. So what's in your message, Cassie?" Jonah Higbie smiled at me.

Now I felt beads of sweat on my folded hands. *I must get away, get out of the boat.* "Please row to the shoreline. I want to get out," I said.

He stopped rowing and pulled the oars into the oarlocks. We started drifting in a circle. Jonah Higbie leaned forward. His face changed completely. He was no more the friendly country lad but a mean, squint-eyed enemy. "Oh, you'll get out all right. If you don't give me the message, I'll push you out. You want a good toss up in the tide."

I was far from shore. We were in the middle of the river. The current was strong. We were drifting in circles faster and faster.

Johnny Higbie leaned on his oars, staring at me. "I ain't gonna row to Newburgh if there's nothin' in it for me. You could understand that."

He meant it. "I shall pay you right now," I said. "Let me out in those marshes next to shore. I have British pounds. Row into the marshes, and I'll get out and give you all the money I have. I won't trouble you any further."

"Ah, I ain't got no more time to waste on you." At that moment, I saw only coldness from him. He reached over and grabbed my reticule. Jonah Higbie laughed out loud. "I've got it, haven't I? The money and the message. Time for you to go."

CHAPTER FIFTY-FOUR

The broad part of the oar hit me smack in the stomach, and I fell backward into the river. I reached out to grab the oar, but Higbie had lifted it and hung it high above my outstretched hand. I dropped into the dense, freezing cold blackness. Splashing, flailing, I plummeted down, down, down, feeling my shoes and my gown pulling me to the bottom. My face stung from the blackness of the swirling water as I wrested one shoe off my foot and kicked the other off. I began to flap my arms and push upward, where I could see daylight through the shimmery water; I saw my bonnet float away from me. Finally, on the surface in the watery blur, I saw trees and earth passing by from the riverbank so far away. But it was I who was moving, not the trees. The current dragged me back so fast that earth and sky seemed upside down like colors in a magic show. Once I turned and saw Jonah Higbie's boat far behind me, a tiny object bumping up and down like a child's toy in the chop. *Keep my head up. Keep my head up*, I repeated it to myself like a prayer.

I began to slip below the surface into blackness again. Feeling the cold water again climbing up to my eyes, I kicked until I was back on the surface. Out of the corner of my eye, something was floating next to me in the current; a dead beaver lay stiffly on its back. I heard a scream, a lonely scream in a watery wasteland. It was I screaming. The beaver passed me by. I became calm. I turned on my back and paddled with my arms. I made slow progress, but I could look up at the blue sky and soft white clouds. The water did not seem so cold anymore. A wet straw nest filled with blue eggs floated toward me. Overhead, a robin dropped close to the water; it flew in circles over the nest, chirping in agitation for its eggs. Finally, it left, climbing into the blue sky, and I lost track of it.

A huge plank drifted at eye level with me. Bouncing up and down along the surface, it headed straight for me. I kicked and flailed my arms to get away from it, but instead of hitting me, it passed alongside of me, sailing by me with the current. I grabbed its edges, hung by my fingers for a few seconds, and then pulled myself up to grasp it. When I had a hold of it, I scrunched and scrambled onto its surface, and I could rest for a moment. I lay on my belly on the flat wood and pushed my arms to paddle myself forward. I was out of the water. The sun, the wonderful sun, was shining down on my back. It was so much easier on the plank. Faster and faster, I paddled, and the plank skimmed the surface. Whitecaps lapped at its edges; showers of foam jumped into my face.

The rush and splash of water became stronger, and a crashing, bashing sound came from beyond where I could not see. I lay still and listened. I could do nothing except hold on to the edges of the plank. The noise grew louder. I paddled just enough to tread water, until I saw a great chasm open up in front of me. The water in its furious, driving, roiling turbulence went crashing down over a waterfall jumbled with boulders. Whirlpools and a maelstrom circled each other down below, pulling my plank closer, faster; the edge loomed before me, came up at me fast. I shut my eyes. Then the plank seemed to spin around crazily until I was hurtled and hurled against something solid. The plank came to a dead stop. I opened my eyes. It had jammed into the hull of a half-sunk dory and was stuck fast in the riverbank. Thick nests and tree branches swayed above me. Minnows darted here and there; little swirling eddies made circles in the backwater pool. But I wasn't saved. I heard the wild roar of the waterfall just inches forward and below me.

CHAPTER FIFTY-FIVE

Buttermilk Falls, New York

"Grab the rope. Grab it," a woman's sharp voice cut blade-sharp through the sound of water cascading down over the falls. A rope dangled over a tree branch. To grab it, I would have to climb up on the ribs of the half-sunk boat, kneel on its tilted hull, and then stand up and pull the rope down. I felt the wet wood of the boat. It was too slippery to climb.

"Get up on top of the hull. Stand up! You got to grab and pull that rope down. Go on!" A woman with white hair stood on the grass in front of a cottage some distance back from the waterfalls. A little black dog wandered nearby.

"I can't stand on the hull; I'll fall off," I yelled.

"No, you won't," the woman yelled. "That boat's been sunk for twenty years. She's stuck fast into the mud. Crawl up the side of the hull. Stand up and pull the rope."

I tried again. "I can't." I knew if I fell into the water, I would be over the falls.

Now the little dog barked furiously at the woman's heels. "Honey, you better do it, 'less you want to spend your day out there." I longed to be standing up there on the green grass. But first, I had to grab on to that rope. I put my head back down on the plank and cried. I punched the plank beneath me.

"Cryin' ain't gonna help ya. That ain't gonna do ya no good! Catch that rope. Kids climb up on that boat all summer long and don't fall over the falls. You can do it too. Come on! I ain't got all day to stand out here."

I got to my knees and inched along the plank, trying to stay centered so it would not tip over. I finally grasped the side of the half-sunk boat's hull, found an oarlock, and pulled myself up, scraping and scratching my knees while the plank tipped way low into the water. No matter how I stretched, I couldn't reach the rope. I would have to stand on my tiptoes to pull down that rope. I could see its braided strands, almost feel its heft, but I couldn't reach it.

"*Jump up, girl,*" the woman commanded me.

I jumped. I felt splinters and barnacles and slime, but I caught the rope, and I held on.

"That's it, honey!" The woman pulled on the rope, and I scraped across the hull of the boat to the shallow water near the bank of the river.

The woman was standing over me when I finally climbed up the banks. "You did it!" I lay there panting. I nodded. I couldn't speak for a few seconds. I was that grateful to be back onshore.

"Thank you," I gasped.

"Don't speak of it! It's fine. Now what's your name, and how did you get on that board? And come to be stranded on the river?"

It was good to sit on the grass. "I'm Cassie Scott from Cow Neck, Long Island, New York. I have to get to Newburgh where General Washington stays. Someone was rowing me there. He pushed me out of the boat."

"Oh, yeah? I'm just guessin', but that someone, was he a tall feller with light hair, blue eyes, lots of freckles, says he hails from North Carolina? Wants to get into the Continental army, right?"

"Yes. He said he could help me to see the general."

"I knew it. You got some kind of message for the general?" I didn't speak. "Good girl. Don't tell me anything. But did you tell him something?"

"Just that I needed to see the general."

"What was this fella's name? Would it be Jonah Higbie?"

"Yes."

The woman put her hands on her hips. Her face got red, and she sputtered out, "I figured as much."

"How did you know?"

"He's a traitor. Come on up the house, Cassie Scott from Cow Neck, Long Island, New York. Right now, you need to put on some dry clothes. I was just cookin' up some bacon. You must be hungry. I'll tell you all about that scoundrel, Jonah Higbie, after we eat. You look like you could eat something." The woman stuck out her hand. "My name is Joanna Collins. I live right here in the proud town of Buttermilk Falls, New York."

"Thank you, again and again and again, Joanna." I shook her hand for a long time. "Thank you, thank you again."

"Stop thankin' me, Cassie. This here's Roper." At the mention of his name, Roper stopped barking from a few yards away and trotted to Joanna Collins. He shook himself off, and we three climbed up the grass to her cottage. The cottage was one room with a hearth and mantle, fragrant with the smell of drying dill, parsley, and rosemary. Two wooden chairs sat around a wooden table, and a yellow bird sat in a cage with a pulled-back cover on a high pole. There were pink curtains on the windows and a braid rug on the floor. A rope bed covered with an Indian quilt lay close to the hearth, and a cot sat in another corner of the room, which I saw immediately was Roper's bed. As I watched, he jumped up on it and established himself almost as if to let me know this was his bed.

Joanna left the cottage door open so we could look across the grass down to the river. It looked so peaceful now, like glass. I shivered. *No one would ever know, like I know, the power of the river, caught in it as I was.*

Joanna told me she lived by herself since her husband, Billy Collins, had died in battle at Trenton. "We won that battle, but my Billy was shot. He only lived a few minutes," she told me as I sat drinking my tea. "I am so proud of my Billy."

"I lost my brother Ernest at Stony Point," I said.

"Another reason to shake hands," Joanna said. She brushed a tear from her eye. At that moment, I felt a kinship with Joanna. "So many of our boys gone," she said. I cried too.

I studied Joanna as I watched her set the table, a chore she would not let me help her with, as though I could; I was as lifeless as a ragdoll. Joanna was a large lady. At first, I thought she was old with white hair, but now, I could see she was a young woman only ten years or so older than me, about Hannah's age. She reminded me of Hannah. There was something about her; she was loud like Hannah, but there was a warmth about her. I almost wished it was she who had taken Mama's place. Joanna told me more about Jonah Higbie as we ate bacon on crusty bread.

"Cassie, Jonah Higbie be always around here, up and down the river lookin' for information he can sell to the British Army. You are not the only one he dumped out of his boat. There are others who trusted him and found their way to the murky bottom. Up here we know him for a bad man. I see you're shiverin' all over again. I never should have told you about the ones he drowned." At the thought of what I had come so close to, I shivered again.

"Now, listen here, you got to get up to Newburgh to see the general. I got a fly and a pretty little mare to pull it. She's smart too, Thomasina is. She trots over when you call to her. 'Course, you have to get to know her first. Tomorrow morning, we start out early, and we ride up there. Take us about two hours, more or less."

After supper, Joanna and I sat outside her cottage to watch the sun go down. "Now, Cassie," Joanna said, "I got to ask you a question. And you can decide how much you want to tell me. I reckon you've got something important to tell General Washington. Is it written down? Or is it in your head? Did Jonah Higbie come into possession of it?"

At that moment, I decided to trust Joanna. "No. He didn't. He thought the paper I am to bring to General Washington was in my reticule, so when he grabbed it away from me and pushed me out of the rowboat, the paper was safe in a leather pouch pinned inside my apron pocket. It's always been pinned to my apron pocket." As I spoke, I put my hand over my pocket and felt the thickness of the leather.

"Good. It's been a long day for you, Cassie. Mayhap you want to go to sleep soon." We sat in the twilight until the sun's last rays faded and the sky turned dark.

"Let's get inside before the gnats come out," Joanna said. Inside, she lit the oil lamp. "Now, you lie down on the cot over there by the bird cage. I sleep on the cot near the fire. It gets cold up here summer nights." Joanna pulled the cover around the bird cage. "Roper will sleep on the rug near me." Joanna handed me a blanket. "Keep the blanket close by." I lay down on the cot and spread my blanket over me. I heard Joanna call out. "'Night, Cassie." *I'm safe.* I slept.

CHAPTER FIFTY-SIX

Next morning the ground was dry. The air was crisp. We left the farm early. Joanna held Thomasina's reins loosely, and the little white mare trotted with her mane flying in the wind and her bells jingling. The fly was comfortable for two people, and the farmers we passed working among their crops of lettuce, corn, and herbs straightened up and waved to Joanna. She waved back. I had to keep reminding myself I was safe. I was glad to be safe, but even so, I kept having pictures of the black water and me falling down, down, down. When that happened, I covered my eyes with my hands.

Soon we were on the main street of Buttermilk Falls, where wooden buildings stood close, almost leaning on each other. Signs proclaiming "James Nugent's General Store," "Wiegand's Tavern," "Mayor's Office," and "Painless Parker, Tooth Puller," painted in large letters, loomed from the stone finials above the buildings. Joanna reined in Thomasina at the post in front of Wiegand's Tavern.

"Cassie, whenever I ride to Newburgh, I stop in here first, have myself a cold glass of cider beer, and get water for my horse. Now, you can come, or you can stay here. Which do you fancy?"

"I'll come, thank you." It was all new and full of wonder to my eyes.

Cool and comfortable inside the wood-paneled tavern, we sat at a table covered with a linen tablecloth. A rug graced the floor. Mr. Wiegand himself served us. Joanna had her cider beer, and I had a delicious root beer. I was content. Every time I thought of yesterday, I felt deep thankfulness that I had survived. I thanked Providence again for Joanna.

"Come on, Cassie, let's be off."

Two hours farther on, the sun beamed down on us without mercy; Joanna announced, "The house is just there. Hasbrouck House, the General's Headquarters. You'll see it better in the next clearing."

We stopped as the trees thinned out and an overlook presented itself, from which we could see Hasbrouck House and the river beyond in all its sparkling surge. The house looked as though it was built of stones from the fields. Green awnings shaded the windows from the noontime sun. A pair of ancient maples shed a few dead leaves that lay scattered across the quilt of green grass.

"We'll just light here a few minutes and rest."

"But why do you turn, Joanna? Is something wrong?"

"Oh, I thought I heard something in the bushes over there. Probably a fox."

"Are you thinking someone is behind us?" Immediately, I shrank into myself.

"I reckon it could be a fox." Joanna's eyes remained glued to the woods off the path. I felt the leather pouch in my apron pocket.

"Could it be Jonah Higbie?" I whispered, feeling horror race through my body.

"I don't know. He could try to find you if he wants that information badly enough. Mayhap not but just to be safe." Joanna reached under the seat, pulled out a pistol, and laid it across her lap. "We'll take no chances."

Within the space of a few seconds, the bushes parted; a man appeared on the path leading a huge white horse. He wore the blue and buff uniform of a Continental army officer, and he carried about him an air of confident authority. I thought he must be a colonel or even a major.

"Good day to you, sir," Joanna said, standing up in the little fly.

"And to you." He nodded to both of us. The officer allowed his horse to graze nearby. I had never in all my life seen a man standing that high before. His hair was gray. His hands were large.

"Where are you ladies bound for?"

My voice sounded ragged with fear. *What if Jonah Higbie was hiding right behind us?* "To Hasbrouck House, sir," I said. "I must see General Washington."

"I see. And your names?"

"I'm Cassandra Scott, sir." I stood and made a curtsy, nearly managing to fall out of the fly in my haste to hide from view.

"And you?" He nodded to Joanna.

"Joanna Collins, sir, from the proud town of Buttermilk Falls, New York."

"And what are you doing with that pistol on your lap?"

"Just in case an animal comes along," Joanna's voice sounded a bit raggedy.

"Put it away, please." Joanna immediately put the gun back under the seat.

"And your business with the general?" he asked Joanna.

I interrupted, "I have intelligence for the general. Joanna is taking me to him. I must get a message to General Washington. Do you know him, sir?"

"Yes, I do, quite well. He's a good soldier."

"He will save our country; we have every faith that he will," Joanna said.

"He's trying, with all his might and main. Now, this intelligence, Miss Scott. You may tell me; I shall see General Washington shortly."

"I cannot do that, sir. I am ordered to give this message only to the general."

The officer seemed to consider what I said. "Well, follow me to the house. The trail is tricky; just stay in the carriage tracks. You'll be fine."

The officer mounted his horse. Sitting astride his horse, he seemed an awesome figure to me. Brambles moved in the bushes. The officer heard the soft noises too; he turned toward the sound at the moment Joanna pulled the gun out from under the seat again, peered back into the shrubbery, and aimed the pistol.

"It's him. It's Jonah Higbie." My throat tightened. My breath was ragged, but I got the words out.

"I know," Joanna breathed. She sat still as a statue.

Next, the barrel of a musket emerged through the shrubbery. At that the officer turned in his saddle, his rifle cocked, and aimed at the bushes. Bullets flashed; white smoke rose in the air. Pow. Pow. *Pow. Pow.* A heavy thud to the ground. Joanna's pistol smoked. Then silence.

The officer got down from his horse. He walked slowly over to the body now face up in the bushes. Joanna jumped down and walked behind the officer. I followed slowly. Jonah Higbie lay motionless. A deep hole oozed dark red blood from his stomach. Joanna stood over Jonah Higbie's body.

"He's dead," the officer said. "His name is Jonah Higbie. He's been a plague to this valley for two years. Does this fellow have anything to do with you?" Pointedly, the officer looked at me.

"He nearly drowned Cassie in the river," Joanna said.

"Joanna saved me." I told him my story.

When I finished, the officer stood thinking for a minute. I supposed he was having a hard time believing us. But when he finally spoke, he said, "Well, you're a brave pair, you two ladies. Follow me to the house. I'll send a detail out for this snake in the grass."

"Will General Washington see me, sir?"

"Oh, yes. He will. I guarantee it."

The officer rode ahead of us down the path to Hasbrouck House. "You saved us, Joanna," I said. I still hadn't recovered from the shock of seeing Jonah Higbie's lifeless body. "You shot straight and killed him."

Joanna turned to me. "No, Cassie, I shot, but my bullet didn't hit him. That wound came from a smooth bore rifle. It was too large for a pistol to make."

CHAPTER FIFTY-SEVEN

Joanna guided the mare along the path carefully. The officer was far ahead of us, but he waited for us at the gated entrance to Hasbrouck House. I looked down at the gown Joanna lent me this morning. It was a yard too big, and my boots were covered with dried mud.

My hands went to my hair. "I'm a sight."

"Nothin' you can do about it. Just pay it no mind. I sure hope they feed us; I'm starving."

I couldn't share Joanna's desire for a good lunch. "I probably smell foul too," I said.

"Cassie, for what you've been through, you need make no apologies. Stand up proud." Suddenly, my hair, my gown, and my boots mattered not at all. What mattered was getting the information to the general. "They will probably feed us in the kitchen or the pantry," Joanna continued. "See, the officer waits for us by the stable. I reckon he'll let us know what he means to do with us." Joanna pulled the reins gently to the right, guiding Thomasina up the carriage path to the outside of the stable.

The officer took hold of Thomasina's reins. He patted her nose. "Beautiful horse," he said. "I shall have her groomed and sent outside to graze. You ladies walk to the door right in front. I'll meet you inside." The officer walked off with Thomasina into the cool, shady stable.

"Thank you, sir!" Joanna sounded confident, even happy. Her gown fell from her waist in a lovely flair. Her hair looked presentable, even shiny. My hair was still a mass of tangles from river water, though I had washed it in well water. It needed a good brushing. *It doesn't matter! It mustn't matter,* I kept telling myself. The front door opened. A servant bowed to us. We walked into a cool, dim interior foyer and waited for directions.

In a minute, a new servant appeared and motioned us to a sitting room. "The general will be along soon. Please do take your ease here while you wait."

Except for the far-off rattle of plates and cups and saucers, the house was quiet. The smell of savory food came from a kitchen somewhere. On the green-and-gold-papered walls, several paintings of palatial homes on high, green hills showed the four seasons of the year on the river. The chairs were soft green armchairs with comfortable seats. A round table stood in the center of the room. Against one wall stood a secretary with an open desk shelf, holding books and papers. A quill in a glass inkwell sat atop a small pile of books. A highboy stood against the far wall, holding dazzling glassware.

The door opened, and the officer we knew stepped in. Joanna and I both stood up and curtsied. I hoped, fervently, the officer would lead us to the general without any more delay. I would hand him the intelligence, and then we could leave and ride back to the pretty little cottage in Buttermilk Falls. "Ladies, I'd like to introduce myself. I'm General George Washington. I am pleased to make both your acquaintances."

My mouth flew open. Joanna recovered from the shock of this news first. "I *thought* you might be the general!" said Joanna. She curtsied. "How do you do, General?"

"I'm faring well. Mighty thanks to you for your help." Joanna's smile was broad at this praise from General Washington.

"And you, young lady, who have come so far and endured so much to get to see me, you have some intelligence for me. May I see it?"

"Yes, sir," Hesitantly, hoping it would be completely dry, I took out the leather pouch, now softened by river water, from the pocket of Joanna's calico gown. I had carried it since I left Cow Neck and I felt immense pride I had not surrendered it to Jonah Higbie or lost it in the river. General Washington took the paper out of the pouch and held it in both hands while he walked to the window to read the smudged handwriting. Joanna's idea to turn the purse inside out, and lay the paper and the pouch on top of the mantle overnight had worked. Though the paper was wrinkled and a bit blurry, the general was able to read the writing with the help of a glass that made the writing larger.

General Washington pulled a velvet cord on the wall. We heard a bell ring nearby, and an aide appeared almost immediately. The general walked to the half-open door and handed the paper to a young officer. *Fast action would happen now that the message got to the general.*

"And now," the general said, "let's have lunch in the dining room." Joanna and I looked at each other. I saw a gleam of enthusiasm in her eyes. I walked with my head up, my gown looking like a sack on me, wearing my big cracked leather, mud-filled boots, I felt like an orphan.

The look on the general's face stopped me in my tracks. "Would you like some moments to refresh yourselves, ladies? It's surely been a disquieting morning for you both, to say the least." Without waiting for an answer, he pulled the velvet cord again. A servant appeared immediately. "Simon, lead these ladies to the baths, and I believe we might have some gowns of Mrs. Washington's, that she left here after her visit last month. Let the ladies each choose which they'd like to wear." Then to us, he said, "I shall wait in the dining room. Simon will bring you there when you feel all refreshed. I assure you we will wait lunch for you."

There was wonderful warm water and fragrant soaps to wash our faces and hands. I washed my hair, and for the first time in two years, I decided to twist it into a French knot. Though wet, it settled nicely into place, and I sank a jeweled comb that lay in a porcelain dish to hold it in place. There were gowns: burgundy, blue, oyster, rose, each prettier than the last. Simon brought them in and dropped them over the backs of chairs in the room he brought us to. Even Suzie at her grampa's house on Beekman Place didn't own such beautiful gowns as these. I chose the peach taffeta gown, its bodice sashed with deep rose satin at the waist and blush pink layers of net falling down to just cover the tops of caked mud boots. Joanna wore a dull, satin, gray-blue gown that contrasted well with her white hair but fell short of her ankles. Joanna's old boots showed dismal dirty too, but she found a silk shawl among the gowns and fastened it to her waist, letting it drop to cover the tops of her boots. She looked in the pile of beautiful colors and came up with another shawl for me. "Voilà!" I said. I think it was my first word of French in two years.

Simon had told us to pull the velvet cord when we were quite ready. He led us along a hallway, from which several doors opened into sumptuous rooms. The last door revealed a blue dining room of large proportions, illuminated by a candle chandelier. A long mahogany table held an abundance of cold meats and salads; a few iced cakes stood on a highboy against a wall next to a silver carafe of coffee, and the whole rested on a pressed linen tablecloth. Glasses glimmered against a dark bottle of wine.

Twenty pairs of eyes greeted us at the entrance to the dining room. The general's aides stood up as one as we entered. I stood as tall as I could and swallowed. Simon announced us, "Miss Cassandra Scott and Mrs. Joanna Collins."

The general ushered us to our seats. "Gentlemen," he said, "we have guests today. I want you to acclaim these two brave, resourceful ladies: Miss Cassie Scott, who endured many hardships to visit with me this morning, and Mrs. Joanna Collins who brought Miss Scott here in her fly from Buttermilk Falls."

After the clapping had subsided for us, to which the general joined in, each young man stood up, walked around the table, bowed to us, and stated his name after which each said, "At your service, ma'am." General Washington proposed a toast to us. It took a few minutes, and it was all so exhilarating I felt "translated" like Bottoms in Mr. Shakespeare's play. Servants then brought us plates of cold, white fish with a tasty dill sauce; hot yams covered in maple syrup; and cucumbers with pickle relish. I ate everything on my plate as did Joanna. When a slice of yellow cake with chocolate on top was passed to me, I ate that as well. Afterward, General Washington himself poured coffee for us from a silver decanter, but not before he asked me if I drank coffee. I assured him I did, since my nineteenth birthday. He smiled at that. I was glad I made him smile.

There was much talk around the table and plenty of laughter. After the coffee, there were little hard candies passed around the table from a red-and-white striped bowl. All his aides waited for the general to stand up first, and when he did, everyone pushed back his chair.

"Ladies, if you're ready, I'll take you out to your carriage."

The general handed us in and seated us himself. He would not let his servant do that. He leaned into the carriage. "Cassie, you have performed your service to your country admirably. I thank you. Miss Joanna Collins of Buttermilk Falls, I thank you for your effort to save your country."

As Joanna guided Thomasina up the long drive to the road, I glanced back. General Washington stood in the middle of the path still waving to us.

"We still have on our borrowed gowns," I said finally. "And this jeweled comb too."

"I think General Washington wanted us to keep them."

"I shall never wear my gown again. I shall save it forever and the comb too," I said, touching my hair and feeling the smoothness of the comb.

"Not me, honey. I'll wear it the day America wins the war and our boys come home. Cassie, do you have a sweetheart fighting somewhere for our freedom?"

"No. My sweetheart turned his coat."

Joanna patted my back. "I'm sorry, honey."

CHAPTER FIFTY-EIGHT

"You going to lie about all this day, like a slug-a-lug, Cassie?" Joanna's voice carried painfully loud to my ear. She turned back the cover of the bird cage, and the yellow bird began to chirp. Sunlight streamed through the window.

I whispered, "It's morning already?"

"Yes," Joanna said. "You've been asleep since seven o'clock last night. Time for you to get up! Have some breakfast."

I left the comfortable cot. When I sat down at the table near the window with the pink curtains, Joanna was already seated eating a big plate of fresh bacon and coddled eggs. On my word, it smelled good.

"Have at it, Cassie. Help yourself; the pan's on the grate." Joanna hardly stopped eating while she talked. "Well, I got to turn the earth over in this field with the plow to give it a rest next year. I got cannin' to do since strawberry season is just beginning, and I got to clean the barn."

I lifted my fork to my mouth. "All today?"

"Much as I can today, plowin' for sure. That field needs to be turned over." Joanna hoisted a forkful of coddled eggs to her mouth.

"I'll help you."

Joanna put her own fork down. She smiled at me. "Well, I was hopin' you might like to stay a bit, and I could use some help. From what you were saying, I'm guessing there's not so many folks left in your little town; You might be a little lonely at home."

"I'd be pleased to stay awhile in this pretty place," I said.

"It's settled. You stay here long as you want, Cassie. If you've a mind to help, I'll be pleased. But it ain't a condition to stay. I think you'll feel better here where the British presence is light." She smiled at me.

"I'll do anything, anything to help you, Joanna. You saved my life. I'll forever be grateful to you."

"Joanna picked up her cup and sipped her coffee. "Anyways, don't thank me too much yet. There's somethin' we got to do first, and you ain't going to like it."

"What?" I said, thinking I would most likely have to feed the animals like I did at home. I wouldn't mind. I was used to getting up before sunrise.

"We got to cut your hair."

"What? Cut my hair? Why?" I dropped my fork. My hands went to my head. "I can't have that. My hair is my..."

"I know," Joanna spoke slowly. "Your hair is your beauty, but this is a working farm, mine and Billy's farm. Now he's gone, I got to work it myself." She hesitated. "There's a lot of farm equipment here, Cassie. Some of it has rusty old chains to make it work. I wouldn't want you bendin' over to fix a chain and your long hair gets in the way . . ."

I pushed my plate away and stood up. All of a sudden, I was not hungry. "Oh no. I couldn't possibly allow my hair to be cut. I can't let that happen. No. Thank you, Joanna, but no. I better go home.

I could never do that, never." The idea horrified me so much I jumped away from the table and ran across the room to pick up my river-sanded mobcap and reticule.

"Well, suppose I cut just to your shoulders. Sit down, will you, Cassie? Wait a minute. Your hair's real pretty right now, long to your waist, yellow as sunlight, but it's dangerous to wear your hair long on a farm."

I did sit out of respect for Joanna, but on the edge of the chair. "No. I can't have my hair cut. I shall go home since I'll be no good to you working on the farm."

"Who said that?" Joanna asked. "For your own protection, I meant for you to wear your hair short. You didn't plow a field or fix a fence with hair that long at home."

"No. I never did. My brothers and my father did outside work. We have a small farm. My father is a judge."

"All right, if you want to go back home, you can go. But do finish your breakfast before it gets cold," Joanna said.

I picked up my fork. *The food is so good. No British soldiers are here to take away my food and my firewood. Here, I have enough to eat and be warm next winter. This nice lady wants me to stay awhile. All I have to do is to submit to having my hair cut.*

"How short would you cut it?"

"Just to your shoulders," Joanna said.

"All right," I said in my lowest voice. "You can cut my hair."

Snip. Snip. Snip. Cut. Cut. My hair fell in clumps on the grass next to the chair. My long golden hair everybody in Cow Neck said was beautiful lay in pieces at my feet. My neck felt naked and so did my ears. I stared straight ahead past the crowd of children gathered on the grass at the back of the cottage to watch the show. When I looked down, piles of hair winked up at me in the sunshine. I felt my head.

Joanna handed me a glass. But I was afraid to look into it.

"Go on. Look. It ain't bad. It looks pretty," Joanna urged me on.

My hair was higher than my ears. "I'm shorn like a sheep!" I wailed.

"Oh dear. I might just have cut a bit more than I intended. But you'll get used to short hair, Cassie. Can't take chances with farm equipment. I've been cutting my own hair for years, ever since Billy went to war in '76." I looked at Joanna's hair. At this new information, I simply sighed.

CHAPTER FIFTY-NINE

July 30, 1779

"I can't get this ox to pull this plow, Joanna." I wiped sweat off my forehead and cheeks. A half an hour of me pulling the ox by his halter in front and Joanna pushing his rump while the hot sun beamed down on us had made me hot and exasperated.

Joanna straightened up. "We'll both have to get behind him and give him a shove. That's all. Here, you get on the right side, and I'll stay here on the left and, on the count of three, push. That usually gets him goin'. One...two...three...push." We two gave a mighty push and had the satisfaction of watching the ox move an inch. Before we could push again, Blaster made his wishes known by bending his forepaws and levering himself down to the ground.

Joanna wiped her face. "Well, maybe the sun's got to him. Let's eat and then we'll get back to it," Joanna said. She tugged at the wooden halter and managed to pull it from the ox's neck, and then the ox found his legs and lumbered toward a shady tree where he dropped his huge bulk down on a grassy patch and slept.

"Blaster ain't cooperatin' today. Mayhap he don't like a new person pullin' on the halter. I'll get in front when we come out. That means you'll have to get behind and push, Cassie. We'll try again after lunch."

The sundial read noon. Not a breeze stirred. Inside the cottage, Joanna poured cold glasses of water from the well bucket, and we ate cucumber sandwiches in the cool kitchen. Afterward, I rested my head on my folded arms on the table and fell to picturing our wonderful lunch with General Washington and his aides yesterday. The gowns we wore, such colors there were! My peach taffeta gown, the officers' uniforms decorated with brass buttons and medals, and the polished highboy on which silver platters rested. Spirited talk, laughing, chatting, and General Washington smiling at me and Joanna. I fell asleep until I heard Joanna say, "We got to go back out, Cassie. Wake up."

Dimly, I heard Joanna; I struggled through layers of sleep to wake up. There was a knock on the door. Joanna faced a soldier wearing the blue and buff. "This newspaper is for Cassandra Scott."

I lifted my head. "I'm Cassandra Scott."

The soldier walked over and put the newspaper in my hand. Across the top in large print were the words "*Mad Anthony Wayne recaptures Stony Point.*" Underneath was a two-column story of the assault on the Point.

"General Washington wanted you to have the newspaper today." He smiled down at me. He shook my hand. "Good-bye, Cassandra." He was out the door and on his horse in a fast minute.

"Well!" Joanna said with an explosion of breath. "Imagine that. A soldier comes here with a newspaper from General Washington for you to read about the battle at Stony Point. I'm not asking a single question, Cassie. But I will say you done good."

Outside again, after I had read the newspaper story out loud to Joanna, the ox was of a mind to move, inch by inch. It took all afternoon to plow the field over. Merciful, cool showers rained down and wet us through and through. "One more furrow to go," Joanna called to me with a lilt in her voice. The furrows were long and narrow, and after all the yelling, pushing, and pulling, I was glad to have helped, and most glad the work was done. The ox remained stoic; he showed no emotion at all, just a mute resistance to hard work.

CHAPTER SIXTY

June 1781

It was the third summer Joanna cut my hair. "Short hair becomes you, Cassie, it does. Now don't frown. I believe you actually like your hair short." Joanna stepped back to admire her handiwork. She was right; I had learned to like feeling the breezes on my neck. My short hair was much cooler in summer. I didn't worry it would catch on a wire or a chain on the farm.

Summers passed peacefully on the farm in Buttermilk Falls. Joanna and I picked wild grapes and made jam. We ate our meals outdoors in the shade of an ancient maple tree, and for fun, we took the fly into town and talked with neighbors while Joanna drank a cider beer and I drank a sarsaparilla. But I missed home. I began to wish for my mansion. I wanted to visit my mama's grave and tell her of all that had happened to me. I wanted to see Miss Hoary and Sarah and have lunch with Mrs. Fanshawe.

In October, there was a great victory for America! The British were surrounded by American troops on land and sea, and General

Cornwallis surrendered to General Washington at Yorktown, Virginia.

The newspapers were optimistic. The tide had turned; the war would soon be over. Now, I began to want to be home in the worst way. Someday soon I would go home. Papa would come home too after the war and so would Hannah.

Hannah. She was a part of Papa's life; I finally realized it, and I began to feel more placid about her. She was necessary to Papa. I would do my best to get along with her. And Max would come home. Suzie will come back from York City! They would marry. Ernest would never go away from me. I held him in my heart. I found I didn't cry for him anymore. I spoke to him every day as I did my mother.

Then suddenly, it was time for Christmas. All work stopped on the farm. Joanna and I rode to church in her fly, its wheels and Thomasina's hooves hurling snowflakes up into our faces! I loved riding on the soft white blanket of snow. Afterward, we dined at Wiegand's tavern, where Joanna made merry with her neighbors and we stayed late, everyone excited and happy that General Washington's army seemed to be winning the war. When I went to bed that night, again I thought of home and how good it would be when I got there.

CHAPTER SIXTY-ONE

May 1782

At eight in the morning, the fields lay quiet; dew shined up the wildflowers by the side of the road. Joanna sent me into town to buy cow balm for Blaster. His hooves were full of pebbles, and he wasn't walking much. Folks out tending their farms now recognized me and waved to me just as they greeted Joanna, which made me feel as though I belonged here, even though I knew I would soon go home. At Mr. Nugent's store, I dismounted and gave Thomasina a carrot. She nuzzled my hand in return.

"Ho! What do you think you're doing?" A voice from the porch of the building next door rang out. A tall fellow dressed in knickers and an old plaid shirt yelled to me from the steps of the mayor's office.

"I'm hitching up my horse to this post," I yelled back. "What does it look like?"

"The mayor ties up his horse there. Don't you see the office sign, 'Mayor's Office'?"

"No. I see the sign that says, 'James Nugent's General Store' above the door."

"Well, look left. You'll see the mayor's sign." He seemed a big, clumsy lump of clay, and he was not going to tell me what to do on public land.

"Why, that sign is on the next building over." This fellow was annoying me. I tossed Thomasina's reins over the hitching post and tied them loosely.

"Move the horse," he said. "This is where the mayor hitches up," he barked from the steps above the dirt road. He double-stepped down the steps and then took long strides over to the post, standing right in front of my face.

"I will not." I stood my ground, not giving an inch.

"Then I will." The fellow quickly moved to untie Thomasina's reins. I grabbed the reins out of his hand and put them over the post again, holding them there. "I'm moving this horse to the public post," he said.

"This *is* the public post," I said. He paid no heed, but being taller than me, he lifted the reins above me and held them tightly in his hands. He pulled Thomasina from the post, not bothering to pat her flank or talk into her ear or do anything pleasant horses like. Thomasina gave a loud whinny of protest; she would have none of it. She reared up on her hind legs and plunged her newly shod hooves into the sandy ground. But the fellow didn't scare easy.

I patted Thomasina's nose, trying to calm her. But she was too excited. "You better get away," I yelled.

Thomasina reared again, and this time when her hooves touched ground, she turned sharply and galloped across the dirt road, dragging her reins through empty lots and off into thick woods. "Now, see what you've done?" I yelled at him. The two of us ran after her, but he ran faster than me. I lost sight of him and the horse when she swerved behind a big barn. I was sure she'd do harm to herself. *Oh, please, please, make her stop, please.* Where could she be? She could be in the next road, or she could be a mile away.

My side began to hurt. I gripped it and stopped running. I had to walk slowly.

She wasn't inside of a barn across the field. She wasn't outside it, cooling off like I thought she might do. She wasn't in the woods, thick with summer foliage. There was no sign of Thomasina. How would I ever tell Joanna? She had disappeared and so had the bumptious, obnoxious fellow. *It came to me he had found her and stolen her.* I leaned against the side wall of the barn, bright red in the morning sun, and saw in my mind's eye Joanna's face when I would have to tell her what happened. Her heart would break over her lost mare.

I looked up just as the fellow emerged from the woods holding Thomasina's reins. She walked calmly beside him. He held the reins out to me and dropped them in my hand. "I found her drinking water out of a brook." He was about to walk away, but I put my foot in his path.

"Thanks to you, I've had all this trouble about my horse." I stood in front of him with my arms folded. He ignored me, walked right around me, and started back to town.

After he took a few long strides, he called back, "She's not your horse." There was venom in his voice. "I happen to know whose horse this is."

"Who do you think you are? What's your name?" I yelled. I would surely tell Joanna just who forced Thomasina to rear up in fear and run away.

"None of your business." He walked right around me and started back to town. When I got back to the post, he was nowhere to be seen. It gave me some satisfaction to tie up Thomasina to the same post. I patted her flank and let her eat a piece of apple from my hand while I talked into her ear gently. When I saw she was calm, I patted her again and walked into Mr. Nugent's store. He had no cow balm left.

CHAPTER SIXTY-TWO

"There you are! I was kind of worried." Joanna looked up from sweeping yesterday's rushes from the floor. You got the cow balm, Cassie?"

"Mr. Nugent didn't have any more cow balm. I have to tell you something, Joanna."

She stopped sweeping. She looked stricken. "Did he say when he would get more?"

"No. I should have asked. Joanna, I do have to tell you something."

"Not now, Cassie. I am so troubled. What will I do about poor Blaster? He'll have to struggle on with stones in his hooves," Joanna went on. She didn't seem to hear me. "The poor beast hobbled like that. So many stones in that pasture. Well, mind you, I'll try putting some bacon fat on his hooves."

"We can do it together, Joanna. I'm sorry I couldn't get the cow balm."

"Ain't your fault, Cassie."

No, Blaster's hooves aren't my fault. But I need to tell you what happened to Thomasina. I heard Papa's voice again in my head. *Think, Cassie. Think.* But I didn't. I let that nasty fellow get me riled up when all I needed to do was move the horse to the other hitching post. Look what happened. But I did wipe off the sweat from Thomasina after we got back to the barn, and I gave her a bucket of water. Wasn't she now enjoying green grass in the pasture, warm under the sun?

"If you ain't too tired from ridin' into town, Cassie, I would like to bake strawberry pies. That will take my mind off poor Blaster."

"No. I'm not tired, Joanna."

"Then I'll get the buckets out, and we can start sifting the flour." Joanna talked while she poked her head around in different cubbyholes looking for buckets. "Thomasina didn't give you any trouble, did she? She can be frisky."

"No. She didn't," I said, feeling my heart sink to my stomach.

"She's high spirited though." Joanna said. She handed me a pail. "I only got two pails. I think that's all we need. And them folks in town, they all waved to you, Cassie?"

"Yes, they all know me now." *How can I tell her? I can't.*

"They're a good lot." Joanna smiled.

There was a knock at the Dutch door. "Hey, Joanna!" I recognized that voice; I'd heard it before. My back stiffened. The same fellow who caused Thomasina to panic and gallop away loomed above the Dutch door. He stuck his head into the kitchen.

Joanna stood stock-still. For a moment, she didn't speak. Then she cried, "Jem, Jem! You're back!" She rushed to greet him. "I prayed for you." Joanna opened the door and gave the fellow a bear hug. "Cassie, Cassie, come meet Jem Clarke, just back from the fightin'. He lives down the road and he fixed things around here before he joined the army." Joanna was beyond joy. "Sit down. Sit down! Cassie, pour Jem some coffee, will you?" When he did, she held his hands in both of hers across the table. "It's good to see you, Jem. What will you do with yourself now you're home, Jem?"

"Well, first, I'm going to fix up things here, and then I'm to start with McCullough & McCullough law firm in September. I'll learn the law from the elder Mr. McCullough and then I'll practice. Won't take me long, Joanna."

"Oh, Jemmy, I know it won't." Joanna was entranced. It was clear to me from the smug sound of this Jem Clarke's voice that he was extremely smug about himself. Taking down two china cups and saucers from the glass-front tricornered cupboard, I poured coffee for them both and put it down in front of them.

Joanna did not notice. She kept on talking. "Think of it, Jem, you being a lawyer. That is wonderful. You've got a great future in front of you." Joanna's whole face lit up. Seeing me standing by with the sugar bowl and creamer, she said, "Cassie, sit and say 'hi' to Jem Clarke."

"Enchanté," I said, remembering my French. I set the pitcher of cream and the sugar bowl next to their cups of coffee on the table and gave Jem Clarke a curtsy.

"Hello." He stared out of slit eyes at me. *He'll surely tell her the truth about the horse. How was I supposed to know he's her neighbor?*

"It's wonderful. I almost can't believe you're sitting here at my table again! I'm that delighted to see you, Jem." Joanna leaned toward Jem Clarke, her eyes shining. "And I to see you, Joanna. I'm here to help." he said.

"Not today, Jem." Joanna glowed with joy.

"Yes. I want to get right back into town doings."

Joanna still held Jem Clarke's hand. I could see she thought of him as a son.

"So come on, tell me, what has to be done?" Jem Clarke persisted.

"Well, Cassie's just back from Nugent's store. He's out of cow balm. I don't know what else I can put on poor Blaster's hooves. I thought of bacon fat. What do you think?"

He laughed. "I think Blaster will be slipping and sliding all over the grass if you do, Joanna. My father has plenty of cow balm at home. I'll go home and get you some." He couldn't wait to be out the door, striding up the path to the road.

Joanna rinsed out the buckets. "Isn't it the greatest thing that Jem's back and all together in one piece, Cassie? All right then, let's cut the tops off these strawberries and bake 'em into pies. Then we'll let the pies set awhile on the windowsill and have 'em for dessert after supper. You'll like Jem Clarke, Cassie. He's a good boy."

"Yes." I smiled. "He seems so, Joanna. I'll groom Thomasina again, after we make the pies," I said. "She had a long trot this morning."

"You'll do no such thing. I forbid it. You'll sit in the hammock and have a little sleep. That's what you'll do. And then later, you and Jem take a walk along the river's edge while I cook supper. You can see the falls from there."

The last thing I want to do on this earth is to see Buttermilk Falls again or, worse, to take a walk with Jem Clarke.

CHAPTER SIXTY-THREE

Around four, we finished baking pies and left them to cool on the windowsill. Jem Clarke had come back with the cow balm from his home, and I found myself walking the trail above the river alongside him. He carried his musket.

"You needn't keep up talking civilized anymore," he said to me. "Joanna can't see us from here. When we get to the falls, I'll head for the woods and do some hunting. I don't care what you do. Be back at the falls at six so she sees us walk back to the cottage together. Do you understand?"

There was something so arrogant about him that I could not be silent. "Yes," I said. "Just so you understand, what happened to Thomasina was your fault."

As if to prove his superiority, Jem Clarke took a few strides in front of me and set off into a copse of trees without answering me. Every now and then, he turned to see if I was still following. I resolved never to speak to him again, except in Joanna's presence.

I heard the falls before I saw them. Louder and louder they roared. My mouth went dry, and my body broke out in sweat. I got to the edge of the grass and saw the furious, plunging waters crashing down over the rocks, pushed along in the current, faster and faster. I clapped my hands to my ears to blot out the noise and splash and watched the raging rapids hurtle down to the rocks below. I couldn't watch any longer; I ran far away from the cliff, laid down on the soft grass, and covered my ears.

He was waiting for me on the path to the cottage, carrying a bloody rabbit he'd shot. "You were supposed to be at the falls at six," he said.

"I chose not to be." I tried not to look at the rabbit he'd shot as I walked a few steps behind him with my nose in the air.

He turned back to me. "I waited for you at the falls. Why did you run away?"

"What do you care?" I said.

He said nothing more but trudged on ahead.

At the door, Jem Clarke offered to clean and gut the rabbit. He would give it to Joanna. "No, Jem. You take it home to your pa." I hated Jem Clarke, but I had to admit to myself these two seemed to care for each other.

"How'd you two enjoy your walk this afternoon?" Joanna asked as we sat down to eat supper, to which, to my horror, Jem Clarke was invited.

"Very fine, Joanna," Jem answered. I had nothing to say. Supper was an effort. I didn't eat much.

Joanna paused. "I thought of it after you left, Cassie. Mayhap you didn't want to see them falls again, leastways not so soon."

"I didn't look down hardly at all, Joanna." I didn't say how horrible it was to see the falls from the cliff. Jem Clarke did not tell her I ran away from them.

"Well, that's all right, then, Cassie. Don't go there for a long while." Joanna said. She filled up Jem's plate again. "I found Blaster resting in a shady spot and painted his hooves with the cow balm.

He didn't utter a sound. After a while, he got up and walked away without limping. I'll sleep good tonight knowing Blaster will be without pain, all thanks to both of you. Ice milk and fresh strawberry pie for dessert, Jem. And Cassie made a pie all herself."

"That's nice," Jem Clarke said.

"I'm tired, Joanna; I think I'll not have pie," I said, desperate to leave the table.

"Save me a piece for tomorrow. Will you, Joanna?" Jem stood up, thanked Joanna, gave her a kiss on the cheek, and left.

"Well," Joanna said after he left, "I never saw anything like it; Jem loves to eat, 'specially pie. Oh, well, I do suppose he wants to be with his pa tonight, after all." But her tone was one of disappointment.

I knew it was on my account he left. And I was relieved.

CHAPTER SIXTY-FOUR

I found it was not hard to keep silence around Jem Clarke. He called in at Joanna's house most days to ask what needed fixing. I started to count the days until he would leave to start his apprenticeship with McCullough & McCullough law firm.

When Joanna came by, Jem was pleasant to me. As soon as she left the room, he took no notice of me or said something mean. I treated him the same way. After that first meal together, Jem made himself scarce at meals.

There were times when I thought Joanna would have noticed a sharp answer I made to Jem. But she didn't catch the dislike between us two. Mayhap because she truly liked each of us, she thought we had regard for each other. Jem Clarke still blamed me for Thomasina running away. I knew he had not told Joanna what had happened. If he had, he would have told on himself.

CHAPTER SIXTY-FIVE

Winter in Buttermilk Falls

Colder than home. Snow covered the lower half of the windows in the cottage. Icicles hung from the barn eaves and the roof of the cottage. Lately, I had been thinking about home in winter. Memories of snowfalls in Cow Neck came to me; how much I loved ice skating on the pond in front of the gristmill. At nights, Mama, Papa, and I would pop corn over the fire in the years before Mama died. How much I missed them all; Papa, Mama, Max, Suzie, Ernest, and David who would bellywhop down Shepherd's hill and then act like he had conquered the world. David. I realized I missed him truly, even though I had vowed to put him out of my mind after the horrible words he spoke to me in Stony Point. Strangely enough, I missed Hannah, too. In my mind, I would picture them all as they were: Papa, sitting at the table reading his newspaper; Hannah, stirring something at the hearth; Max and Suzie together walking the roads; and David putting his mother's opal ring on my finger and kissing me that last morning when he left. Soon, I would go home and see them all again, except for Ernest. But he would never go away from me.

On a brilliant day, when icicles hanging from the barn roof started to melt and the sun was warm on our backs, Jem Clarke and I cleared a path from Joanna's door to the barn so we wouldn't have to trudge through the ice and snow. "Now, you will have less trouble to feed the animals at dawn," he said to me, as though he were doing me a favor.

"Thanks so much," I muttered, hurling the snow from my shovel an inch from his feet.

"What did you do that for?" He shook the snow off the top of his boot.

I kept quiet, and he then hurled a shovel full of snow at my feet, which I ignored. Jem didn't know Joanna took turns with me to feed the animals. And he wouldn't know it from me. If he did, he would have insisted to Joanna that I do the barn chores every single day. I knew he felt I was not doing enough to earn my keep.

Late that afternoon, a few wagons got through the icy ruts in the road, and Jem Clarke rode Thomasina into town and brought the Albany newspaper back. I read the paper that night to Joanna in the light and warmth of the fire. Jem Clarke stayed too, sitting in a chair close by the fire. *Why was he here? He could read the newspaper himself at his own home.*

The news was much better from the battle fronts. "Since Patriots had defeated the British at Ramseur's Mill in June 1780, and at Hanging Rock, South Carolina, in August 1780, and American troops at King's Mountain, led by Isaac Shelby defeated one-third of General Cornwallis's army," the newspaper said, "taken together with Cornwallis's defeat at Yorktown, the end of the war would come soon." Joanna and I danced around the table, causing the dishes on top of the mantle to rattle. Jem Clarke sat without moving by the fire. *What was the matter with him? He was always glowering.*

Joanna and I celebrated with chocolates and tea. "We're winning, Joanna. We're winning the war!"

"Have chocolates, Jemmy. Will you take tea? Cassie, will you? I'm out of breath from that romp around the table."

I poured for Joanna and me. "Will you take tea, Jem?" I held the tea kettle up for him.

"Yes, I will, thank you, Cassie." *Speaking civilly to me; I knew he would say something horribly nasty to me later. Soon I'll go home. It doesn't matter.*

CHAPTER SIXTY-SIX

March 1783

"Did you have a brother at Stony Point?" Jem Clarke came in from the cold, stamping his feet and shedding snow and sleet on the kitchen floor, dropping off his coat and boots.

"Yes." I stopped rinsing dishes and dried my hands.

"He died there?"

"Yes," I said, "in the first battle of Stony Point." I saw Ernest's grave in my mind and felt a stab of grief when Jem reminded me of his death.

"General Washington is awarding him the Military Badge of Merit posthumously. You see? It's in the newspaper. I guess we didn't notice it last night." Jem handed me the newspaper.

The piece was on the front page with Ernest's name and rank and an account of his heroic actions at the first battle at Stony Point. The paper said he was one of those running down the hill as the British gained the summit. When Ernest saw a fellow soldier lying on the ground with a bullet hole in his shirt, he stopped, picked him up, and carried him. His progress was slow, and bullets pinged all around him, but he kept up until he was all the way down the hill. There he put the soldier down gently in a doctor's tent. As he walked out of the tent, a bullet from a Brown Bess aimed at him from the top of the hill found him.

"I thought you would want to know," Jem Clarke said. "The paper says the medal will be sent to Ernest's next of kin. That would be you."

Now I knew what had happened to my brother. I sat down and cried. After a while I heard the chair scrape. I looked up. Jem Clarke was still sitting there.

"I'm very sorry for your loss," he said. "Would you like a cup of tea?" He washed his hands in the bucket. "I can make it for you."

"Yes." Because I couldn't cry forever.

That night I brought writing paper and a quill to the table and began a letter to Max, who was with his unit in Charleston, South Carolina. I cut the piece about Ernest out of the newspaper and put it in with the letter.

Six weeks later, I received a letter from Max in Charleston. He had finished up his army time and would stay in Charleston for a while because it was warm and he felt at home there. About Ernest, he wrote: *Thank you for letting me know about the Military Badge of Honor for our Ernest. I miss him but at least the country will know of his courage and compassion. Cassie, your brother loves you.—Max*

I felt my heart drop at reading those words. Max wasn't coming home. At least not at present. Now my mind was made up. I told myself I would leave Joanna's cottage and go home to Cow Neck

That night the cottage was quiet. After Jem Clarke set a cup of tea in front of me, he left quietly. I must have been grieving; I didn't know he was gone. Jem *was pleasant to me, today, almost as if he liked me. Is it possible?*

CHAPTER SIXTY-SEVEN

"Cassie, the snow and mud is pretty much gone now. Before we get another late snowfall, and if it's a nice day tomorrow, I'm going to treat you and Jem to dinner at Wiegand's Tavern. We need a bit of joy."

But it wouldn't be joy for me. Jem Clarke found out about Joanna's and my arrangement of barn chores. He saw Joanna's wet cloak hanging on a chair near the fire early one morning and asked why she had been out so early. When told, he was not pleased. He found a moment to speak to me alone.

"Cassie, Joanna has plenty to do without feeding the animals. There's no reason why you can't collect the eggs from the chicken coop every day, Cassie, and bring feed to Thomasina and Blaster? Do you good. Get rid of some of that snobby York City air you carry about with you."

"Really, that's laughable coming from such a country bumpkin as yourself!" I said, tossing my newly long golden hair all the way to my shoulders. He walked away sputtering something I didn't hear. Good. I was grateful I could toss my hair to show my disdain for what he had to say. I was also grateful that after years of haircuts twice a year, Joanna had forgotten to cut my hair this spring.

But I did go out to do the chores every day after that. Just to annoy Jem, I had the animals fed and the eggs collected by six-thirty every morning. It made me proud that my work was finished before he began his work. He never got here to fix anything before nine in the morning. He was lazy; even Joanna said so. Still, she thought the sun rose and set on him.

"Will you have some of Mr. Wiegand's biscuits, Cassie? They are crusty. Here, try one." Jem Clarke leaned across the sparkling linen tablecloth at Wiegand's, holding the bread tray out to me. The only thing worse than Jem Clarke finding fault with me was Jem Clarke patronizing me. At least he was sincere when he was mean to me. At the lunch, he sounded more like a superior, overbearing country squire than the twenty-three-year-old farm boy he truly was.

"Thank you," I said, wanting to throw it at him as I tried to remove a biscuit delicately from the tray he held. *This lunch was going to be awful if it goes on this way with him baiting me. If I give it right back, Joanna will be unhappy.*

Joanna was happy. She was happy to be here, happy to greet her neighbors, to see smiling faces all around her in the dining room of Wiegand's Tavern. I looked at her face and felt glad to see her so spirited. This was the woman who had saved my life. I would never be able to make it up to her. Joanna was shaking hands and kissing people she hadn't seen since the snows had set in, in November. All around us, people were chatting, laughing, and greeting one another. Oil lamps and candle lamps lit the room. Pine cones surrounding candles sat in centerpieces on the table. There was a festive feeling in the restaurant. I understood Joanna's mood; she was exuberant.

Jem Clarke's father sat at a table nearby with his neighbors. I hoped against hope Jem would sit with his father, but he didn't. He sat with us. After a time, he got up and walked around to my side of the table. "Will you come and meet my father, Cassie?" he asked me in the humblest way. Of course, I could do nothing else but to follow him to his father's table. For some reason that I couldn't define, I was scared.

The introduction to Jem's father was pleasant. He seemed to be a genuinely nice old man, and so were his friends who sat around the table with him. I noticed Mr. Clarke wore a jeweled tie pin that I thought extremely elegant. He greeted me with a solid hand-shake and gave me a kiss at parting. I liked him.

"How is your law learning coming along?" I forced myself to ask Jem when we were back at Joanna's table. I felt thoroughly thawed out after meeting his father, so dignified was he, and so eager to impress me. It was easier to talk to Jem.

"Mr. McCullough is very pleased." Jem could hardly keep the smugness out of his voice. "I expect I shall be practicing before the two-year course is done," Jem answered me, smiling down at me from the heights.

Joanna looked at Jem with warmth. "Jemmy, how fast the time's gone by since you began to study the law. I'm sure you will be a great lawyer." She took a sip of her cider beer. "I wonder if Cassie would like to follow that path. She's excellent with words."

Jem laughed out loud. "I doubt that."

"Why?" I asked, putting down my fork.

"Well, it's, shall I say. . .?" He paused for words. "It would be extremely unusual for a girl to be in the law. It's not done. Besides, women can't do law."

"Is that so?" I said, not bothering to hold back the sarcasm in my voice. "My father is a judge. When I told him I might want to study law, he urged me to do so."

"Name a female lawyer," Jem smirked.

Responding to the turbulence in the air, Joanna intervened, "I'm sure there are some women lawyers, Jem. Cassie, I wish you to be one if it is what you want. But Jem is right when he says lawyering is much more a man's profession."

"Joanna," I said, "with all the thinking and planning you do to run your farm successfully, do you believe women don't have the brains to be lawyers?"

Joanna swallowed a forkful of her roasted beef, lifted her glass, and took another sip before she said, "Now, Cassie, I didn't say that, did I?"

"But do you believe so, Joanna? I need to know."

"Let go, can't you, Cassie? You can see Joanna is not in favor of the whole premise."

"Indeed. I see you're quite the barrister already, Jem, with your high-sounding phrases!"

"Not at all, Cassie." He was feeling victorious, I supposed. He didn't even know enough to take offense at my words. "Comes naturally to me." Jem managed to sound pompous and humble at the same time. How I longed to punch him right in the nose!

There was alarm on Joanna's face. "Look what I started. I never meant for you two to fight. Neither one of you is eating, and I'm paying good money for this nice meal. I want to enjoy myself. Now, come on. Be friends." Joanna leaned toward both of us. "Come on now." Just as though we were little children, she took my hand and Jem's and joined them together.

Silence and hurt feelings on my part. Silence and overbearing annoyance showed on Jem Clarke's face.

"Do try some of these mashed potatoes, Cassie." Joanna held a serving spoon of the buttery potatoes out to me. She heaped a dollop of the buttery, soft potatoes on my plate. I knew she was trying to placate me.

"Thank you, Joanna. They are very good," I said, picking up the bowl from the table and trying to pass it to Jem.

"No, thanks." He smiled at me. *Ugh!*

We were plunged into silence again. I did not want Joanna to feel unhappy. I saw it was up to me to fix things. She was already sad and had stopped eating.

"Jem," I said, "that new pasture fence you put up for Blaster is a marvel. It is straight and the cross ties are all even. The paint is gleaming white. I do like to sit on top and view the whole country-side from it."

"Do you? Well, thank you, Cassie. Pass me the beef, please."

I looked over at Joanna. Her face softened as Jem spoke. Disaster was averted. The rest of the meal passed pleasantly.

I am so tired of this war. I want to go home. Over and over in my head, I thought about home. *I saw the mansion, the yard, and the fields with wheat and corn. In my mind's eye, I saw my friends. I just couldn't seem to tell Joanna I wanted to go home. Please let this war end soon.*

CHAPTER SIXTY-EIGHT

Late March 1783

Up with the rooster's first crow one morning, I walked among Joanna's daffodils out to the barn. I didn't bring the candle lantern; I thought I could manage without it. In the dimness, I made my way to Thomasina's stall and hitched up a pail of oats to her post. I knew the inside of the barn well. I threw grain to the gawky rooster, crowing so loud his red wattles shook. I went inside the chicken coop where the clucking, brooding hens waited for the mash I had boiled up yesterday to be spread around their nests. I collected the eggs and left the sticky warmth of the coop. The cow was agreeable to being milked. Across the field, Blaster lay sleeping in his shed. I left the pail of feed for him on a low hook hanging just inside his stall. Soon, soon, I told myself, I would go home to Cow Neck. The war was winding down. Even the newspapers said so.

Finished with barn chores, I plodded back to the springhouse and stored the perishable milk and eggs. I felt so confident of my own powers this morning, I added a chore. I lowered the bucket into the well and fetched up water for coffee; then I brought it into the cottage. Joanna would be very pleased when she awoke.

The sun was just beginning its rise. Outside, I paused for a moment to look out at the woods in the silent morning. These woods reminded me of home, before the war. My heart longed for home. I walked through the silent woods. I wanted to see the sun shining through the newly green leaves. The sugar maples' tall trunks and high branches green with blossoms against the deep, blue wash of the early-morning sky made me feel great ease, and I formed a plan.

I would tell Joanna as soon as I got back to the cottage I was going home. I walked on and on in the woods until the sun was fully up. Then I turned for Joanna's cottage.

I was startled to see Jem Clarke facing east, outlined in sunshine. He could have been a Greek citizen paying obeisance to the oracle at Delphi or an ancient sun-worshipper in a prayer ritual. I walked ahead. *How dumb of me to have such fancies.*

Jem heard me. He turned. "Oh, Cassie. It's you."

"Yes. I interrupted you. I'll go back." Suddenly, I felt a strange confusion.

"No need. I was simply looking through the trees at the branches. Do you see, over the top branch of this tree, there's a star pattern, those three branches? Look up to your left. Now, do you see it?"

I moved toward him. "Yes, yes, I do see it. It's beautiful," I said.

"I shall walk back with you," he said. He walked to my side, and we started back out of the woods. "Cassie, I…"

I looked up. It wasn't often that Jem Clarke was stuck for words.

"I uh…" He took my chin in his hand. Whether I put my face up or he leaned down, we kissed. I was suddenly full of joy and shock all at the same time. Did that happen? We walked back in silence together, not speaking.

Joanna was up frying eggs. There were three plates on the table. Joanna ate. I did not. Jem ate little.

"What's wrong? Are these eggs not to your liking? I give up with you two. Was there another fight?" Joanna was annoyed. It showed in the frown around her mouth.

"No." I picked up my fork and ate with a vengeance.

"Will you weed the garden today, Cassie? And pick me more daffodils, while you're at it."

"I will, Joanna." *I was very happy to weed the garden and pick daffodils and, strangely enough, to feel again the wonder of Jem's kiss this morning. Why did that happen?*

"And, Jem, I'm not feeling up to a ride into town. Will you take Tomasina and ride to town for flour and a tub of sweet butter?" Joanna said between forkfuls of coddled eggs.

"Today's the day. Got a list?" Jem put his fork down and stood up from the table.

"I didn't mean right this very minute. Finish your eggs. What are you doing? You haven't eaten nearly enough." Joanna looked up at Jem.

"I'm going to ride into town as you asked. Where's your list, Joanna?" Jem smiled at me. My heart leaped.

"On the mantle, but you don't need to go so early." Joanna was agitated.

"You know what the early bird gets, Joanna." He loped out the cottage door.

"What's the matter with him? And you too, Cassie?". Joanna looked across the table art me, her blue eyes round and not understanding.

"Growing pains?" I said.

"Hmph!" Joanna responded.

CHAPTER SIXTY-NINE

Next morning, I walked to the clearing in the woods, where we had kissed. Jem was there, waiting for me. We walked down a path to a quiet part of the river, and there we talked.

"I like you, Cassie. You have spirit." Jem was gazing into my eyes. I was thrilled.

"I think I liked you, but I didn't know it," I told Jem.

There was so much to talk about to Jem. I discovered Jem had always wanted to study law. He was learning from the lawyers in the firm. He didn't seem pompous anymore.

I saved up things to tell Jem. When I was alone, doing my chores, I thought of him. Knowing I would see him in the early morning, every morning, I brushed my hair over and over again at night.

I wore the pretty gown Joanna gave me for Christmas to the dance in the grange hall in Buttermilk Falls in August. We danced, Jem and I, all evening long, except for the times we talked to each other. When we walked out twilights in summer along the paths holding hands, I liked Jem more and more. Those times with him became my favorite times.

But I was troubled, no matter how I felt about Jem. I longed for home. I must go home. I must. But I couldn't tell her. I would miss Jem more than any other living human being. Besides, what would Joanna do without me, anyway? I was now part of her family. *Someday, I promised myself but not quite yet. I could not leave yet. Not yet. Soon I will leave. I will kiss Joanna good-bye and Jem! How could I kiss Jem only one last time? But I knew I would.*

CHAPTER SEVENTY

Jem and I met in our clearing after the day's work was done. "Marry me, Cassie."

"Marry you!"

"Yes, in a church facing an altar, marry me."

"But I. . . I can't". It grew quiet in the glade; leaves on the trees were silent and still; grass stood at attention; the birds did not chirp.

"Why not?" Jem said. "Cassie, things are different after the war. You're grown-up. Do you want your father's blessing? Is that what you're worried about."

"I do want my papa's blessing, Jem, for when I get married."

"Then it's settled." Jim threw his arm around me and kissed me roundly. Unless you feel mayhap a summer wedding is not to your liking. Is that it?".

"I'm leaving soon. I want to go home".

"Well, then, you feel it's too fast to get married. But, it's not, Cassie. It's not too fast. Not for people who feel strongly about each other. Just say the words." Jem's face was becoming agitated. His brown eyes glowed like hot coals. But the look on his face changed. "Do you want to marry me, Cassie?"

"I haven't thought of it, Jem. I'm too busy liking you."

"Will you at least think about it now that I've asked you?"

"Yes, but I know I shall go home. Once the war is over, I want to go home."

Jem kissed me; everything else floated away. "We shall marry, Cassie. I know we shall."

But in my mind, I wondered. I wasn't settled; I needed to go home.

"What's that?" The noise from the road was raucous and loud with shrieks and clapping and the banging of pots and pans.

CHAPTER SEVENTY-ONE

September 3, 1783

"The war is over! The war is over! The peace treaty is signed!" Joyful noises grew louder and louder as we ran out of the glade to the road. "We've won the war! It's over!" People marched; clapped pots and pans together; lit off fire crackers; and played fiddles, drums, and fifes. Church bells pealed. It was a rollicking, joyous expression of gladness from all of us. "The war is over! The war is over! The war is over!" Jem and I dove into the crowd; we kept repeating it and marching to the drumbeats.

Joanna beat a stirring spoon on her tin pail when we found her in the crowd. At the junction of the Old Post Road, we joined up with another marching crowd on their way to Wiegand's Tavern. When we got there, the doors were wide open, and people were dancing on the green. All the fiddlers in the neighborhood stood together and sawed away. The ducks waddled over to the side of the pond in front of Wiegand's to watch these curious goings-on, and the swans on the water glided among them in a confused mass of feathers and noisy squawks.

I was crazy with happiness! Everything was forgotten! We all got into a big circle and danced with great abandon almost until darkness, when Mr. Wiegand invited everybody outside to come inside the tavern for supper. For the ones who couldn't fit inside, he brought out trays full of tasty food for us.

A great big bonfire was built to celebrate our freedom. The British, after seven long, brutal years, would leave us in peace. It suddenly came to me while Jem and I and Joanna sat on chairs with plates of food, watching shadows from the bonfire darken the faces of the dancers, that I could go home tomorrow! Home!

Jem and I stayed sitting until the bonfire became sparks and embers. Joanna walked back home with neighbors, among them Jem's father.

"Are you tired, Cassie?" he asked me. "Will you walk a bit?"

"Surely," I said. It was a beautiful night. The moon was out, and the stars were so close they looked as though you could catch them.

"I've been a bit intense, Cassie. I realize, sometimes, I can be a bit too emphatic. Have you thought about what I asked?"

"Yes. But..."

Jem bent down and kissed me on the cheek. "Meet me tomorrow in the glade. We'll talk about it then."

"I will," I said. "Good night, Jem." I opened the cottage door, listening to Roper's welcoming barks. When I passed, Joanna was sitting up in bed, reading.

Joanna smiled at me. "The war is over, Cassie! For you and for me."

"I am so happy. My papa will come home now." I walked over to Joanna's cot and could not contain myself. I kissed her cheek.

As I walked to my own cot across the room, shadows flickered over Joanna's face. I could have sworn she wore a look of expecting some words that didn't come. But of course, that was my dramatic fancy, which my papa has told me never to rely on.

It was a dark night full of jumbled thoughts and twisting and turning. Now, I could *go home. Papa would come home from Connecticut with Hannah soon. Suzie, the neighbors, I want to see them all. I want to be home. I've been yearning for home for a long time. Jem, Joanna, I love them both. But I must leave.*

CHAPTER SEVENTY-TWO

"I'll come back, Jem." The day sparkled around us in the clearing. "I did think about marrying you. Jem. Again and again. I can't say what you would like me to say. My father, my friends, my home, they're waiting for me. But I'll come back, Jem."

"No. You won't." Jem looked away from me and didn't speak for a moment. Then he said, "I see no point in waiting for a visit from you. You've had time to think. Your answer is no."

"I will come back, Jem. I will."

"Don't say that. This is good-bye, Cassie. If you do come back, I won't be here."

I ran after him. "Where will you go?"

"Never mind," he said. In that instant, Jem became the person I met that day in front of Wiegand's Tavern. Mean.

"But the law?" I was almost out of breath; he was walking so fast.

"I can be a lawyer in any big city, New York, Philadelphia, Boston. It's nothing to you. You're going home," Jem hurled back at me.

I waited for a while, hoping he would relent and walk back, but the clearing was silent around me. Just like that, Jem took leave of me.

CHAPTER SEVENTY-THREE

"Isn't Jem with you, Cassie?" Joanna looked up from cleaning pots with ashes. A bucket of water rested on the floor to rinse out the pots.

"I don't know where he is." I knelt down on the floor next to her, picked up a pot, and started to rub the inside with ashes; then I plunged it into the large, round tin pail full of cold well water.

"Are you crying? What's wrong?" Joanna sat back, wiping her hands on a towel.

"Everything." I kept on scraping the pot.

"You want to leave Buttermilk Falls, Cassie, and go home, don't you?"

"Yes, I want to see my home again, Joanna."

Joanna nodded. "It's right. You should. Don't cry. Be glad you can go home. I'll miss you, but you need to see your folks. You've been very special to me. You know that."

"Thank you, Joanna. But it's not only that."

"What is it then?" Joanna sat back, still holding a wet rag in her hands.

"Jem asked me to marry him. But I want to go back to Cow Neck. I told him a little while ago. I offered to come back here. But he thinks I won't. He says he's going away; he'll not be here if I come back."

Joanna sighed, sat back, and took a moment before she spoke. "I hoped, but I did not know you were considering marriage to each other."

"I wasn't." I scrubbed the inside of the pot with vigorous brush strokes.

"Cassie, Jem is impetuous. He doesn't listen at first, but he will mull it over. And he will change his mind. You will see. He will be here when you return to Buttermilk Falls."

"No, he won't, Joanna."

We were silent while Joanna washed her hands. I put the pots away. She stood near the fire, stirring porridge, as though it took all her effort to do so. She sat down again, and I poured tea for us.

"I shall stay and help you for the reaping, Joanna." She was downcast, looking above my head, out of the window.

"There's no need for that, Cassie, although I do thank you for offering to stay. I have hired some fellows back from the fighting to help with the harvest. You see, I thought you would go home soon. But I shall miss you."

"Joanna, what if Jem does go away?"

"He promised to work for Mr. McCullough for five years after he became a lawyer. He will never break a promise. He is not going away. I think, Cassie, it is time you should go home and be united with your family in Cow Neck. You must." Joanna gave a small smile. "I will say, it would have been pleasant if you and Jem had made it to the altar."

"I'll groom Thomasina and collect Blaster's feed bucket." I got up from my chair and ran toward the door so Joanna would not see me cry.

The harvest season was upon us. All day the boys from town, along with Joanna and I, toiled to bring in the wheat. At noon, we trooped back to the cool cottage to eat our lunch. There was time for a fifteen-minute nap, and then we were out again until suppertime.

I was grateful for the hard work of reaping and bunching wheat even though my hands were cut and chafed. Jem never once came near us in the fields. I stayed on and on, hoping to see Jem once more yet longing for home, still not able to leave Joanna. She never told me again to leave. "Stay on, Cassie," she said, "as long as you like, but someday, you will go home, someday soon."

In the end, I simply left a note for Joanna on the kitchen table and tiptoed out the Dutch door, closing the bottom first so that animals could not get into the house and then the top. Outside, I took one long look at Joanna's kitchen through the curtained windows, as I had seen it the first time and left. At dawn, the roads were empty, and I began the long walk to the ferry that would take me down to York City.

CHAPTER SEVENTY-FOUR

November 23, 1783

Mud splattered the dirt roads next to the East River. The ferry to Long Island would leave the east-side pier at high tide in the afternoon. I was not tired; I had slept with my rucksack under my head for a pillow on the ferry down to York City. Too agitated to be still, I struggled against the crowds of Tories rushing to the wharves to flee York City. They carried their babies, their pots and pans, their clothing, their silver, and their blankets. Some even carried their beds to the ships that would take them away from York City to new starts in Nova Scotia, Bay of Fundy, St. John's River, Fort Frontenac, or even back to England—away from the Patriot revenge they feared—now that America had won the war.

And it was fast in coming. Abandoned by the British Government, Tories were afraid for their lives as Patriots stormed back to the city to reclaim the houses and the jobs these Tories had taken away from them seven years ago. It was clear to me: "Tory City" was no more.

At the head of Wall Street, blackened tombstones from the great fire of '76 still cluttered the ruins of Trinity Church, where the English Captain Stonecroft had followed me. Lettering on the doors of *Rivington's Gazette*—Papa's and my favorite newspaper, even though it was a Tory paper—was chipped and flaky. Inside, Mr. Rivington's printing presses lay in heaps of broken metal, his fonts scattered, thrown about, and stepped on by the heavy boots of Patriot thugs. His precious fonts could not be replaced. The newspaper was dead. Mr. Rivington went back to England. If he knew, Papa would be sad about that.

Everything was changed. I hoped to see Hercules Mulligan handing out broken clumps of bread to the pigs in front of his shop. But his shop was dark, and he was nowhere to be seen. The pigs, though, did not desert him. They waited patiently in the road outside his store window. Mayhap Hercules would come by and feed them. But I couldn't wait. I wanted to go to 82 Beekman Place. Was it possible that Suzie and her grandparents were still living there?

CHAPTER SEVENTY-FIVE

The breeze had stirred up in the afternoon sun. I boarded the ferry to Cow Neck at three o'clock. The tide carried us along at speed. Tired though I was from struggling through the crowds, dirty and dusty from the trip, I loved seeing the towns again. Hugging the shoreline, the ferrymen used their poles to make a wide turn from the East River into the Long Island Sound. They whipped past villages and small towns until they turned into the Flushing inlet, where a great commotion could be seen onshore. While ropes were tossed from the ship and knotted around tree trunks, crowds of villagers shouted, "Huzzah!" to the returning soldiers. Single file, the soldiers marched down the plank. I was thrilled when men and women who hadn't seen each other in years embraced. Children were thrust into the arms of soldiers who hadn't seen them since they were babies. Then we were off around the peninsula to all the little towns, and finally, north, to Cow Neck.

The ferry turned in at Berry Cove and hovered about ten yards from shore. In a fever, I jumped off ahead of some soldiers whom I did not know. After splashing and wading to the banks, I climbed up on a patch of weeds and hard mud, shook water from my gown and my rucksack, and stood in the warm sunlight.

I was home. The stillness, the eerie silence. On the ground surrounding the mansion, the remains of hastily extinguished fires—tankards still spilling coffee dropped on the ground in haste, half-eaten plates of food, seared logs—all spoke of rapid flight. Camps were flattened, their tent poles at crazy angles to the ground. I stopped and listened to the quiet. No more did British soldiers bend over their tasks—shave, eat, chop firewood, call out to one another, squat 'round the campfires at twilight, smoke, or swap war stories. A whole company of British regulars gone. The regiment itself gone from the homes and properties of our town. Nothing but the empty swinging of the barn door back and forth. Back and forth.

I was home, and I was free! The British waited in York City to set sail for England. I walked halfway up the hill and saw the shack and our house still standing on the summit of the hill, its white columned portico and black shutters leaning dully against the November sky. I had only to climb another few yards on the hillside and walk across the sandy lot filled with debris to enter it.

CHAPTER SEVENTY-SIX

"I'm home!" I stood on the mansion porch and shouted it out to the sky.

"Good afternoon, miss, we've been expecting you. Captain Stonecroft sent me to welcome you back," the red-coated soldier greeted me from the ground below.

"Not man enough to face me himself. Never mind, just leave. Now." The gall of this redcoat standing there on our property.

"Yes, ma'am. I'm to tell you our regiment is established in quarters in York City until we sail. Our company left this morning; the captain stayed to welcome you home." The officer smiled. "Will you have a cup of tea?"

"I will not." I glared down at him. He was slim and young; a summer breeze would topple him.

"Of course, miss, you'll direct the tea, won't you, in your own home?" His head bobbed slightly as he spoke in an effort to please me. He smiled.

"I'll pour no tea while there is a British soldier anywhere on the property. Tell your captain I'm home, and he does well to leave the premises now."

He inclined his head toward me as if I were royalty. "Yes, miss." He turned and walked into the mansion. I would not lay eyes on Captain Stonecroft. I would not enter the mansion until the very last redcoat was gone.

Instead, I walked to the shack that was now overgrown with a jumble of tall grasses. Weeds grew up around the rose bush that I had tended so carefully before I left that day in '79 to carry out my mission in Stony Point. The door was closed and stuck to its threshold when I tried to open it. After a good push, I managed to open it and walked into its dark interior. The rocker was still in its place. I gave it a tap, hearing its familiar whine as it swung on its hinges. Everything seemed to be as it was, even the jug on the table except for the thick covering of dust that neither Mama nor Hannah would have ever permitted.

A knock. Captain Stonecroft stood before me. "Miss Scott. Welcome home. I thought there should be a presence here until either you or your father returned. But I shall say good-bye to you now. It was a privilege to know you. I hope someday to meet you again." He waited for a second or two. But I had nothing to say to him. He bowed to me, turned, and walked out the door.

Though I had hated his presence in our mansion, he was going home too. I shouted across to the road, "Wait, Captain." He turned, about to step off the property onto the road. "I'm sure you will be happy to meet with your family too. Good fortune to you, Captain."

"Thank you, Miss Scott. And to you." He walked away to the Long Island ferry which would bring him to his regiment in New York City for the long journey home to England.

They were gone. Every last redcoat.

CHAPTER SEVENTY-SEVEN

Our mansion. I walked from room to room. The velvet sofa sat in its usual place in the parlor, but dirty and stained. The piano keys sounded dull and sour to my touch. The window drapes were torn, hanging at odd angles from their rods. The colors of Mama's Persian carpet had faded from bright reds and deep blues to a drab, uneven brown. Its flower patterns were filled with mud.

It was late afternoon when I lay down on the sofa, exhausted. When I awoke it was night. Outside, a full moon shone down white across the fields, barn, and fences. Nothing to eat but a bowl of something gray on the table in the kitchen. I opened the door to the back porch and threw out the bowl and its contents. It landed somewhere nearby in the brambles. Hungry, with not a morsel to eat, I tried to sleep. Silent and dark, the night wore on.

But when the sun rose, I jumped up and pulled all the drapes back from the french doors and saw all the way across the yard to Fanshawe's house and Comerford's house, even down to David's cottage sitting at the bend in Berry Creek where his rowboat was tied to a tree. For long minutes, I gazed out at his cottage; I was stern with myself and was able to walk away from the windows without a tear.

The mansion, warmed by the sunshine beaming down, reminded me how glad, glad, glad I was to be home. Nothing was impossible. I vowed to myself I would fix up the house until the very moment I opened the door to my room and saw the desecration there. But what did I expect? There was nothing of its old prettiness left. Even the bed was a broken old rope bed. The dresser was gone, probably used for firewood. A mother-of-pearl handle to my brush and comb set stuck out of a floorboard. I did cry then.

CHAPTER SEVENTY-EIGHT

A ghost stood in the kitchen doorway late in the afternoon of
the next day. Framed by sunshine, but so thin, Sarah Harkens
carried a lit candle in a lantern and a bag of potatoes.

"Sarah!" I ran to her. "How good it is to see you."

"Aye. And I to see you, Cassie."

For another minute, we stood and looked at each other. "Have
you been living here in town all this time, Sarah?"

"I have. I've brought you some fire, Cassie, and potatoes for
supper. It's all I have for the moment."

"Fire! And food. And I'm so hungry. Do you know, Sarah,
there's not a burning ember left in any of the fireplaces, and there
is nothing to eat here."

"Mean-spirited blokes, aren't they! Not to leave one hearth
alight, nor a scrap of food," Sarah said, laying her bag of potatoes
down on the table.

"I am so glad to see you, Sarah! I came home yesterday afternoon. I haven't eaten since yesterday."

"You must eat! Quickly, let's get the fire going. Grab some wood
chunks and chips out of the bag and spread them out in here,"

Sarah said, her voice muffled, kneeling at the grate and holding balled-up paper to spread over the wood I threw into the grate. She opened the door of her lantern, pulled out the lit candle, and held it to the paper covering the wood, and in seconds, we had a fire and heat. I dropped the potatoes in among the flames for roasting.

"I'll draw water. Sarah. I'll be back in a minute."

"I'm not going anywhere. I'm that glad to see you, Cassie. I've been lonely," she said.

When I came back in, I noticed again how thin Sarah looked. Her gown hung on her. I stared.

Sensing my eyes on her, Sarah said, "There was never enough to eat, Cassie."

"I know. I was always hungry, too," I said, "until I left Cow Neck." The kettle was boiling. I got up and pushed a couple of Mama's china cups, chipped and without handles, in front of us. Out of them, we drank boiled tea from sassafras leaves. The roasted potatoes smelled delicious from the grate when I turned them over.

"Where did you go?"

"I was in Buttermilk Falls for the past two years living with a war widow who owned and worked a farm."

"That's best then. And you look healthy, Cassie. I'm awfully glad for you to be home. Awfully glad."

"Sarah, tell me how it's been since I left."

"Dreadful. Miss Hoary and I have been hungry and cold most of the time; no one is left on the lane. We were fortunate to have each other for company."

"Where did the neighbors go? All the cottages are dark on the lane."

"The Comerfords and the Fanshawes left when food became scarce; they went to York City. But now they're back and living in Jesse Prouty's barn until they can fix the damage to their houses."

"I suppose nothing will ever be the way it used to be, will it, Sarah?" I said, looking out at the empty cottages on the lane.

"For me, it won't. My papa and my mama left for England. I've been alone ever since."

"I remember. You told us on the day of my nineteenth birthday."

"You left the next day, and my parents left only a week later. I was miserable for a while; I missed them so much." She swallowed and began again, "Yet my papa loved America, too. He didn't want to leave; he was convinced the Patriots would take revenge on Loyalists. Papa was right, for the state has just confiscated the homes and properties of all Loyalists. My house is padlocked."

"Padlocked!"

"Yes. Padlocked and boards are up against the windows." Sarah wiped her eyes with the tip of her apron.

"That can't stand." I was more than angry; I was furious. "You're very brave, Sarah; you could have gone with your parents. Instead, you chose to stay. You are no Tory; you're a brave Patriot."

"I'm not brave; most of the time I was hungry and scared. Help came to Miss Hoary and me from a British soldier who brought food and wood to us. If it hadn't been for him, we would have perished. "At first, I didn't trust him. I wouldn't open the door. But he left food on the path for me. When he came around the next day, I met him outside. He told me Suzie Mancks had left for England with her grandparents, and if I would move into Suzie's cabin, he could keep his eye on me and help me with food and wood. I didn't know what to do. Here was a British soldier offering to help me. But there wasn't much choice. I had almost no wood left, and I was living on scraps and crusts and what I could steal from the British after the cook in your mansion threw out the leftovers from the officers' suppers. I moved into Suzie's cabin that very day. The soldier moved Miss Hoary into Eban's cottage next door to Suzie's cabin. Cassie, the English soldier is one of us. He stayed here after the evacuation."

But I heard none of that. "So Suzie's gone. I thought so. Well, it's best, I suppose, Suzie went to England with her grandparents."

"It's just another rumor," Sarah said, when she saw the sadness on my face. She looked as though she would say more. But then we were both silent.

"Do you know anything else?" I asked her.

Sarah hesitated. "Yes, but it is all rumor, Cassie."

"Tell me, please."

"She was in love with a British officer, I heard. She waits for him to come home to her in London, and they will marry."

"Well, at least it is resolved." *For once, I am thankful for Max choosing to stay in Charleston;* he would be spared this news.

As though she read my thoughts, Sarah said, "Max knows." She put her hand over mine.

"How could he?" I said.

"It was right after the peace treaty had been signed and David Van Essen came home from the fighting. David wrote to Max and told him that Suzie had gone to England to marry."

"David is home?"

"Yes." Sarah sat very still. "David is home from the war."

"I see." I swallowed hard.

Sarah went on, "I'm sorry, Cassie, to tell you about Suzie."

I lowered my head into my hands. I am sad. I would be lying if I denied it, but I feel better knowing it was David who told Max. They were best friends."

Sarah had brought her knitting today, and she took out the soft wool from a sack and began to knit and purl. "Try not to be sad, Cassie. This is a new day for us. We're the first generation of citizens in our country, the first to taste the joys of liberty."

"You're right. I'll get plates for the potatoes." Trying to sound cheerful, I said, "Who is he, Sarah, this British soldier who helped you and Miss Hoary?"

"His name is Tom Doggett. You might remember him, Cassie."

I began to scrub the table down before I said, "Tom Doggett. I surely do remember him."

The look on my face must have taken her aback. "What's the matter? Why do you look so angry?"

"Why? He hit me in the back with his gun, and he robbed me of my ring that David gave me. That's why."

Sarah gasped. "Cassie. That can't be true."

"It is true, although he did return my ring." I went back to scrubbing with a vengeance.

Sarah stood still; her needles rested in her hands. "Tom Doggett has done everything to keep us alive here. He's taken risks that could have gotten him hanged for a traitor." She looked away. Her cheeks had turned red. "We are very good friends now, Cassie. I think very highly of him."

I sighed. Everything was so topsy-turvy in my life, "Never mind, Sarah; if he's been kind to you and Miss Hoary, I shall welcome him into my house."

"I know you'll like him, Cassie, when you talk to him. Why don't you come to the cabin this evening? Tom stops by about eight."

"No. Thank you. I want to stay here, Sarah. Father and Hannah could come home anytime. Have you heard anything about where they stay?"

"No, only that they are in Connecticut." Sarah bit her lip and looked away. "I better go. Miss Hoary is expecting me for supper. She told me to ask you for supper, too." Sarah was at the door, holding it open. It seemed to me she couldn't get away fast enough all of a sudden.

"You're going to Miss Hoary's cabin for supper and then you're going to be at home for Tom Doggett's visit?"

"Yes, Cassie. I've suffered too long from loneliness. I try to keep as social as I can. Come with me; you need company too."

"Sarah, if you know where my papa and Hannah stay in Connecticut, please tell me."

Sarah closed the door and walked toward me. "I don't know, Cassie. I didn't hear where they stay in Connecticut. I did hear your papa is too weak to travel."

"Then I'll go to Connecticut and bring him home myself."

"Cassie, do not do that. We have no idea where they are. And you might make trouble looking for them. There are still angry Tories around with guns on the roads and in the woods. Why not let your papa be for a while until he gets his strength back and can travel? Meanwhile, you can get the mansion ready for him. Besides, Hannah can help him when he's better able to travel. You have enough to do here."

The logic of Sarah's argument didn't escape me. She didn't say it, but I could be responsible for Papa's death if I went looking for him.

"I won't go. I'm sure they'll be back, he and Hannah. But it's scary by myself in the mansion."

"I do promise I shall come every day, and we can do wonders here fixing up the mansion. Meanwhile, I mourn for my house taken from me. I am not Tory. Why should I be punished?"

"My papa will help us when he gets back, Sarah. There must be a way to let the authorities know you're a Patriot so your house and property will be returned to you. It's unjust. You'll get your house back."

"And, Cassie, you won't be lonely anymore, and I won't either. We'll have each other for company. We're friends now."

"We are, Sarah."

CHAPTER SEVENTY-NINE

But the mansion was too big. Too silent. Gloom shrouded the rooms. There were spirits everywhere. Again, I woke up to the sun streaming in through the french doors. I opened them, and cold air freshened the room. I had slept overnight again on the rubbish-strewn couch with the comfort of a dirty blanket. Morning had just broken. I had slept straight through the night.

Shaking out one of the dried, stuck-together drapes, I watched a family of field mice scurry out over my feet and leap through the open doors. A noisy woodpecker bored holes into a fence somewhere on the property. Outdoors, later, I felt the rising sun on my back. It looked as though we were to have a rare mild November day. *I'm home and I'm free! And no English are about.*

I surveyed the wreckage in the yard. Where to start? Not now. It was too much to think about on this beautiful, sunlit day. I walked across the dirty sand to the chicken coop. Even though I knew there were no chickens left there, I wanted to see the inside of the place again. Oddly, there was feed on the ground. Generous handfuls of grain. I opened the door of the green-shingled coop and bent over to walk between the shelves filled with nests of straw. Hens were pecking and clucking amid the feast of eggs. I could not believe my eyes. Four warm eggs lay among the straw from the hens' nests.

"Ah, now ye've found me out, Miss."

Startled, I edged against the wall. "Who is there?"

"Doggett, Miss . . . Tom Doggett."

"Doggett!"

"I've stayed behind, I 'ave." He carried a bag of feed.

I stepped forward. "Sarah has told me of all the good you've done for her and Miss Hoary. Thank you for all you did during the war."

"Brilliant that the war's over, miss. But there were times these past winters when we were all so hungry, the people here were worn down to skin and bones. Myself I was so cold some days, I felt like I didn't have a bit o' blood left in me."

"And yet you looked out for Sarah and Miss Hoary. It was splendid of you," I said, and as I did, I felt all traces of my resentment melt away.

Doggett was clearly embarrassed. "Ah, well. The Brits are all over with, now."

I felt a bit of awkwardness too. "Praise be," I said. "It's true. How did you manage to stay behind?"

"Hid in the barn. Wasn't hard. When I saw Captain Stonecroft turn his back, I simply dropped off the line and slipped inside the barn. At night, I slept in the woods and waited till sunup and then went over to Heatherton's barn, where I had been keepin' the chickens. I caged them up and brought 'em here. They're happy as clams now."

"I owe you so much, Doggett. I don't know how to thank you."

"As for owin', miss, we'll call it a draw, won't we?"

"Yes. We shall." And then after a few seconds, I asked, "You didn't want to go home to Dublin?"

321

"There's nothing to go back to, miss. Sellin' meat pies from my cart? I'll take my chances here." Doggett paused for a few seconds. "America is my country now; it's the new world."

"Then welcome, Tom Doggett. America is pleased to have you," I said.

"Your father said something like that when he took me into his spy network. Thank you, miss."

"I'm gobsmacked! You worked for my father?" All this time I had hated him for picking up information about Papa and reporting it to the colonel. "I thought you were a spy for the redcoats."

"I did spy work for your father. He was a good man. I hope to see him back here soon. But the war is a memory now." Doggett shifted uncomfortably in the small, damp coop. "I was thinkin' you might need somebody around the place till you get settled, Miss Scott."

"I do, but I have no money."

"Neither 'ave I. Neither has anybody. But ye won't be needin' money to make some order out of the mess, will ya now?"

"No. Thank you for the offer to help, Doggett."

"I've led the cows to Heatherton's pasture for grazin' as well. Grass is still plentiful there. I'll bring 'em back this evening."

"Do you mean Jamie and Jubie are still here?"

"Yes, miss, here and producin' milk."

There was no reason to cry, but I could feel my face crumple. Hot tears started to roll down my cheeks. I was truly ashamed; I covered my face. Doggett looked away.

"How do I say thank-you, Doggett?"

"No need Miss. If I can be of help. And if it's all right with ya, I'll be livin' here in the shack till you're fixed up proper."

"Yes, but do come live in the mansion. There's so much room."

"In the shack, if you please."

"I've got four warm, fresh eggs. To start off with, come over in ten minutes to the mansion. I'll have them coddled."

Both of us fell into silence. I was conscious that Doggett was no longer the young Irish tough; I was no longer the selfish, pampered girl I was at the start of the war, and this house was no longer the shining white mansion on the hill that I loved so much, but a dirty, old, broken-down pile.

"We'll fix the old place up. I'll help you, miss. This house will be lookin' good afore long."

"Doggett, do you think you could call me Cassie, and I could call you Tom?"

"If you like, Cassie."

"Good. Come over in ten minutes, and I'll have these eggs coddled."

CHAPTER EIGHTY

That was the first of many breakfasts for Tom and me. We worked in the mansion every day. We moved my piano away from the french doors and cleaned the sofa as well as soap and water could do. I washed the drapes, and Tom rehung them. Not warm and soft anymore, the material was clean and spare. The mansion was beginning to be comfortable. The throwing out, the knocking, the hammering—it was all music to my ears.

One evening, just before twilight, I sat in the parlor of the mansion with a stray cat I called Smokey purring softly next to me on a pillow. A soft snow fell on the barren ground. Through the french doors, a darkening shadow hid part of an orange streak crisscrossing the sky. I looked up. A man stood outside, peering into the parlor.

The cat jumped away in fear, and I stood up, frightened at the sight of the bent, bearded stranger in dirty knickers. An old homespun shirt hung loose from his shoulders. There were so many soldiers returning from the war, bodies bent, eyes haunted. Mayhap this one wanted just a bite to eat to hold him till he got home.

I opened the doors. Before me stood David Van Essen.

"Hello, Cassie. Yes. It's me. I saw you from the road. I just stopped to say welcome back."

He was a scarecrow of a man. He was not the boy I knew. Thin, bearded, his hands were blackened as he fingered his cap.

"It's hard to get used to me. I know. I'm different."

"Sit down, please." It was all I could manage to say. I gestured him to the easy chair.

"No. I'll stand." He laughed, a short, not funny laugh.

"David, do sit down."

David Van Essen looked at me steadily but sat on the edge of the chair, twirling his fishing hat in his hands. "You look very well, Cassie." He smiled. "Your hair is shorter."

"Your cap is new?" I said.

"I gave the old one to Mr. Harkens to give to you to save for me." He hesitated. "Did he?"

"He gave it to Sarah to give to me. I put it away in the shack. I shall look for it tomorrow. Will you have tea?"

"No need. I was walking. I saw you through the glass. It's good to see you again. I'm glad you've come back." He nodded and smiled. It felt to me as though we were talking to each other through a long tunnel.

I cast about for something to say. "Are you all right, David?"

"Yes. I'm home since the peace treaty has been signed. But I don't live in the cottage. The government has it."

"Yes. I know. The government has confiscated the homes and properties of all known Tories."

"True. But I'm one not of them. I'm a Patriot. I worked for my country, and I shall be vindicated." David got up from the chair. "Keep well, Cassie."

"You don't have to leave yet, David. Stay. I have food in the springhouse. I can get something for you to take home with you."

David laughed, a bitter laugh. "I'm not accepting charity this evening. Thank you, ma'am."

"I didn't mean it that way. I just…"

"It's all right. Good-bye, Cassie." He went down the steps slowly, like an old man, holding on to the wooden railing. As he walked away, I saw him signal to a dog. A black mongrel picked itself up off the ground and followed him.

CHAPTER EIGHTY-ONE

"David isn't the same. You didn't tell me, Sarah." Sitting in my newly cleaned and sweet-smelling kitchen, Sarah's fingers flew over her needles to shape the deep reds and yellows of a skein of wool into a scarf, while I polished my mama's silver. Bent, twisted, and scratched as the pieces were from the rough treatment the British officers gave it, the silver set was still my mama's and precious to me.

Sarah crossed her needles and rested her knitting. "I didn't know what to tell you. David's different. He's sad. He's not himself. I think he needs time to heal." She paused, looking at me. "People here are awful to him. Some accuse him of being a traitor. Most go out of their way to avoid him. Tom and I don't want him to suffer anymore."

"I don't want him to suffer either. He's so changed, Sarah. I do feel badly for him." I lifted a teaspoon of sugar out of the silver bowl I had resurrected from the debris in the dining room and stirred it into my tea.

"He's still David, Cassie. Remember that. You couldn't get enough of his company before the war." Sarah picked up her knitting. She was silent now; there was just the click of her needles as her fingers flew across the rows of wool.

"He spied for the British during the war," I said.

Sarah lowered her knitting. She spoke slowly and did not look up. "David Van Essen is not a traitor. He's as true a Patriot as you are, Cassie."

"No. He is not. I saw him and spoke to him in his British officer's uniform."

"He was working for the American cause, Cassie."

"He would have you believe that, Sarah, but the opposite is true. I know." More than that, I could not say without giving away my own part in the struggle for independence.

"It is not true. David did spy, but for the Americans. He is a hero, and someday, everyone here in Cow Neck will know it. Aside from that, you used to love him, Cassie."

"Yes. I did; I don't now. But I would like to know where David is living now that his house is locked up. I didn't like to ask him."

"He lives rough in the woods. He has built himself a shanty and made it quite comfortable. Tom and I have been bringing him what food we could spare."

"A shanty in the woods?"

"Yes. The government has made a mistake in calling out David a British spy and padlocking his cottage. He will be vindicated. That will happen, Cassie, for David is a Patriot and not one of 'the disaffected.'" Sarah knotted the last row of knitting and then cut through the strand of yarn with a vengeance. "And I'm no Tory either. Why was my house taken? My papa deeded it to me before he left for England. Where is the justice for that?"

"That house is yours, Sarah. And the government will realize its mistake. For David, it will be different. David had a choice, and he chose wrong. He is being made to pay," I said.

Sarah ran her knitting needles through the ball of yarn and took a sip of her tea. "You can't be so hard as all that, Cassie. Go and see David; he is alone. It would be so good of you if you would. You'll understand more if you visit him, no matter how you feel about him."

"No. I'm sorry for him, but I hate what he did. I could not go and see him, especially as he's living in the woods. It would be more than awkward."

"He came to see you." Sarah stood up, putting her knitting in her cloth bag. "Whenever did you get so hard-hearted, Cassie?"

"You judge me wrong, Sarah."

"I think not," Sarah said in a clipped tone. "I shall see you tomorrow."

CHAPTER EIGHTY-TWO

Winter. Every evening when Tom came to see Sarah after his work day, merry candlelight lit up Sarah's cottage. Even though Sarah invited me, it was too hard to see them so sweet with each other and myself so alone in the mansion. I began to take walks by myself sometimes on the path alongside the woods; "bare, ruined choirs" Mr. Shakespeare had called the skeleton trees, and so they were. Bare and without song.

Twilight came early, and once I saw a camp, a dull, brown, discarded old British soldier's tent, and I was sure David lived in it. But I didn't stop. I never stopped, never looked deeply into the woods. I hoped he was warm enough and had food. But when the winter turned so very cold and bleak, I worried for him living rough in the woods. I felt selfish, and at the same time I wanted to see him again, to talk to him again.

It became December 31. I dressed warmly and walked out on the empty road separating the woods on both sides. I carried a plate of hot stew, in a covered bowl, inside my tucksack. Dark clouds scudded across the sky, making afternoon seem like twilight. There was no one else on the road. When a camp became visible to me through the skeletal trees, I pushed my way through the dead limbs and tangled bushes; stepped over dead branches; and slid through cracked, dried leaves lying on the slippery ground. I found the way treacherous and slow.

The camp was roofed over by a discarded piece of British broadcloth. I pushed the flap aside; in the gloom, an upended barrel made a tabletop on which a lit candle in a holder rested. A blanket of woven, matted tree leaves and dead grass provided a covering for the dirt floor.

"David?" I called softly. The man sat with his back to me, warming his hands over a brick fire.

Aware of me, he turned. "Cassie, come inside. Here, you must be cold. Sit down here by the fire. I've coffee. I shall pour for you."

"Hello, David." I let go of the flap, and it snapped back against the tent. "How do you keep?"

"I'm well. Tom and Sarah are helping me with food until I get back into my cottage."

I held a bucket of stew and biscuits I had baked out to him. "I made the stew, and I baked the biscuits myself."

"Thank you. I'm glad to have them."

"They're not as good as Sarah's or Hannah's, but they are not too hard and tough."

"I shall like everything you brought, Cassie. I thank you."

David's voice held so much warmth, he gave me courage to sit down on top of the upended crate he had put for me on the side of the fire where it was warmer.

"It's not what you're used to, but it is the best what can be got," David said.

I tried to make sense of the inside of David's camp. Gloom penetrated every corner except for the light from the spitting fire that he kept low to keep the smoke down. David stood up but bent his head so as not to disturb the cloth roof. He poured boiling coffee from a can hanging from a hook over the fire into dented pewter tankards.

"Do you hear from your father or Max?" David sipped his coffee, and I sipped mine, which was hot and warmed my insides.

It seemed ages before I could swallow and answer. "No. I pray that soon they will be home." We sat silently staring into the flames. "It feels comfortable in here." I said, and I sincerely meant it.

"This will have to do me for a bit until my cottage becomes my own again." David reached over and put the can back over the fire. "There's a New York lawyer, name of Alexander Hamilton, close to General Washington in the war. He's interested in taking on cases defending Tories' homes and property. Hamilton's a powerful man and a great lawyer. I'm hoping he will take my case, to prove to the government I'm a Patriot and don't deserve this confiscation of my cottage." He stopped talking and looked directly into my eyes as if he was challenging me to believe him.

"But you did go over to the British." I could have bitten my tongue the instant I said that.

"No. I never did. I am a Patriot and not loyal to the king, never was; I worked for General Washington. But I'm sure you have a hard time believing that."

I looked down, saying nothing.

"I see you don't believe me. Except for Tom Doggett and Sarah, most folks here don't believe me. You seem so sure I spied for the British. I won't try to convince you." He reached down at his feet and lifted another log to drop into the fire. Sparks flew upward. *But it is too hard to continue saying nothing when I knew he was a British spy.*

"David, I more than anyone else have reason not to believe you. Do you forget I had dealings with you wearing the red coat up at Stony Point? You said you owed your loyalty to the English king then, now, and forever."

"I said the words that would keep you alive, Cassie. I knew you were spying. I was a spy in General Washington's spy network planted at Stony Point by Major Tallmadge. I swear it. I never gave over my allegiance to the British."

"You wore the red coat and managed the king's business. How can I believe you when you say you worked for General Washington?"

"Except that it's true." David looked at me. He took both my hands in his and said in a soft tone, "Cassie, I need you to believe me. I want you to believe me because I want to marry you, as much as before, more so I think now. And how can I do that if you don't believe in me?"

The fire jumped up in the grate as he spoke, and I saw his face in the glow. A muscle in his cheek twitched. I saw how troubled he was.

"I don't know how I feel anymore, David; I'm betwixt and between." Both of us stayed quiet; I studied my hands. "I saw too much in the war," I said finally.

David didn't speak for a moment. Then he said, "Why did you come here, Cassie?"

"I wanted to bring you some food and to make sure you weren't suffering from the cold."

"I suffer from want of you." David's eyes glowed in the firelight. "Believe me, Cassie. I speak the truth to you when I say that I never spied for the British. Never."

"I want to believe you," I whispered.

"You must. Otherwise, otherwise, there's nothing left for us."

I felt this voice coming from inside me that was low and harsh, as if it was wrenched from me. And it was an angry voice. "You did this, David. You convinced me you were loyal to the British king that day in Stony Point. Now you try to convince me you were working for General Washington."

A change came over him. David stood up; he faced me with a grim look. "I am not that person you saw in Stony Point, no matter what you think." We faced each other in silence. After a few seconds, he reached the poker into the fire and pushed it around, scattering the embers. "But it's no good; I can see that. Come on. I shall walk you through the woods to the road."

"I shall find my own way," I said, walking to the makeshift tent flap.

"Just as you say." David loosened the tent flap, and we stepped out into the cold. The wind gusted swirling snow into our faces; I pulled my cloak tight about myself. I looked at David full in the face; then I stepped away and began the walk through the woods to the road. I turned once and saw him standing at the open flap of the tent. I wanted to run back to him, but I didn't.

When I got home, I lit all the candles. The mansion was cold. I stirred the fire and saw it leap up in the kitchen hearth. I made tea. *He wants me back. I want to go back to him. I would forgive him if he told me the truth. He's had excellent training in deception, but then so have I.*

CHAPTER EIGHTY-THREE

Spring 1784

The daffodils were out. Around them green blades of grass shot up from the ground. Noises from the shack were excruciatingly loud. For two weeks, as soon as the snow melted on the ground, Tom Doggett hammered away inside the cottage. Three times a day, I walked across the grass, knocked, and left pails of food hanging on the doorknob. I knew he heard me because the hammering stopped for a while and then resumed, but I couldn't see inside the cottage window. The rough burlap he'd put over the glass shielded the kitchen from the light. It didn't concern me. I had enough to do in the house. And if he could fix up the shack into a real cottage, mayhap I could put it up to let. Lots of people coming home now from the war needed shelter. And I needed money desperately.

I had not seen David at all. Not on the roads or in Mr. Douglas's store or down at the water fishing. I wondered if he were still living rough in the woods. I missed him dreadfully, and I missed Suzie. I missed her working in the schoolhouse and walking home from school, stopping to sit on Jesse Prouty's hillside in the afternoons after school. But I accepted it: she was gone forever, just as David was gone from me forever. Sarah came for walks with me, and I was glad for her company, but she just was not a friend like Suzie and she believed in David.

Neither of us spoke of David, but I knew Sarah and Tom still brought David food, and when I asked about him once, she told me he still resided in the camp in the woods. By now, there were a good number of returning soldiers living in the woods in camps like David's. They stayed for one or two nights to sleep and then left to pick up the trail home. Other soldiers took their places, and then they left to go home.

The knocking and hammering continued for days on end in the shack. Tom didn't appear at my door at all. Then, at noon of a sunny day in early May, he came to show me the new interior of the shack.

CHAPTER EIGHTY-FOUR

Cassie's tea shop

"Come and see, then." Tom Doggett gave me a wide, satisfied smile. I walked briskly ahead of him to show him I was annoyed with the long wait; I could have seen the improvement anytime. Instead, he insisted I wait till it was done. Tom followed me. "I've been busy a fair piece," he said.

"I noticed. I don't see why I had to be kept in the dark." Keeping up my irritation was futile. Sarah stood at the shack door, holding a big box.

"Don't go in yet until I…" Tom said.

"Nonsense, I'm going in." I pushed my wheelbarrow with new seedlings up against the shack and then wiped off my hands.

Since Tom hung back and didn't follow me, I entered the kitchen, or what was the kitchen. It was now an immense sitting room. Walls had been knocked out, and I could see clear through to what used to be the bedrooms to the road outside. I saw white, gauzy curtains hanging from the windows, framing the early-afternoon scene with our cows, Jamie and Jubie, grazing in the front yard.

Inside, small, round tables with rough-hewn chairs were placed at conversational distances from each other, and candles rested on pewter saucers on each table. The walls were whitewashed until they gleamed. On a large, unbroken wall hung the painting of three young girls walking through a flowered meadow in ruffled pinafores, a painting that had always hung in our parlor, and for some reason, I had not realized was gone. The floor was dusted with clean sawdust.

It took my breath away; I turned and looked for Tom. He was nowhere to be found. I walked outside slowly. He was standing with Sarah. Both of them stood smiling at me.

"You wanted a tea shop, Cassie," Sarah reminded me.

"But it was just a thought; I never meant for you to build it. I can't believe it. I can't. Thank you, Tom, thank you."

"Come on!" Sarah walked through the door, carrying the box. "Cassie, come back inside; here's another surprise." Once inside, Sarah laid the box on one of the tables. She opened up the linen and uncovered a set of white, translucent china bordered with gold rims.

"They're yours, Cassie. Use them for your tea shop."

"But this is your mother's beautiful china." I sat down on one of the polished wooden chairs. Sarah and Tom sat opposite me. "Sarah, Tom, I..." My words failed me. "You've been too good to me." I jumped up and hugged them both.

Sarah lifted a cup. We watched its gold rim glisten in sunlight. "Thank you, Sarah, but I can't take your mother's china. Thank her for me." I wiped my face of tears with the edge of my apron.

"I'll not be in England for a while, Cassie, to thank her. Come on, let's unwrap the dishes." My eyes still watered. Sarah was already removing the pale, shimmering porcelain cups and saucers from the box that had sheltered them for most of the war years.

There were tears in Sarah's eyes too. "It's all right about my parents, Cassie. I'm sure my mama has new china by now. Someday soon, I'll go to visit them."

"And you'll go with me," Tom said. "I'll have a chance to show off my American wife." He smiled broadly. "Now, I got work. I'll see you ladies later."

"You will marry Tom?" I wasn't surprised though. I had seen the loving looks between the two.

"Yes," Sarah said, "I shall, for I love him."

"Sarah, we shall have your wedding in the mansion." Lately, I had stopped calling it the house and optimistically gone back to calling it the mansion. "You'll wear a white silk gown and golden slippers. We shall all eat strawberry cream cakes and toast you and Tom with French wines. We shall all be so happy at your wedding."

"Oh, Cassie, I wish! But we have no money. I shall wear that yellow gown of Suzie's, and Tom will wear his serviceable homespun. Tom is helping Jesse Prouty construct chairs again, and he is saving up what Jesse pays him for a used carriage to get us to Ohio territory."

"To Ohio? So far away, Sarah."

"I know, Cassie, but there is good, fertile land to be bought cheap in the Ohio valley. And once we're settled, we shall come back and visit with you."

"Yes, Sarah, and I shall go out to visit with you too. I hope it isn't soon that you leave Cow Neck. But I'm happy for you both, Sarah, even though I'm sad you're going. We can make your wedding lovely with flowers from the fields, and we can sew up your pretty wedding dress ourselves. We shall do it, Sarah. You will have the wedding of the year."

"Good. Let's accomplish the washing and the drying of the china, first," Sarah said, ever the practical one. It took the better part of an hour to wash and dry each piece of porcelain, and when the job was done, I ran home to the mansion and pulled down one of the packets of Darjeeling tea left behind by the British. We sat and drank a cup out of Sarah's mother's china tea cups, feeling the newness of it all, watching the way the sun gleamed on the pretty tables.

Over tea, Sarah said: "I must go, Cassie, over to Jesse Prouty's barn. He's taking ten families in to live in the barn until houses can be built for them. I shall do what I can do. Why don't you come with me?"

"Ten families, Sarah? I hadn't heard of anything like that."

Sarah hesitated. She looked at me a few seconds. "They are Loyalists, Cassie, some English, some American. But all homeless. They need to escape from Patriots just back from the war, who want to drive them from their homes and beat them in the streets. It's ugly in New York City, Cassie."

"Oh. Are they the same people who waited for our boys to leave for the fighting, and then stole their houses for themselves at the beginning of the war, Sarah?" I went on. "Aren't they, many of them, British loyalists who spied on Americans for information to give to the British?" I picked up the tea things and brought them to the pail of warm water in the shack kitchen. I didn't try to hide my hard feelings toward those Tories with warm feelings for George III.

"That was a long time ago, Cassie."

"And I have a long memory, Sarah. I have no sympathy for those people. I shan't have anything to do with those who betrayed our country in the war. I won't go with you, Sarah, and I most certainly will not serve them in my tea shop."

Sarah stood at the door. "I'm sorry you feel that way, Cassie. I truly am. These are homeless and hungry people. I've never known you to turn away a needy person."

"They made their own beds, Sarah. Now they will have to sleep in them." Sarah was silent. I felt her judgement, but I knew I was right to feel the way I did. "I do thank you for helping me, Sarah."

She half smiled, and we continued to work in silence until our elevenses tea outside on the grass, when I saw from Sarah's silence that trouble was brewing between Sarah and me over the Loyalist families, and I felt bad about this disagreement with my friend.

CHAPTER EIGHTY-FIVE

Within a week, news that Jesse Prouty would build houses on his hillside for the ten disaffected families was all over town. Impossible. "How could Jesse have invited them here to his hillside, to his barn, and now this new outrage, to build new houses for them here in our town of Cow Neck? It's unthinkable, Sarah."

"Yet Jesse did offer to house them, and we'll have to help them. What's more, Cassie, there are many others here who will help the families." Sarah wore a fixed look. Her mouth tightened into a thin line as she spoke.

"I won't. You won't." I looked into her eyes; something made me ask, "Will you?"

"Yes. I will. I found they needed someone to cook for them. I shall cook. The war is over, Cassie. We've got to get used to it. Why not help them? Why do you feel they are our enemies?"

"Because, because...they worked against us in the war."

"And they lost. And now because they have been thrown out of their homes and off their property, all their worldly goods confiscated by the government, they are without shelter, landless, and without money. Isn't there such a thing as compassion?"

"Those homes belonged to Americans, who left to serve their country in the war for our independence. Have you forgotten New York got to be known as Tory Town during the war, Sarah?"

"No, but there is a great need right now for forgiveness and redemption."

I stood up and gathered my reticule. "I can't find either of those virtues in my heart for those disaffected ones," I said. Sarah picked up her shawl and left.

CHAPTER EIGHTY-SIX

At home in the mansion, dullness of the day cast a gray pall over the porch, and inside, over the rooms, the furniture, and even the silent kitchen. I might have been too harsh with Sarah, I thought, but I certainly could not help them, nor allow the families to come here to my tea shop after they had betrayed America in the war. No matter if I did understand Sarah's feelings of pity for them.

It was a week now that Sarah had not come to the tea shop. The day being so wet and chilly, I set about baking pies that were as good as Sarah's. The gloom outside made me feel worse, and my pies were runny; still they tasted good. I thought Sarah would approve them. Soon, Sarah and Tom would marry and leave Cow Neck. It would be lonely without Sarah. I missed her already. I so wished she weren't going, nor Tom. I wish they would both stay with me. It occurred to me that both Suzie and Sarah had gotten sweethearts, myself not. The word for me was drifting.

I went on and on looking out through the French windows at the rain coming down in torrents: *What has happened? Why am I alone? I must see about finding a husband. Wait! What about Jem Clarke? I had completely forgotten about Jem.*

With a start, I sat up. I hadn't thought of Jem Clarke since I came home. But how could I when there was not a day, nor an hour, that I didn't think of David and yearn for his company. Yet I could not marry David. He wouldn't marry me the way I felt about his spying for the British. I couldn't marry a traitor. And Papa would never allow me to marry a British spy. David was a traitor and a British spy.

I decided to give my pies to the families on Jesse's hill. Meantime I would put them in the springhouse for safekeeping. The day we had the fight and Sarah left, she had said that I was improving in my baking. Now I imagined she was cooking and baking over at Jesse's place. I struggled to get things ready for our opening, but it wasn't as much fun as it was when Sarah was coming to help. *Oh, how I wish Sarah would come back and help.*

And as if she had heard me, the door opened, and Sarah walked in. "I'm glad you came back, Sarah. What should we do first, Sarah? Look at these pies. They're awful."

Sarah laughed. "No, they aren't. Let's have tea and taste them. You go get napkins and tablecloths for the tables. Your mama must have had plenty. I'll start baking awhile."

"Tablecloths. Mama has tons of them. I'll wash them out here and spread them on the grass to dry, just to get the English smell off them."

"Good. Better get some more apples from your root cellar and peaches if they kept good from the winter."

I raced out the door and across the grass to the mansion, thanking Providence over and over again that Sarah had come back.

Later Tom Doggett came in very pleased with himself. "Look here, ladies. I found a wooden board, and I've painted a sign on it in big letters: STOP AT CASSIE'S TEA SHOP *** CAKES, PIES,

COBBLERS, BISCUITS with DARJEELING TEA. OPEN JUNE 15."

Tom was happy, "Later on, you can walk over to Mr. Douglas's store and see it for yourselves hanging from the porch railing."

"I didn't know how I was going to open so soon. But thanks to you two, it's going to happen." I took a deep breath. No longer was I filled with panic

Tom and Sarah never stopped helping me. Every day Tom came around to fix a faulty leg on a table or to sweep the tea-shop floor and change the rushes to keep the shop sweet-smelling. He was heaven-sent. Sarah's pies were mounting; there were five keeping cool in the springhouse, and she brought armloads of tiger lilies just beginning to bud. The best was that Tom was so generous with the money he got from Jesse for helping to build the houses; he insisted on paying me board, for which I did everything I could to dissuade him, but his attitude was that as he lived on our property, boards must be paid. It was so good to have some money again.

The night before the opening, surveying Cassie's tea shop at its best, I decided to make a surprise supper for Sarah and Tom. The evening was a success. Boiled cabbage and potatoes along with mutton and gravy was a treat. And what's more I had watched Mama prepare this dish since I was little, and I knew how to do it. Sarah and I talked all the way through the evening, and then Tom left to take a walk.

"He'll be back in a little while. He most likely will be stopping at David's camp," Sarah said. We sat on the porch. After the early rain, the breezes were soft and mild; soon we saw Tom run across the fields. He ran up the porch steps. He stood on the top step, and his words tumbled out.

"All the padlocks have been taken off the front doors. You can take possession of your house, Sarah. David just told me."

Sarah's eyes flew up to Tom's face. "Is it true?"

"Yes. It's true. We have Mr. Hamilton's word for it. He has kept up his arguments against confiscation of Tories' houses in the Legislature and in the newspapers. He believes punishing Tories by putting them out of their homes will only weaken our country. The news is all over town!" Tom stopped for breath.

"Go home, Sarah. You must be aching to see your house again," I said.

"Yes, to see it and to sell it, Cassie."

"Sell? It's a beautiful house. Why?" I asked.

"So Tom and I can have more money when we marry."

"You can't sell your house, Sarah." Tom's lips became a thin line.

"Why not, Tom?"

"I haven't got enough put by yet. We are not going to marry with your money."

"But we could marry now and move if I sell the house, Tom."

"No, Sarah."

Tom sat with his shoulders sagging, and Sarah stirred her coffee until little whirlpools formed. She pushed a lock of hair from her face.

"You look as though the sky has fallen in, Sarah." I sat down opposite her at the dining room table.

"In time, we'll leave and not have the trip be paid for with your money," Tom said, looking up.

Sarah looked at me for support; I couldn't help but agree with Tom. "I see nothing wrong with that plan, Sarah. Tom's got character. That's why he won't spend your money. He wants to work with Jesse to earn money building chairs and houses for the Tory families. Then he can take care of you, not the other way 'round."

"But I want to go; I want to make a new start. Besides, Cassie, when did this new-found liking for the families begin?"

"I feel the same way about the families. They were traitors to our country. But if Tom can earn money working for them, I say, that's good."

"Yes, I reckon so," Sarah had to admit. After a while, we three took our coffee down the porch steps and sat on the grass in front of the tea shop, which was cool and dry. The evening was full of fireflies and soft sounds, which prompted Tom to nap on the grass.

Sarah looked over at me in the shadows. "Cassie, David will be back home in his cottage soon, probably by tomorrow, if he isn't already. Don't look away, Cassie; you do hear me. I know you do."

"Yes. I hear you, Sarah. But it does not signify for me."

"Why not?"

"Because when I saw David last, we said good-bye, not in so many words, but still I knew it, and so did he."

Sarah gave a deep sigh. "I wish things were different, Cassie, between you and David."

"I wish it so too, with all my heart, Sarah."

"You do? Then I think I must tell you something." Sarah leaned closer to me; she hesitated and then spoke. "All the time that Tom was fixing up the shack and making it into a tea shop, David Van Essen was working right along with him. Tom told me David did most of the work, but he didn't want you to know," Sarah said, mercifully not looking at my face.

"I don't know what to say. I shall thank him," I said, but my heart was beating fast; I felt elated.

"Do thank him, Cassie."

Waking from his nap, Tom sat up. "You've told her, haven't you, Sarah?"

"Yes, I did."

"Well, mayhap it's for the best."

Sarah smiled at Tom. "Yes, Tom, it is for the best. Cassie should know who her best friend is."

There didn't seem to be anything more to be said; we three sat in silence with our own thoughts. Tom drank his cold coffee. After a while, Tom and Sarah said their good-byes; Sarah whispered to me, "Think about it, Cassie."

I did think about it. Sitting on my porch in the twilight, I watched Sarah and Tom walk across the fields to home.

CHAPTER EIGHTY-SEVEN

Opening day! Sarah knocked at the door of Cassie's tea-shop a minute after seven in the morning. By nine o'clock, her mother's china graced Mama's crisply stiffened embroidered tablecloths.

Here Sarah was, and we were like two magpies, chattering, laughing, and working at the same time to bake lemon cakes and chocolate cookies. Then we sat down and admired my cheerful, pretty tea shop. My dream had come true.

Sarah looked around. "It's so lovely in here, Cassie." Tom appeared at the door, carrying bunches and bunches of lilacs, and he put them in Sarah's arms, which she placed in jugs as centerpieces for our tables. Next, I set the freshly washed porcelain sugar bowls and creamers on the table. Found in the yard among a jumble of throwaway, odd shoes and broken pots, their painted flowers and sprigs of green brought the magic of new growing life to my tea shop.

We hadn't mentioned David since Sarah told me of his work on my tea shop, so my heart leaped when Sarah said, "Tom says he met David as he picked the lilacs this morning, Cassie."

"How does he keep?" I tried to sound as though I wasn't interested.

"He's well. He's home in his cottage. Have you seen him yet?"

"No. I'm not sure I should go there. If he doesn't want me to know he did the work on the tea shop, mayhap he doesn't want to see me again. We did part, Sarah. You know that."

"Cassie, what happened to you?" She sighed, a deep sigh.

"The war happened to me."

"It happened to all of us. Go on and say 'thanks' to David. Before Tom and I leave Cow Neck, I want to know you're happy."

"It's not that simple. I just don't see myself anymore marrying David."

"Who's talking about marriage? I thought you were going to thank him for doing all that work on the tea shop."

"No, not now. I shall write a note to thank him." I picked up a bent fork and replaced it with a shiny straight one. "Happiness is a fleeting thing, don't you think, Sarah?"

"No. I don't. You must pursue happiness, as it says in the Declaration. Remember 'the pursuit of happiness' in the Declaration?"

"I'll think about it, Sarah." Sarah gave another huge sigh.

Two hours later we opened Cassie's tea-shop door. Both Sarah and I had no time to speak of David. We had dressed ourselves in whatever finery we could find. Sarah wore a calico gown of Suzie's, and I wore the gown given to me at General Washington's lunch.

When I saw Sarah in Suzie's gown, I thought of Max who hadn't come home yet. I hoped the soft warmth of the South was comforting for him.

"All my gowns are still too big to wear. I'm so glad for Suzie's gown today," Sarah said.

"Yes, and you look so pretty in it too. I'm sure Suzie would be happy to know you wear it, Sarah."

"I'm not so sure as you, Cassie," Sarah said.

"You heard something more about Suzie?" I asked.

"Just another rumor flying about, that's all."

"What was it?"

Sarah hesitated. Finally, she said, "That Suzie married her British officer in a London church." Sarah stood ready to pour sugar into a fancy bowl. "That is something you should do, Cassie."

"Get married?"

"Yes. You do know David is helping to build small houses for the families. I just thought you might like to know when you stop by to thank him."

"I don't care anymore, Sarah. I wish David the best. And Suzie too. I don't want to see either of them again."

"All right, then, if you feel you must be a mule," Sarah said. "Let's go sit outside for a while. It's beautiful out." It was still early. Sarah had made both scones and apple pies for today's tea, since my pies were still flat, half-baked, fruit-filled dough. They were pitiable. But it was a new day.

"We must move on, Sarah."

"I don't agree. You don't have to move on so soon. Can't you stop and let David know you appreciate what he's done for you?" Sara turned her face to me, waiting for me to answer.

When I did, she turned silent. "David and I are finished. Done, Sarah. I let it go."

We walked in uncomfortable silence in the sunshine a while longer.

Midmorning, we had finished our walk. Sarah put loose tea in strainers over kettles. I cut the cakes into slices and arranged them in a circle on top of a deep blue plate I found in the dim recess of a forgotten cupboard. To myself, I gave thanks that we were able to find and use so many of the tea things, not broken or thrown out or stepped on by the redcoats.

"Well, it's getting toward teatime," Sarah said, too brightly. "The ladies should be stepping out soon. I think we might have every table filled, Cassie." I could see she was putting on an effort to be cheerful.

I laughed. It felt so thin and brittle after our talk. "Every table? We should be rich by afternoon!"

"Cassie, I invited some people." Sarah put down her tea strainer on the warming hob. "I think the ladies might come for a cup of tea, Cassie."

I turned silently from my plate of cake slices, proving I had learned something from our last fight. "Sarah, if they do come, you serve them. All right?"

"I shall," Sarah said. "You won't regret it, Cassie. The ladies will be so happy to have a bit of social tea and talk."

I moved to the mantle, reached up to the vase on the mantle, and lifted a purple lilac down from the cut flowers. I made a space on the cake plate for it. *Fine way to open a tea shop. Serving tea to a roomful of Loyalists. Who would have thought it?*

In they came, more than ten of them, in their gowns worn out with wear, not wearing aprons, and their sleeve ruffles rolled up. Their fingers reddened, they still smiled. All of them. They did look happy to be here. And they wasted no time jumping from topic to topic over their tea and telling each other memories of London. They were eating their cakes with relish, laughing and having a superior good time. They looked around in wonder at the brightness and cheer of the room. I could tell they hadn't had any niceties in a long while.

"Come and meet the people, Cassie." Sarah put her arm through mine and led me to the tables. Some of the ladies' speech sounded London-like. I tried not to frown at them. But after a while, I found myself serving them tea and smiling myself, listening to their comments.

A large lady, who sounded as loud as if she were calling her friend from a hillside two fields away, told her seatmates of an experience she had in London.

"Maeve, d'you remember that corner coffee shop on Curzon Street? I stopped in one day, ordered myself a coffee, and sat down at a table next to two fine gentlemen. Ooh! Didn't they look like they belonged in Parliament? Thinkin' I might learn somethin', I listened to 'em talk. One 'ooz white 'air was down to his shoulders had on a fine waistcoat, made outa broadcloth; I'll bet me last ha'penny on that, and he kept droppin' crumbs all over it 'cause 'e wasn't lookin; he was busy winkin' and smilin' at me. When he did look down over his spectacles to brush off his coat, I couldn't believe it! I was sittin' across from Mr. Benjamin Franklin!" She leaned forward. "Ya could a knocked me over with a feather. Flirtin' with me, the old geezer was. How do you like that, girls?"

"Whud he have to say then, Jackie?"

"Ow! Not much that I could 'eah. Wasn't long after that I read of 'im comin' back to America. Too bloody bad about that, I say. I was wearin' the dress I wore to have a look around in 'arrod's. Sometimes, I do miss me London, though, don't you all?" Jackie trailed off. I kept listening and pouring.

"I don't," answered the lady named Maeve.

"I don't," said a second lady, and most all the ladies agreed.

But one lady speaking very softly said, "Anyway, it wouldn't do to be missing London right about now, would it?" She glanced up at me, waiting for my response.

I surprised her. "Free country now, ladies, speak about anything; our politicians are fair game."

"Well, I never heard you speak so eloquent, Cassie." It was Sarah, passing through. I continued on, pouring tea and slicing up cakes. We were very busy, Sarah and I. The water basin on the pine table in the kitchen was full of china cups and saucers by the time the ladies said good-bye.

"It's over," Sarah said and plopped into a chair. "Here, Cassie, take this."

"What's this?"

"Money. Five pounds sterling. They were too shy to offer you money. The ladies paid me. I never asked for a cent. Did you?"

"No. Happy day, Sarah. Now we can buy new cake plates. Huzzah!"

No matter what Sarah said, I could not make myself go and thank David. But I was lying when I told her I had let the romance with David go. I had not. Every time I thought I would go to Jesse's place and see David to thank him, I got butterflies in my stomach and couldn't do it. But the day came when I could put it off no longer; Sarah told me the houses were all built, and David would leave Long Island to find work somewhere else. He was leaving Cow Neck; I had to go.

First, I would have to make myself pretty. How to accomplish it when the only glass left in the mansion was contorted with a crack down its middle? Then the gown. In the farthest reaches of every closet in the mansion, I looked, but didn't find any old gowns. And I certainly wasn't going to wear the gown I brought home from Hasbrouck House because it was too fine for an afternoon visit to Jesse's barn. There was one place I hadn't looked, a small store room in the shack used as a closet for Hannah when we lived there. Not that she had anything decent, but when I opened the door to the store room, a gown fell out. A taffeta solid rose color gown with a daisy pattern appliqued onto its silk sash. I had never seen the gown before. Papa must have given it to her. It fit me.

A group of children sat on the grass in the sunshine writing in their hornbooks while Miss Hoary stood over them like a watchful mother hen. When she saw me climbing the hill, Miss Hoary ran down the hill and kissed me.

Sarah waved to me from the barn door, calling out to me across the wide expanse of grass. "Cassie. Come inside. I'm right glad to see you. How do you keep?"

Sarah waved me inside the barn. "Come and see the ladies. They haven't stopped talking about the tea you gave them." Sarah led me into the barn where the women sat in little knots, peeling potatoes for the evening meal. Sarah got tea things out for all of us, and the ladies claimed it was their turn to pour for Sarah and me.

Twilight. I stepped out of Jesse's barn, wondering which way was the cabin David was building. But all work had stopped. Candles glowed from the windows of houses on the hill. Everyone was settled in for the night. Whatever was I doing here? I couldn't go through with my plan to see David and thank him.

Early the next morning, I finished up tidying Papa's study, which had been used by one of the British officers for a bedroom. In my pocket, I had put a folded paper with writing I picked up from under the bed amid empty bottles of Jamaican rum, old newspapers the British officer had dropped on the floor, and even an old spittoon full of dried spit, which disgusted me. It was gloomy in Papa's room, and I decided to read what the paper said later on outside in the sunshine.

It was good to sit outside and feel the summer breezes. I thought of the homeless families, now homeless no longer because of people like Jesse, Sarah, and David. People were in need; my friends helped them. *Where have I been?*

I felt in my pocket for the paper I had picked up in Father's study. The writing was unusually large and was no one's that I recognized.

Tom Doggett came loping up the porch steps. I stuck the note back in my pocket.

"Lo, Cassie." Tom Doggett sprawled in a chair.

"Tom! Will you take a cool drink?" He mopped his face with his sleeve, a good, solid homespun.

"No, thank you, Cassie. I wanted to stop to tell you, I just wanted to talk to you about something."

"What is it?" I said. *Why is my first feeling always dread when someone tells me something?*

"First, is your house livable enough now, not perfect the way it was? There's more work to do but…"

"It is perfect to me." *He and Sarah will be leaving soon.*

"Cassie, Sarah and I will leave on October fifteenth, before the roads become impassable."

"I knew it would come soon. Sarah must be very happy," I said, feeling my stomach drop.

Next evening, Tom, Sarah, and I sat in my dining room, planning her marriage to Tom in the little wooden church down by the water. "I shall wear my mother's wedding dress. Think of it, Cassie. On October fifteenth, we shall set out for Ohio. I can't wait." Sarah's eyes danced in the candlelight.

"And we two shall be married!" Tom said.

"Yes, Tom." She reached over and caught Tom around the neck and then kissed him. Sarah wore a lavender taffeta gown that framed her deep blue eyes, and she had fixed her hair in a mass of curls around her face. Tom Doggett could not seem to take his eyes from her.

"What about your house, Sarah?" I asked.

"I'm not selling it after all, Cassie. Betsy Rose Thayer and her mother and father will live in it for now. So it's all settled. And I'm so pleased."

That night I stayed up late sorting Papa's papers. I felt in my pocket for the key to his secretary; the paper I had put in my pocket yesterday and forgotten to read fell out. I held it up to the candle light; the handwriting was unfamiliar. The note was dated July 24, 1783, written over Hannah's signature.

Cassie, I cannot forbear to tell you of the grief I feel and the grief I know you will feel at the passing of your father. Your father did not recover fully from his time on the prison ship. Even though the best doctors attended him here, the harsh treatment he received on board the prison ship caused his death yesterday, July 23, 1783. His last days were filled with thoughts of you. He missed you dearly. I miss you too. I shall stay here in Essex, Connecticut. I live in the household of a very fine, amiable couple. I am their housekeeper. I do intend to go back to New York City and hope to get work at Mrs. Curry's Inn, when I feel up to traveling. I hope you are well and prospering now that the war is over. Someday I hope to see you again.

I sat with the paper in my hand. *Papa is dead almost a year. And I didn't even know.*

Hammering from the barn. Next day after I put a CLOSED sign on the tea-shop door, I walked into the barn, holding the letter. Tom Doggett was replacing a plank in the floor. I sat down on a milking stool opposite him. I handed him the letter.

"My father is dead, Tom; he has been for a year."

He set down his tools and wiped his hands on his thick overalls; he then took the letter I held out to him and read silently. "He was a fine man, Cassie."

"He was, Tom. Papa's been gone a whole year, and I never knew," I said, feeling again the awful knowledge. I felt the tears falling. I felt I couldn't breathe.

Tom shook his head in sorrow. "Let me go and get Sarah, Cassie. She'll stay with you awhile."

"No. I'm going to walk." I stood up and took the letter from Tom's hands.

Nothing mattered anymore, not for days, not for weeks.

I read and reread Hannah's letter until the water marks from my tears completely smeared the words so I couldn't read them. I couldn't come up out of the darkness. My time was spent sitting in the rocker hours each day, seeing no one, even though Sarah and Miss Hoary and Tom came by every day. They knocked and left food inside the front door for me. I only left the mansion to tend to the animals. Some days I didn't wash my face or run the brush through my hair. But I did eat the food.

On October 15, David and Sarah married. I didn't have the spirit to attend, but I watched from the porch as the decorated farm carriage carried them away from Cow Neck. They waved and waved; I waved back. It was useless to cry at their leave-taking. I had no more tears.

It happened while I sat on the porch. Squeezed in, winking pink and purple, between two planks in the porch floor, was my opal ring. I stared down at it and then ran to get a knife to fit between the planks. The stone, when I was finally able to slide it out and hold it in the palm of my hand, was not injured, but the metal part framing it was twisted . . . *I shall give it back to David. It was his mother's ring, and since we were apart, he should have it.* I must walk to Jesse's barn and hand it to David, and at the same time I would thank him for his work on the tea shop. I must.

Suddenly, so bright was the sunlight when I got out on the road the next day, I had to close my eyes for a few seconds to get used to the splendor of it. Papa's death had knocked everything else from my mind. Yes, I needed the bright sunlight to get away from sorrow.

The families were still on Jesse's hillside. Up and down the hill, children played and ran, threw balls to one another, and raced each other across Jesse's grass. Higher up on the hillside, men hammered pegs into half-built cabins and huts.

Watching from the shelter of an old crumbling cabin storing rakes and hoes, I watched the men work and the women hang clothes on a wash line while children ran, playing tag through the wet sheets. Mrs. Fanshawe came out of the barn and rang a cowbell. Instantly, children stopped running after each other; they dropped their sticks and balls; men put down their tools, and all hurried across the grass to Jesse's barn for a midday meal.

One fellow stayed behind to shovel out some dirt in front of a just completed hut. He wore pressed overalls with a faded red flannel shirt and a woolen cap. My breath came quickly: it was David—tall, clean shaven, and full of strength.

He came striding down the hillside still holding his shovel, jolting to a stop in front of me. "Cassie! What are you doing here?" He waited, his face a study of what? Hope? annoyance, interest? I couldn't tell. He dug his shovel into a mound of dirt.

"I was passing." I tried for a cheerful tone.

"Would you like to see the inside of one of these little cabins?"

"I would, but won't they be missing you in the barn?"

"They'll save me a plate. Come on." He walked me toward the little house. Once inside, I was struck by how tight and comfortable it looked. "Will you sit?" He motioned me to sit down at a hand-hewn table. "What do you think?

"I think anyone would be proud to live here. It's cozy."

"Jesse and I built it in a week." There was pride in David's voice. "I like helping these people; they're very grateful." Conversation became scarce between us.

I felt I must say something. "You look very well," I said.

"I am very well. Thanks to Tom and Sarah, people in town accept me now. They know the truth about me; I worked for America in the war."

"I'm glad for you, David."

"Thanks. Well, you walked quite a way down here."

"Actually, I didn't just pass by. I've come here to say thank-you for rebuilding the shack into my tea shop."

"Oh, that. I asked Sarah and Tom not to tell you."

"Why?"

"I wanted you to have a good start." David looked at the floor. "No need to blast it around."

"I'm very grateful to you," I said. "Thank you."

"You're welcome. By the way, knowing what you think of Tories, it must have been hard for you to come here."

"I feel these people have paid the price for their betrayal."

David nodded. "You still think they betrayed us, Cassie. You're wrong; they were loyal to their king. But never mind; I reckon my telling you will not change your mind." He opened the door for me.

"Wait. I wanted to give you this." I held out the opal ring in my palm.

David looked down at it. "Why, it's all twisted. What happened?"

"I don't know. It was stuck between two floorboards on the porch. Probably, some redcoat stepped on it." We both looked down at the opal reflecting the sun. "It's a survivor," I said and smiled at David.

"I'll fix it." He hammered out the twists in the gold and fitted it on my finger where it shined luminously. "You wear it, Cassie." For a second, a look of tenderness came into his face. The feelings I had for David came back to me, and I looked at him with all the love I used to feel.

"David, couldn't we just step away from what's happened to us, as though there never was a war? Couldn't we forget?"

"I don't think we can," he said, looking at me.

At the door, I turned to him. "I don't care anymore what you did in the war."

He shook his head. "Yes, you do. Everyone in town believes me except you. You will always think of me as a traitor."

"But it doesn't matter to me," I said, looking up at him.

"It matters to me." He closed the door. We walked down the hill. We parted at the barn doors. "Good-bye, Cassie." It was easier this time to walk away from him.

CHAPTER EIGHTY-EIGHT

David Van Essen got off the ferry at Coenties Slip and went to stand on the corner of Wall and Nassau Streets. He realized how rustic he looked in his overalls and homespun shirt, wearing boots whose soles were papered with cardboard, but the sight of soldiers like himself walking the streets was common to the people of York City since the war had ended. Here on Wall Street, he couldn't quite meet the eyes of men in top hats, morning coats, and polished boots, as passing opposite him they looked supremely confident before disappearing through the huge glass doors of stores and restaurants. Sometimes, these men searched in their pockets for coins. David saw what was coming and would shuffle along with his head down and hands in his pockets to avoid the hand-out.

To his right, the pillars of City Hall gleamed in the sunlight. To his left, the Tontine coffee shop beckoned to him. He was hungry. The coffee shop was just as good a place to begin looking for work as any other.

The shop was empty except for a young man who stood with his back to David, over a huge pail of soapy water resting on a long wooden counter set off on each end with a candle lantern. The fellow washed pewter tankards and bowls with care, setting them down carefully on a clean, dry cloth, then dried each of them. The soft splashes of water against the pewter were the only sounds in the room. The interior of the shop was cavernous, filled with a deep gloom relieved only by the flickering light of the candle lanterns. Another pile of dirty dishes waited on the counter for the washing tub.

"Say, mate, got any coffee left?"

"Might if you wait." The fellow didn't look up. But the sound of his voice was familiar.

"I can wait. Just got off the ferry. Got no place to go. I'm looking for work."

"Been tough here. Lots of people looking."

David still couldn't see the fellow's face, just his back. *Where had he heard this voice before and this clipped way of speaking, not giving away a spare word? In the army, yes. That's where. There was a fellow spy in the kitchen of the Morgan House to whom he passed on information. What was his name?*

"Say, you wouldn't be Luke Welch?"

"I be him. Who be you?"

"David Van Essen." The fellow turned. David stuck out his hand. "Staten Island, the kitchen of the Morgan House. I passed you stuff."

"Right. The kitchen." Luke Welch wiped his hands on the rough wool of his shirt, turned, reached over the counter, and stuck out his hand. The two men shook. "I reckon we were damn lucky not to get caught in that little adventure."

"Amen." David said. "Say, let me help you, Luke. I got nothing else to do."

"That's all right. Sit down," he said, while pouring coffee into two pewter mugs. One he set down in front of David, the other for himself. He straddled the long bench opposite David. "This here coffee comes by way of the swells who pay through the nose for breakfast," he said.

"Thanks. It's good." David took long sips of the hot coffee.

"I've got nothing much to do here. This job is just what you see, washing dishes and sweeping the floor. I'm out of here by ten o'clock."

Over cups of coffee and leftover muffins, each told his story. Luke, not dismissed from duty, simply slipped away from Staten Island in a stolen rowboat in the disorder that followed the cessation of hostilities. He never went home to Huntington but stayed in the city, drifting from menial job to menial job. He could never seem to connect for long, he told David. "What about you?"

"I got back to Cow Neck a month before Evacuation Day, November twenty-third, 1783. There was a girl there. We planned to marry when I came back from the fighting. But I was recruited for General Washington's spy network early in '76. It was made known around town to protect me that I was a turncoat for the British so if I met any Loyalist from Long Island when I arrived on Staten Island, I would be believed. When I came home after the war I was a pariah in Cow Neck; no one spoke to me. The girl I loved didn't believe that I worked for General Washington. She thought me a spy for the redcoats. Simple as that. Even now, when the town has accepted me as an American soldier, she believes I spied for the British."

Lucas Welch folded his arms and looked down. He finally looked up. "And here we are."

"Yeah. Here we are," David said. After a time, he asked, "What do you do with yourself all day? Look for work?"

"I did for a while. Now, I mostly sit in the park, nap, read the paper, think. I meet a lot of people like myself, down on their luck after the fighting." Luke gave a short laugh. "I'm lucky I got some kind of work." He took a last sip of his coffee and then looked around at the empty tables and chairs. His half-smile was almost an apology. "This kind of life sure don't have the same excitement as you had spying for General Washington."

"That's all gone. Say, I have some money. I saved it working as a carpenter after the war. Why don't we team up and see what we can manage to do?"

"Only thing I can do is cook. And I know how to run a kitchen. I did it in the war." Luke Welch resumed washing the pewter plates and coffee things.

"Right! I can do carpentry. Together, we could make money." David looked up at the ceiling timbers and the planked walls; here and there knots of wood had eroded and left holes open to the air. "I could do even better than this," he said.

Luke smiled. "I'd have to find something to do in the way of cooking and you in carpentry."

"What about an abandoned shack or a driftwood house we could fix up and sell?"

Luke gave David a penetrating look. "If you could fix it up, an abandoned cabin would do nicely. We could open a restaurant, mayhap."

"We could, but not here. I'm thinking mayhap some town along the North River just getting built up."

"That's it then. Let's go find some kind of falling down, bone-less wonder out there."

David sipped his coffee. He waited a few seconds. "Bet north of here there's plenty of lots with standing structures ready to cave in."

"How far north?"

"Upriver. I'm thinkin' of a place called Ward's Bridge. You got your taverns there. Some of 'em built way before the war, in 1710's; and '20's, in the '50s. You got your lumber yard there. And you got stands of trees just waitin' to be cut down and built into houses. It's a growin' place. I heard tell of a book store there." David took out a small pocket notebook he used when he worked for Jesse Prouty. He wrote down: *Land, wood, hammers, saws, levelers.* "Well, what are we waiting for? Let's go," David said, pocketing his notebook.

"Yeah. First, I have to pick up my stuff in the shelter. I got a bed there. Twenty-five cents a night."

CHAPTER EIGHTY-NINE

Night. Deepest, darkest night. "Where are we?"

"We'll have to climb this hill. Ain't no way of gettin' around it. You can just make out the river down there. It's kind of a darker dark than the land. We should be close to the town." They spoke in soft voices, neither admitting to the other that the noises and branch-cracking sounds coming from the woods surrounding them struck fear of wild animals through their very bones.

Finally, dawn. Luke rummaged around in a pack he had brought, pulled out a thin homespun shirt, and shouldered himself into it. Together, they made their way down the hill.

"This town looks good. Don't it?" He picked up David's pack from the ground and handed it to him.

"Ward's Bridge. We're here." They dropped their packs on a shelf of rock jutting out under the bridge and looked to where the river snaked off into a wide creek as long as the eye could see, banked on both sides by thick trees, bushes, and swamps and enveloped by a cobalt-blue sky. The bridge they stood under held a sign tacked up on a wood stanchion lettered "Ward's Bridge, home of General Montgomery, late of these parts and an American hero in the war." The bridge itself was a leaky wooden pile.

"Glad I'm goin' under it and I ain't crossin' over it," Luke muttered. "Come on, we'll look for an abandoned cabin."

"Don't have to look far. See beyond that maple tree?" David began to walk across a cornfield to the maple tree. "It faces on the water. C'mon, Luke."

"Why, that wreck don't have walls or framing posts. What could we do with it? It's just a floor."

"It's a start. Let's get the trees down first; then I'll make posts, and we'll set them up. I can turn this thing into a prize winner. Have you got an adz, Luke?"

"A what?" Luke said.

"Just joking. Never mind. Can you fetch me my axe stickin' out of my pack? Meantime, I'll start peeling bark."

"Yes, sir! I'll get that axe." Luke took it on the double and was back in a few seconds; by then David had a quarter of the bark peeled. It was a small-size tree, almost still a sapling, but when it was safely cut down and they counted the rings, it measured twenty-five years.

David whistled. "She sure didn't look that old. Good wood. Maple."

The house on the water in Ward's Bridge was their first house. They lived in it for six months while they built two more houses and were in contract for another two. By then, David had a new suit and new shoes, and Luke had new knickers and plenty of homespun shirts that girls in town had sewed up for him.

CHAPTER NINETY

Spring Beekman Place, 1785

"I don't like whortleberries." Cassie stood in the center of the dining room in her New York City mansion, with the palm of her hand pressed flat against the grain of the polished mahogany table, looking down at the dish of berries and cream sitting there.

"Sorry, milady." The young servant, Lucy, stood biting her lower lip, struggling to hold on to the morning newspaper, half of which had fallen to the carpet from her trembling hands.

"This is America, Lucy. Please leave off the 'milady' and call me 'Miss.'" Cassie pulled out the chair and sat down, straightening the silverware that had been laid clumsily on the gleaming white lace tablecloth. "Will you bring eggs, please?"

"Yes, miss. Coffee, mi'lad...Miss?"

"Yes, please."

The servant, Lucy, hurried over to the coffee urn on the sideboard and poured coffee to the very brim of the cup so that it sloshed all over the saucer as she set it down on the table. Lucy stepped back and tried to mop up the coffee spill already staining the tablecloth. "Saints preserve us! I'll pour another cup, Miss."

"It's all right. Just set about the eggs, will you, Lucy?" Cassie looked up and saw a tear roll down Lucy's cheek. *It's only two days since she stepped off the boat from Ireland. She's trying to get things right. Where will she go if I dismiss her? She'll be on the street.* Cassie gathered up her napkin under her saucer and wiped up the spills. "Don't worry, Lucy, you'll be fine here."

"Yes, miss. I shall get the eggs."

"Do. That's a good girl." After she watched Lucy's back retreat from the room, Cassie added cream and sipped her coffee while looking out the windows at the carriages following each other in stately procession along Beekman Place, most of them destined for Wall Street, carrying men of the moneyed class. *The class I now belong to,* she thought. Early on this warm June day, a few young mothers sat out on the grass with their babies and chatted. Soon they were joined by others who sat their babies up to enjoy the spectacle of boats sailing up and down the river.

Through the open windows, Cassie felt the soft breezes and heard the mothers' laughter. She rested her elbows on the table and then dropped her head into her hands. At first the blue sky, the green grass, the mothers—colorful in their fine calico shifts, playing with their babies on the grass while chatting in the glow of a brand-new summer day—presented such a pretty tableau out on the lawn it had made her smile. No doubt, the women were children of Dutch landowners. Did they know hardships during the war? She didn't think so. They spoke English and Dutch fluently and must have spent the war years in leisure and indolence in the great houses of the Dutch landowners upstate. Most likely, these ladies had not seen the bloody battlefields and stark cemeteries with makeshift crosses and never hunted through garbage looking for scraps of food either.

Yet here I am, as rich as anyone of those girls. Papa had left me the mansion and a trough of pounds sterling—enough money to keep me in wealth for all my life. The envelope had been dropped off informing me of my inheritance by the post rider from the lawyers in Connecticut. Filled with thick pages of small print, I learned I was heiress to half of Papa's fortune built through years of practicing law. Hannah was bequeathed the other half. Max had been bequeathed the Mansion.

I was leaving Cow Neck for York City, where I had bought a house facing the river in the same block as Suzie's grandparents. Everyone I held dear was gone from Cow Neck—my father, dead; Max, settled in Florida; my Ernest, killed in the war; Suzie, married to her redcoat in London; Sarah and Tom, to Ohio; Old Eban, dead.

When I found out Hannah had been remembered by Papa, I was actually glad, for Hannah had taken good care of Papa; *she must miss him just as much as I do.*

Buying the mansion on Beekman Place was an irresistible impulse. I had to leave to get away from the places that reminded me of David. He was gone from Cow Neck, but every time I walked along the creek I saw his rowboat still resting up against the outside cottage wall. Every time I passed his cottage from the road, I saw the same empty chairs on the porch.

After Tom and Sarah left, I finished restoring Scott Mansion to its former beauty from the great damage inflicted on it by the British; I then closed the mansion up, not taking the furnishings or the pictures on the wall or any of the valuables. That day, I left a note in the tea shop, ceding the shop to the Tory ladies I had befriended at Jesse Prouty's place. I cut off all ties to Cow Neck the day I left with only the clothes on my back.

At first, when I moved to the city, I attended all the salons and chatted with all the young men. I even went with them to the plays of Mr. Shakespeare in the John Street Theater. I bought silks and satins to be sewn into formal gowns from the tailor Laboyteux, who, when I came into the store now, brought out a velvet-covered chair for me to view selections from. I dined out of Limoges china and drank wine out of crystal glasses in City Tavern now with all my young admirers. I wished Hannah would come and see me. I was bored, bored, bored.

This beautiful mansion facing the river I bought with Papa's money was to be a brand-new start for me. But in the end, it failed me because it was not mine. There were no memories here. None of my people had been entertained here. I pushed my coffee cup away, laid my arms on the tablecloth, dropped my head into my hands, and cried, I had not done so in years.

It was something about the mothers out on the grass; these ladies had married rich men with homes on the river and lived on estates up north of New York. But I was rich too. So that wasn't why I cried. It didn't matter if a man was rich; David wasn't rich, neither was Jem Clarke. Both were hardworking; both had loved me.

What happened? I was rich, but was not married, and I had not a child. I should be married, and I should have a child. I was twenty-four years old.

Enough. Most importantly, I have money. The ladies had moved with their babies, following the river. I stood up and began to clear the table. And it was in the act of cleaning up that Miss Hoary found me.

"Good morning, Cassie." Miss Hoary's eyebrows shot up. "Isn't that Lucy's job?"

"Yes. I keep forgetting. You slept well, Miss Hoary?"

Miss Hoary sat down at a place setting across the table from me. "I did. It's lovely here, Cassie. This house was a good choice."

"I suppose. Let me get you some coffee." I brought the cup and saucer over to the urn and poured. For a few seconds, there was just the soft clatter of spoons stirring sugar into porcelain cups of coffee.

"What shall we do today? Would you like to walk down Wall Street and have lunch at a restaurant there?"

Miss Hoary didn't answer right away. She lifted her cup and drank. "Cassie, would you think it amiss if I go home? I've been here two weeks."

"But I love having you here. Don't go."

"Truthfully, it's been wonderful here in New York City, seeing all those plays with you and chatting at the salons, and even buying new gowns at the shops. Meeting new people...but Cassie, I miss Long Island. I miss home." It was then that Miss Hoary looked into my eyes. "You've been crying, Cassie. Why"

I lifted my lace-edged sleeve to my face. "It's nothing."

"It's something if it makes you cry. Come home with me, Cassie. Stay with me and my sister."

"I don't think going back to Cow Neck is the answer for me."

"To what?" Miss Hoary laid her cup down carefully. "The answer to what, Cassie?"

"That I'm terribly bored. I bought this house, and all these beautiful furnishings, with the money Papa left me, thinking it would make me happy. I gave the tea shop away, and I'm not sorry. It didn't hold my interest after it became successful. But I'm not happy. And I have nothing to do, except to go to all of those silly salons and balls and dancing, with all those tiresome, leftover Englishmen, and watch plays, though I do sometimes let them distract me."

On the river, boats sailed up and down under a peaceful blue sky. Cassie picked up her cup and drank. "Come, Miss Hoary, let's go out and walk. There's so many places to eat lunch around here, and then we can watch the boats come in from Europe. I believe the *Globe* says the *Oceania* is due into the bay this morning. Shall we?"

CHAPTER NINETY-ONE

"Buttermilk Falls," Miss Hoary said at dinner, though neither she nor Cassie had spoken in the moments before. "I've been thinking all afternoon about Buttermilk Falls. You must go back, Cassie. That's where you must go."

Cassie's mood this evening was different from that at breakfast. She had napped two hours in the afternoon and then brushed her hair until it shone in the sun. She was wearing a new shift of pale lavender muslin.

"Why do you say that?" She stopped and looked directly at Miss Hoary.

"Because you left there with unfinished business. Go back and take care of it; you'll feel better, I believe." Miss Hoary got up from the table. "I shall sit on the porch and take in the air for a while," she said smiling, "while you think about going to Buttermilk Falls."

Miss Hoary's sabbaticals in the sun, as she called them, usually lasted for an hour or so. Cassie had time to walk through the rooms of Crow's Nest. With its enormous high ceilings, two huge kitchens, one for baking and one for preparing meals; a parlor twice the size of the parlor at home in Scott Mansion; four bed-rooms; and a birthing room, the house was enormous. Richly fur-nished with velvet drapes, Parisian carpets, and fine mahogany dressers, Crow's Nest had china closets that held fine Limoges dinner sets and crystal goblets as well. Cassie moved from room to room, smoothing a bedspread and placing a vase of roses to show to better advantage on a dresser, but just under the surface of her thoughts was the phrase Miss Hoary used: "You must go to Buttermilk Falls." *But should I? Yes. I should. Joanna. How could I have left her alone for so long? Of course, I should go. I will go.* Now, sitting at the burnished teak secretary with all its pigeonholes filled with of-ficial papers from her purchase of Crow's Nest, gazing out on the twilight, some sun streaks still resting across the horizon, she knew she must go to Buttermilk Falls, if only to see Joanna and yes, to see how Jem Clarke was keeping.

The coach to Buttermilk Falls left from Cedar Street at six o'clock the following morning. Cassie was on it, her portmanteau so full Miss Hoary had had to sit on the cover to make it close while Cassie snapped the locks.

CHAPTER NINETY-TWO

David Van Essen struck his axe into the deep cut he'd already made into the trunk of an ancient sugar maple, straightened up, and wiped his face with his shirt.

Luke stumbled down the path to the grove of maples, breathing hard. "I've got us a job. We're to build a cottage downriver a way for a man who owns property facing the river. It's to be ready for his family in three weeks."

"When do we start?"

"Soon as you draw up the plans."

"That'll be right now. You take over chopping; I'll draw up the plans. How many rooms?"

"Just the kitchen, parlor, and two rooms for beds. They have two children, the father told me when we signed the paper in the General Store." Luke fished the paper out of his pocket and handed it to David.

Signed by one John Fallows and by Lucas Welch on the line underneath, the agreement provided for a cottage of four rooms to be built fifty feet up from the banks of the river on the site of the big bend in the town of Ward's Bridge. The amount to be paid to the builders was written in both numbers and words—$200.

David whistled, long and loud. Both David and Luke found it hard to believe their good fortune so soon after the war when so many soldiers returning to Ward's Bridge were poor as church mice. Luke had found someone to love. But David had not.

Well, this was the new life that I picked for myself. Money coming in. Yet I miss the old one before the war, when Cassie and I were sweethearts. I have got to get over this constant thinking of her, this longing to see her. After all, I sent her away. And then I went away. His sorrow about Cassie knew no bounds. But still he was grateful for the work. Work was the only thing that saved him.

On paper, the new house looked livable. On the ground, it looked prosperous and well placed. Built of maple, its chimney of brick, ancient trees shading the roof, the view from the porch across the river was peaceful. Inside, David planned a kitchen hearth to fill up one entire wall with stones from the fields. The clean smell of the outside brought by the fresh wood and stone inside appealed to anyone who came into the house. "The best cottage on the water," Luke said to the workmen who rode out from town to fit the last fieldstone into the fireplace.

Word got around. David and Luke found it hard to keep up with the demand to build cottages both near the water and in the town. *It's an odd feeling to have earned so much money over the course of only three summers and autumns,* David thought. And it didn't seem to make much difference in his living style. He lived much as he lived in Cow Neck.

Books, a fire, walks in the woods, work—in this way a year passed. David's main interest was in reading anything written about the war he could get his hands on.

Luke took to riding into town on Saturday nights when snow was packed down well on the paths and trails. He never missed a grange dance if he could help it, for there he knew he would dance with a certain young lady.

"Might as well come with me to the grange sooner than stay home and listen to the wolves howl," Luke said one Saturday night.

"No. I've got stuff to do. I'll be busy."

Luke persisted, "What stuff?"

"Contracts. I've been studying contracts."

"Why?"

"Because I'd like to buy more land myself here. Most of this land was under charter to the king of England.

"The king is done here." Luke stood by the door. "Come on, ride into town. There's pretty girls there." Luke stood in the doorway, eager to get riding himself.

"I'll study, but thanks," David said, looking up. "Next week I'll go."

After a while, Luke brought the young lady to the Forge—as he and David had christened their house—to meet David, who looked at Tessa Mobray with her long, sun-bleached hair. *So much like Cassie's hair.* With a jolt, David turned away from Tessa to hide the quick sadness in his heart. Only weeks after that meeting, David and Luke were building a cottage for Luke and his bride-to-be, Tessa, on the water a mile downriver.

June 4, 1786

Inside the country church on a hazy Saturday morning, Luke and David waited for Tessa. Soon, a flurry of bejeweled and bedecked girls with shining, glittering barrettes in their hair and brooches pinned onto the bodice of their gowns of silk and taffeta arrived to stand in the back of the church to welcome Tessa and to guide her parents to sit in the front pews to be close to the bridal couple. And then the ceremony was over and the party afterward, and David was alone in his house.

Every year on Fourth of July, the town celebrated the Declaration of Independence with fireworks, fairs, and music. David and Luke with Tessa and their one-year old George were a great part of the festivities, along with other returned soldiers of the American Revolution. *It is a good life,* David reflected, as he sat on his porch in the evening of July 4, 1787, watching the stars come out. He still harbored the old longing for Cassie; for three years he had missed her with his whole heart, but now he was able, not to forget her, but to face his memories of her with a gentle recognition that they two had somehow just missed each other and had gone past each other in life. Someday soon he would, as Luke had done, look for a wife for himself up here in the country.

CHAPTER NINETY-THREE

"All off for Buttermilk Falls!" the horses' clopping stopped. There was dead silence on the road: even the tree branches filled with summer foliage stood silent and still. From the gloom of the carriage interior, Cassie saw lying just ahead small farms with fields of green corn as far as the eye could see. It had not been an easy ride; ruts and holes in the winter-weakened dirt road jounced the carriage up and down so that the other three passengers in the stage slept with their heads lolling against each other, mouths open. In the crowded nearness, Cassie inched herself along to the door held open for her, trying not to bump into knees or dislodge shoulders. She stepped a foot down to the lower step, where she allowed herself to be helped to the ground. The coachman pulled her portmanteau from the space between his seat and the carriage itself and dropped it on the path. He tipped his hat, sat in his box seat, and gave the whip to his horses. "Town's just there," he yelled back, pointing to the left with the back of his hand, "beyond the cornfield."

There was no carrying the portmanteau: she stowed it behind a bush and began to walk through the rows of corn, waving her arms to disperse the bugs flying through the corn, until the rows ended and a road emerged where stores and offices vied with one another for the brightest, most vibrant signs.

McCullough & McCullough, the sign said in dignified six-inch letters, putting one in mind of black robes, powdered wigs, and low, dignified speech. A sense of reassurance seemed to flow from the stately sign, giving the illusion to passersby that everything wrong could be set right if one were just to consult the lawyers in the gloom-shrouded offices behind the burnished teak doors. Next to the sign was a row of portraits of lawyers of the firm, one of which was a smiling Jem Clarke. Cassie stared at it for a moment, remembering . . .

Next door to the law firm, Painless Parker's dentist sign jutted out, revealing an upper and lower set of overlarge wooden teeth inside a red-roofed tunnel seeming to have a dark throat behind it.

The last stone building spelled out the title MAYOR'S OFFICE in large black letters on the pediment. *It was right here that Jem Clarke called me out for hitching Joanna's horse to the mayor's post.* Cassie didn't know why, but she had the most insane urge to cry and felt tears squeezing from her eyes. Wiegand's Tavern still stood in isolated splendor next to the mayor's office, and more memories flooded her mind: *How many times had she been here with Joanna, with Jem, in the winters at Christmas, the day the war ended, or just for a glass of sarsaparilla with Joanna on the way to somewhere?* The sign was new since she had left, and it stood out from the wooden structure with its painted glass of amber cider beer along with little flecks of lacy foam flying around the glass held up to the lips of a smiling, jovial head, the whole mounted on a blue board.

How much she had missed this town of Buttermilk Falls; how glad she was to be back. She must hurry along the path to Joanna's cottage. She must get there soon. She must tell Joanna she was here to stay a long, long time.

CHAPTER NINETY-FOUR

B ut when Cassie walked along the road and finally came to Joanna's cottage, she found it quiet, empty, and dark. She peered inside the kitchen window and saw the bird cage, its door flung open as though the little canary had just flown out of it. The path down to the water was completely overgrown with weeds. In the back of the cottage, the kitchen garden lay fallow with burnt dead stalks sticking up from the ground.

"No need to look any further; she's not here." Jem Clarke came walking around the corner of the barn, smiling. "How are you, Cassie? I was working real early in my office and saw you from my window walk out of the cornfield. I decided to come out here after you. I surprised you, I . . . think. Sorry."

"Jem." She swallowed. Sound came out. "I'm very glad to see you."

"And I, you. Come inside. I'll tell you the news."

"Where is Joanna?"

"She's at the Old Place. It's a falling-down house where people go when they get too old to take care of themselves."

"I shall go and get her and bring her home, and I shall take care of her. I don't know how I could have stayed away so long. She took care of me once; she saved my life."

"She can't come home, Cassie. She's...she can't walk."

"Oh, Jem, I should have come sooner."

"Don't blame yourself. It's no one's fault. She's old and she's sick. I don't think she realizes what kind of place she's in. I couldn't take care of her because I work for McCullough now, and I've got plenty of cases. Come, I'll take you back to town, and you can have lunch with me at Wiegand's. Then I'll take you to see her. Will you come?"

"Yes." Cassie felt as though she had no limbs. She followed Jem back to town, barely speaking.

Inside Wiegand's, it was lunchtime, and many of the people who worked in Buttermilk Falls, now sitting at the little circular tables covered with white cloths, remembered her and waved to Cassie. She waved to them all while fresh tears wet her eyes, which she struggled to hide. Soon she had a plate of fried oysters and hot buttered cabbage, which she picked at while Jem ate his mutton chop with gusto.

"So, Cassie, tell me what you have been doing since the war ended and you left Buttermilk Falls." She couldn't help but admire Jem's avoiding any talk of his destroyed marriage plans or her leave-taking of Joanna.

Cassie strove to answer Jem with enthusiasm. "I opened up a tea shop. And I put my father's house to rights after the British had almost ruined it. After I learned my papa died the last year of the war, I sold Scott Mansion and bought a house on Beekman Place in New York City."

Jem put his fork down and reached across the table to put his hand on top of Cassie's. "I'm sorry about your father."

Cassie nodded. Papa's death was still too new in her mind to bring up and talk about. "And you, Jem?"

"I'm a lawyer."

"I'm glad you stayed and did that." She stirred the cup of coffee the waiter brought to her. "And you married?"

"No. I didn't. Not yet, anyway. Are you married, Cassie?"

"No." Cassie stirred her coffee.

After a pause, Jem said, "Just about everyone else I know is rushing to the altar. Are we war casualties, Cassie?"

"No. We're survivors."

"How bleakly you say that."

"It's true, but I feel bleak sometimes." She looked up. "I'm sorry. I'm so upset Joanna's in a bad way. I can't…I can't. I want to see her, Jem. Can we go now?"

"Yes. We shall." He got up from the table. "And tomorrow, if you're still intent on taking Joanna home, I'll help clean up her cottage, and when that's done, we shall bring her back home."

They walked out the door of Wiegand's. "You can make the decision to take her home after you see her, but I warn you; it won't be easy for you to take care of her. Come on." Jem Clarke stood up. He took Cassie's hand as they walked uphill to Old Place. There was no thrill as there used to be when Jem took her hand. "I shall make arrangements for a room for you after you've seen Joanna." He smiled down at her.

Walking, Cassie looked at Jem with new eyes when most of the folks they passed on the road waved and shouted "hellos" to Jem. "They all like you, Jem. You've done well."

"I've probably defended all of them in local disputes," Jem said. Cassie looked at the cut of his suit. The way he wore his jacket, swinging away from his slim body in the European style, was the way she'd seen prosperous men walk along Wall Street. Cassie let her thoughts idle. *I could have married him. But I didn't love him. I didn't know it then, but I do now. Joanna, dear Joanna, how could I think of anyone else at this moment? I shall take care of you.*

Jem took her arm as the two wound their way up the squeaky steps of Old Place's wooden porch. Cassie heard a low, muffled sound as though someone inside closed something with finality. Otherwise, all was silent. Around the low, narrow entrance door, rooms squirreled crookedly at different heights from each other, giving the appearance that at any moment the whole structure would topple in on itself. Old Place surrendered to creaking and moaning as if protesting the suffering it was obliged to bear in its final journey to destruction.

Jem knocked. From inside came a vicious pull: the jammed door swung open with accompanying wrenches, guttural sounds, and muttered curses. A woman dressed in a servant's shift, cap, and apron led them to Joanna's room, where she lay under a faded, ripped cover full of holes, most of it falling to the floor. An empty glass sat on top of some boards doweled together to form a crude dresser. A spotted mobcap hung over the edge of a dry sink, its once white strings rested on the floor. Joanna's eyes were trained on the ceiling. "Joanna. It's Cassie." She picked up the cover from the floor and put it over Joanna. "I shall come to get you tomorrow."

Joanna turned her head, looked at Cassie, and whispered, "I knew you would."

When Jem and Cassie came to take Joanna out of Old Place next morning, she was sitting up in a soft chair, wearing a clean shift and mobcap. Her face was washed and her eyes were clear. *She's so small. I remember her being tall and healthy.* Cassie smiled down at Joanna. "Are you ready to come home, Joanna?"

"More than ready." Both Jem and Cassie noticed her voice was still loud and vigorous.

CHAPTER NINETY-FIVE

The grange hall on Saturday night was crowded with farmers wearing work shirts, clean breeches, and boots polished up to a shine, free of the stiff, dried mud acquired from the day's herding of cows. *They could be boys from home, farmers,* Cassie thought. Jem Clarke waved to them but steered Cassie away to a knot of young men dressed in string ties, white vests, and waistcoats over broadcloth knickers. *Lawyers, like Jem.* She wished she could pass some time with the homespun fellows. But it was not to be; Jem's interest lay with the lawyers.

The band played. All chatter stopped as couples stepped out for a rousing horn blower; the crowd went wild with dancing until the crossbeams shook with the motion and energy of a hundred pairs of boots and silk shoes jumping, hard-stepping and skipping, and then parading across the wooden plank floor. Even the wildflowers in their bowls waved back and forth.

Girls, some wives, some sweethearts, some on the edge of spinsterhood, their faces bright, their eyes shining, and their gowns swirling with the energy of the dance, commanded attention.

Cassie saw Jem watch the dance, tapping his shiny black lawyer's boots to the rhythm of the music. He seemed very removed from her as he trained his eyes on a girl with black, curly hair dressed in a red gown standing quite alone on the edge of the crowd near the door, almost as though she were waiting for someone.

Jem looked down at Cassie. "That's Rebecca Quiney. Would you take it amiss if I danced with her, Cassie?"

"No. Go, Jem. Dance with her." For a second she felt hurt. But it was all right; after all, their romance was in the past. *Still, what might have been had I not gone home at the end of the war?* The question loomed large but soon forgotten.

"Thanks, Cassie." Jem was gone in a shot across the dance floor, and Cassie saw him bend over, take the hand of the girl in the red gown, and lead her out on the dance floor. Cassie was not alone for long. Out of the corner of her eye, she saw one of the fellows detach himself from the others dressed in homespun. He walked to her, and she was glad to be singled out. It had been lonely standing by herself. Over the dancers' din, he said, "I'm John Lyon; I overheard your name. It's Cassie, isn't it? Would you care for a glass of lemonade?" The two walked to the table where cupcakes sat in pewter plates and pitchers of cold lemonade sweated through the glass.

It turned out John Lyon constructed houses as did others in his circle. "You are not farmers?"

"We used to be, but this construction work pays more. At present, we're building a house fronting the river for one of our friends from Staten Island, name of Luke Welch, about to be married to one of the girls up here, Tessa Mobray. He came up to these parts couple of years ago with a friend, and now they build houses for a living. Pretty smart, hey?"

Jem Clarke, holding Rebecca Quiney's hand, joined them, and then they were four. John Lyon proved eager to dance with Cassie and Cassie with him. When the evening ended, Cassie knew she hadn't had as good a time as she had tonight for a long, long while. "I'll see you again, Cassie," John Lyon said to her.

"Yes," she said. "I enjoyed your company, John."

The musicians put away their instruments; the dancers left the floor and the grange hall emptied. It grew very quiet in the carriage after Jem dropped Rebecca off at her house. On the way to Wiegand's, Jem said, "We never got to dance, did we, Cassie?"

"No, but it was fine, Jem. I enjoyed dancing with John Lyon."

"He's an excellent man, Cassie. I can vouch for him. I know him." He spoke casually, as though he and Cassie were good friends and never had loved each other.

"About Joanna, Jem. You heard me tell her I would take her home tomorrow to her cottage. I can start to make her more comfortable there, the sooner the better."

"I'll help you." Jem was true to his word and more. After Cassie cleaned up the cottage, he had Joanna's cottage painted and put a new singing canary into the old, chipped cage. A few logs from the cord of wood Jem brought lay next to the grate to crackle in the hearth, and the cottage came to its old life. With Cassie to take care of her, Joanna came home. Her spirits soared.

All that is wanting to me is someone to share this contentment. A long-ago, faraway dream, Cassie reflected one evening after supper in late September as she sat outside the cottage, gazing down the slope of green grass at the placid, peaceful river, while Joanna slept. Though she took her embroidery and needle out with her, very little needlework got done.

Instead, pictures of her life long ago during the war kept intruding into her mind. The terrible dousing in the North River at the hands of Jonah Higbie always came first, still causing her to cringe, but then Joanna had called her from the grass to grab on to the rope; it was Joanna who had saved her. It was Joanna who now lay inside, growing more fragile by the day, yet hanging on to her life holding Cassie's hand, smiling weakly up at her. As the weeks and months rolled by, Cassie saw there was nothing more she could do except to keep Joanna comfortable.

There came a morning when Joanna's eyes stared unblinking, when the chirping of the canary went unheard, when her body became still.

"It's over, Cassie. Joanna's gone." Jem had stopped by the cottage that morning on his way to his office, just as he did almost every day. He arranged for the sawyers in town to construct a pine box for Joanna. Cassie arranged a church service, and people from all over Buttermilk Falls came to say a final good-bye to Joanna. Invited by Cassie, all of Joanna's friends and Cassie rode from the cemetery to Wiegand's Tavern to share a meal out of respect to Joanna. When it was over, people left, giving Cassie their good wishes for her future. Jem Clarke's fiancée, Rebecca Quiney, the girl in red at the grange dance, stood a little apart from Cassie and Jem, giving them room to say farewell to each other. Tonight, after her supper she would rent a room at Wiegand's and buy a ticket for the morning stage back to York City.

"It was good what you did for Joanna, Cassie," Jem said softly.

"Joanna gave me back my life, Jem."

"You don't mind about…"

"You mean Rebecca?" Cassie looked up at Jem. His face was a study in confusion.

"No, Jem. I'm happy for you both."

"That's all right then. Isn't it, Cassie?"

"Yes, Jem, it's fine."

CHAPTER NINETY-SIX

April 1787

"General Washington is coming to York City today to visit. Taking a tour of the northeast. Meeting people here," Luke said. "We're going down to York City, Tessa and I. You going? You can ride down with us."

"I'm going down, but I'm taking the carriage," David said. "Afterward, I'm heading out to my cottage on Long Island just to see if it's still standing. I'll be back in a couple of days. Time enough to see you get married."

"Yeah. Sure. It's really going to happen, too." Luke smiled.

"See you on Saturday in church." The two men shook hands.

"Try and get onto the corner of Wall and Nassau Streets. That's where we'll be," Luke yelled back as he closed the door behind him. David watched as Luke and Tessa drove the carriage out to the road and out of sight. He had to check Luke's house before he left to make sure the windows didn't rattle, the doors fit their frames, and the beams were settled into place. And then he could ride down to New York City, where this new life he had fashioned

for himself had begun. When he thought about it, David was relieved he would be traveling alone. It was hard to be with Tessa
and Luke lately for their talk was about their wedding and the
new house Luke and he had built for them. He must really go to
the grange dances, as Luke had done, and try to meet a girl. But
somehow, Saturday nights came and went, and David found himself alone with his books and contracts.

CHAPTER NINETY-SEVEN

Flowing from the steps of City Hall and the surrounding streets, a dense crowd four or five feet deep grew, as a parade of farm wagons, carriages, and horses carried people from as far away as Montauk at the very tip of Long Island to the southerly reaches of New Jersey. The crowd worked its way along the strand, pushing to get as close as possible to the corners of Wall and Nassau Streets. David tried to inch his way into the crowd lumped together into every square foot of space between street and waterfront in the squishy April mud—but it was no good. If Luke and Tessa were in front, he couldn't possibly get to them. He would have to get a glimpse of General Washington from a better viewing spot.

The moment she had been waiting for had come for Cassie. Preceded by two matching pairs of cream-white horses, General Washington's carriage waited at the entrance to Nassau Street for a path to be cleared for his carriage. Through her lace-ruffled half gloves, her fingers bedecked with a lapis lazuli ring and wrist bracelet to match, Cassie found it impossible to move. She felt herself being pushed forward by the crowd. Helpless in the midst of its relentless movement, she was thrust forward into the road. She felt the embroidered silk streamers of her dress pull away from her waist, but she could not lift her hands to hold on to them. The crowd was now surging toward Wall Street, and just as suddenly, she found herself stopped in the very middle of Nassau Street, as an honor guard of Continental army regulars riding black horses galloped forward of General Washington's coach and six white horses. Cassie tried to lift her hands together and pull them up beneath her chin to yell out with the huge crowd, "Excelsior! General Washington." As the general passed, he waved to the crowd, and Cassie felt the dense, solid wall of people surge forward. The black horses bore down upon the crowd, raising a cloud of dust and mud that coated their very bodies. Just behind them General Washington's coach-and-four stopped. He stood up in his open carriage and waved to the crowd again and again. Cassie saw he was wearing his uniform of blue waistcoat shining with brass buttons fronted by eagles. Then, from the roofs of houses on Nassau Street, descended thousands of tiny pieces of colored paper like multitudes of butterflies landing on his coach. While church bells pealed and bonfires on surrounding hills burst into flame, Cassie stood entranced. When the general signaled his wish to move forward, the honor guard astride their black horses continued to beat a protective path ahead of his open carriage, spewing sand, dirt, and pebbles into the faces and bodies of the people crowded in the road, much the way ships foment turbulent, angry waters in their wakes.

Sparklers in children's hands glittered; foghorns out on the water blared their nasal tones; the crowd roared; and the metal hooves of the black horses clattered closer, their sweat grazing Cassie's hair. Deafening thuds rang into her ears, and clumps of mud hit her in the face, forcing her eyes shut. Wet pebbles and dusty swirls of earth flew in her mouth, and a strong wind tumbled over and about her. In a heartbeat, the black horses split apart, turning away from the crowd at the last second. Stillness. The ground ceased shaking. Quiet. Cassie lay silent for a moment. There was nothing else to do but pull herself up from the ground.

Finally, able to stand again, seeing the general had passed in the interval, Cassie still saw the sun shining down onto the back of his carriage. Yet she had seen him and gazed at his face. The wideness of his smile gave her joy. She had heard the shouting and the calling out to the general as he passed along. She looked down at herself standing in the middle of Nassau Street. Dirty as she was, she was unhurt. Her gloves lay limp on her hands, the lace full of holes, and the lapis lazuli ring and bracelet grimy with mud; her gown, now an all-over gray, shot with horses' spittle and sticky brown mud, with not a spot of its blue color left, felt stiff to her touch, showing road dust from the top of her bodice to the tip of her hem. Her beloved shoes, one missing a heel, lay on the ground next to her begrimed feet, overturned in the dirt. But the most wonderful thing was that she had seen the general again. She only wished David could have been here with her.

At that moment, David Van Essen turned the corner onto Nassau Street and had a glimpse of General Washington as he rode on down to City Hall. The crowd running to keep up with his carriage emptied out of Nassau Street into Wall Street, except for a young woman standing in the midst of the muck of sand and mud, trying to put a shoe back on her foot. Her dress was a shamble of rips and tears; her hair held more sand than the street did. Her other shoe was missing its heel. But on her face was a growing smile. As David Van Essen approached, she looked up at him.

"I knew you would be here," he said. Then there were two people standing in Nassau Street, full of sand and mud, smiling at each other, their kisses notwithstanding.

The End

ACKNOWLEDGMENTS

A great, abundant cornucopia of thanks goes out to all the people who made my story better! To Bobby Eilbacher, Matty Eilbacher, Ellie Eilbacher, and Dominic Eilbacher, for their editing suggestions and manuscript work; to Mrs. Donna Serpico for reading my manuscript and for her knowledge of chocolate-eating habits in colonial times; to Gina Ardito, whose suggestions to develop the characters were very valuable; to Katherine Ann Radigan for her meticulous reading of first and second drafts of my story; to my two writing groups, the Forest Hills Women's Writers and the Manhasset Scribes for listening to, and making rich suggestions on how to improve my drafts of the story, and to Bob Eilbacher for his computer and editing skills which helped enormously when technical difficulties -- read: I'm stuck!-- presented themselves.

To all of you: Thank you.

Made in the USA
Lexington, KY
31 March 2018